PARADISE INTERPRETED

THEMES IN
BIBLICAL NARRATIVE
JEWISH AND CHRISTIAN TRADITIONS

VOLUME II

TUTA SUB AEGIDE PALLAS · 1683 ·

PARADISE INTERPRETED

Representations of Biblical Paradise
in Judaism and Christianity

EDITED BY

GERARD P. LUTTIKHUIZEN

BRILL
LEIDEN · BOSTON · KÖLN
1999

This book is printed on acid-free paper.

Library of Congress Cataloging-in-Publication Data

Paradise interpreted : representations of biblical paradise in Judaism and Christianity / edited by Gerard P. Luttikhuizen.
p. cm. — (Themes in biblical narrative ; v. 2)
Includes bibliographical references and index.
ISBN 9004113312 (alk. paper)
1. Paradise—History of doctrines—Congresses. I. Luttikhuizen, Gerard P. II. Series.
BT846.2.P37 1999
291.2'3—dc21 99-13596
CIP

Die Deutsche Bibliothek - CIP-Einheitsaufnahme

Paradise interpreted : representations of biblical paradise in Judaism and Christianity / ed. by Gerard P. Luttikhuizen. - Leiden ; Boston ; Köln : Brill, 1999
(Themes in Biblical narrative ; Vol. 2)
ISBN 90-04-11331-2

Cover design: TopicA (Antoinette Hanekuyk)

Detail of '*Carte de la situation du paradis terrestre, et des païs habitez par les patriarches*', by: Pieter Daniel Huet. Edition: Pieter Mortier, around 1700.

ISSN 1388-3909
ISBN 90 04 11331 2

PRINTED IN THE NETHERLANDS

As Good as a Feast

She didn't eat much, really.
Indeed was barely hungry.
And when she had gone, taking
her small noontime shadow
with her, the apple lay
on the upright grass; both,
of course, perfect but the apple
as red as arterial blood.
There was dew, of course,
even at noon: the entire garden
like the produce section of
a fancy grocer's—the world was good
enough to eat—and the blades
of grass upright as spears
held the apple on a hundred
sharp points. (The grass, unbent,
stood up like thorns.) No apple
had ever fallen before
and the perfect grass pricked
small wounds, like the elegant circle
left by her teeth, where the flesh,
now poisoned by the perfect air,
turned brown. That, of course,
was death. And that wavy
dark line, leading nowhere
in the dew, was the serpent.

(Arthur Lindley)

Reprinted by permission of the author, after original publication in *Westerly* (Perth, Australia, 1988) 33.3, p. 59

CONTENTS

PREFACE

This book contains twelve papers given at a conference of the research group "Early Jewish and Christian Traditions" of the Faculty of Theology and Religious Studies, University of Groningen, held in June, 1998. The conference was devoted to Paradise accounts in the Hebrew Bible and to their reception in Judaism and Christianity. As the actual research of the team is centred on the interpretation of biblical texts in early Jewish and early Christian traditions, the emphasis in the conference was on these traditions. But it was decided to include also some later receptions of the biblical Paradise. A number of scholars were invited to comment upon views of Paradise in Rabbinica and Kabbalah, in the Christian Middle Ages, and, finally, in John Milton's poetic works about Paradise.

The proceedings of the conference open with a historical investigation of the Greek loanword *paradeisos*, used in the Septuagint version to render the Hebrew word *gan*, "garden" (J.N. Bremmer). A second fundamental chapter discusses the two different concepts of Paradise in the Hebrew Bible: the orchard where Adam and Eve lived, in Genesis 2–3, and the garden on the mount of the gods in Ezekiel 28 (E. Noort).

Post-biblical views of Paradise elaborate mainly on the Genesis story. The third chapter deals with the motif of the Paradise garden in early Jewish literature, particularly Enochic texts and some fragments found in the Judaean Desert. The Enochic references to Paradise seem to be dependent on traditions that are older than the final version of the Genesis story (E.J.C. Tigchelaar). In this chapter the *Book of Jubilees* is mentioned only in passing. The rewriting of Genesis 2–3 in *Jubilees* is analysed in more detail in a separate essay (J.T.A.G.M. van Ruiten). This chapter is followed by a discussion of two texts known from Qumran, the Damascus Document and 4Q365, in which elements of the biblical Paradise narrative are used in order to base halakhic rules concerning man and woman (F. García Martínez). The part of this volume dealing with Jewish Paradise interpretations is concluded with a discussion about Paradise as a paradigm for good and evil in Rabbinica and Kabbalah (W.J. van Bekkum).

A chapter about Paul's visit to Paradise in the early Christian *Apocalypse of Paul* marks the transition to Christian views of Paradise. Moreover this chapter pays explicit attention to the emergence of the idea of a Paradise in heaven (A. Hilhorst). Two further chapters deal with early Christian Paradise interpretations, the first one with the highly critical treatment of the Genesis story in a Christian Gnostic text (G.P. Luttikhuizen), the other with various ideas about Paradise and Paradisiacal life in early mainstream Christianity (H.S. Benjamins).

The last three chapters pursue later developments in the Christian perception of Paradise. Chr. Auffarth shows how the biblical Paradise imagery was conceived and put into actual practice by medieval Christians, including married lay people as well as monastics and priests. S. Brouwer focuses on late medieval Russian views, particularly on the idea of Paradise as an accessible region somewhere on earth. The volume concludes with the interpretation of the story of Paradise before the fall in Book IV of John Miltons's epic poem *Paradise Lost* (H. Wilcox). As the author of this chapter emphasizes, Milton's work is a milestone in the modern interpretation of the Genesis story of Adam and Eve: "Milton's interpretation of Genesis (. . .) resulted in a powerfully persuasive text whose impact across the centuries has been enormous". It would be worthwhile to study the reception of the idea of Paradise after Milton. An investigation like that must, however, be left to others, who may be encouraged by what Wilcox observes in the first sentences of her essay: "Paradise is all around us. This is not so much a theological statement as an observation on a contemporary preoccupation of literature in English".

The conference was held under the auspices of the Rudolf Agricola Institute, the Groningen Institute for the Humanities which is the present home base of the research group "Early Jewish and Christian Traditions". It is a pleasant duty to thank this Institute as well as the Faculty of Theology and Religious Studies for all the help provided to enable the organization of the conference and the publication of the proceedings. It is also a pleasure to thank the colleagues, students and other delegates who attended the conference and by their comments on the various papers have contributed to the final results.

The present book is the second volume of the series *Themes in Biblical Narrative: Jewish and Christian Traditions*. Thanks to the competent and energetic support of Freek van der Steen and Brill Academic Publishers the present volume could be published shortly after the conference.

Gerard P. Luttikhuizen

ABBREVIATIONS

AB	The Anchor Bible
ADPV	Abhandlungen des Deutschen Palästina Vereins
AH	Acta Historica
AHw	Akkadisches Handwörterbuch
AJ	Josephus, Jewish Antiquities
AOAT	Alter Orient und Altes Testament
BG	Berolinensis Gnosticus
BHS	Biblia Hebraica Stuttgartensia
Bib	Biblica
BJ	Josephus, Bellum Judaicum
BK	Biblischer Kommentar
BKAT	Biblischer Kommentar Altes Testament
BT	Babylonian Talmud
BZAW	Beihefte zur Zeitschrift für die alttestamentliche Wissenschaft
CBS	Catalogue of the Babylonian Section
CCSL	Corpus Christianorum Series Latina
CD	Cairo Damascus Document
COT	Commentaar op het Oude Testament
CSCO	Corpus Scriptorum Christianorum Orientalium
DJD	Discoveries in the Judean Desert
DSD	Dead Sea Discoveries
DSS	Dead Sea Scrolls
DSSS	The Dead Sea Scrolls Study edition
En	Enoch
EthGen	Ethiopic Version of Genesis
FGrH	Die Fragmente der Griechischen Historiker
FOTL	The Forms of the Old Testament Literature
GAG	Grundriß der Akkadischen Grammatik
Gen r	Midrash Genesis Rabbah
HAL	Hebraisches und Aramaisches Lexikon zum Alten Testament
HSCP	Harvard Studies in Classical Philology
HTR	Harvard Theological Review
JAOS	Journal of the American Oriental Society
JBL	Journal of Biblical Literature
JJS	Journal of Jewish Studies

JNES	Journal of Near Eastern Studies
JSJ	Journal for the Study of Judaism
JSOTSS	Journal for the Study of the Old Testament, Supplement Series
JSPSS	Journal for the Study of Pseudepigrapha, Supplement Series
JSS	Journal of Semitic Studies
JTS	Journal of Tamil Studies
Jub	Jubilees
KBL	Lexicon in Veteris Testamenti Libros
LAB	Liber Antiquitatum Biblicarum
Lev r	Midrash Leviticus Rabbah
LXX	Septuagint
Macc	Maccabees
MMT	The Making of Modern Theology
MPL	Monumenta Polyphoniae Liturgicae sanctae ecclesiae Romanae
MS	Mediaeval Studies
MT	Masoretic Text
Nag Hamm	Nag Hammadi
NTS	Supplements to Novum Testamentum
NTT	Nederlands Theologisch Tijdschrift
Num r	Midrash Numbers Rabbah
PAM	Palestine Archaeological Museum
PFT	Persepolis Fortification Tablets
PL	Patrologia Latina
PT	Palestinian Talmud
P. Tebt	Ptolemaic Tebtunis
PTT	Persepolis Treasury Tablets
1QapGen	1QGenesis Apocryphon
RB	Revue Biblique
RE	Realencyclopädie für protestantische Theologie und Kirche
RevQ	Revue de Qumran
RSV	Revised Standard Version
Sanh	Sanhedrin
SBL	Society of Biblical Literature
Songs r	Midrash Song of Songs Rabbah
STDJ	Studies on the Texts of the Desert of Judah
SUNT	Studien zur Umwelt des Neuen Testaments

TestTr	Testimony of Truth
Tg Ps-J	Targum Pseudo Jonathan
ThWNT	Theologisch Wörterbuch zum Neuen Testament
TRE	Theologische Realencyclopädie
TSAJ	Texte und Studien zum Antiken Judemtum
TU	Texte und Untersuchungen zur Geschichte der altchristlichen Literatur
TUAT	Texte aus der Umwelt des Alten Testaments
UPZ	Urkunden der Ptolemäer Zeit
WBC	Word Biblical Commentary
WMANT	Wissenschaftliche Monographien zum Alten und Neuen Testament
ZAW	Zeitschrift für die alttestamentliche Wissenschaft
ZNW	Zeitschrift für die neutestamentliche Wissenschaft

PARADISE: FROM PERSIA, VIA GREECE, INTO THE *SEPTUAGINT*

JAN N. BREMMER

The first chapters of *Genesis* mention a landscaped, enclosed park, full of fruit-trees, planted by God himself, with a river running through it and possibilities for walking. The translators of the *Septuagint* have called this park *paradeisos*.[1] The enormous impact of the Biblical description of Paradise has been often studied and its main lines are now well known.[2] Less familiar is the development of the term "paradise" itself. Recent studies are not really very informative in this respect. According to Joachim Jeremias, *paradeisos* is an Old Iranian ("Altiranisches") loan word which first means "tree garden", "park" and is subsequently used to denote the Garden of Eden as "*Gottesgarten*" in order to distinguish it from profane parks.[3] Although his explanation, which is representative for most modern approaches to the problem, is not totally wrong, it is not really fully right either. In order to provide a more exact answer to this question I will look at the term in the early Achaemenid period (§ 1), the later Achaemenid period (§ 2) and at its development in the post-Achaemenid era (§ 3), and conclude with a discussion as to why the translators of *Genesis* opted for this specific word to translate the Hebrew term *Gan Eden* (§ 4).

1. *The early Achaemenid era*

The etymology of Greek *paradeisos* is not disputed. It most likely derives from Median **paridaeza*, "enclosure", **pari* being "around"

---

[1] The basis of any investigation of the term must now be the rich study of C. Tuplin, *Achaemenid Studies* (Stuttgart, 1996) 80–131 ("The Parks and Gardens of the Achaemenid Empire"), to which I am heavily indebted. The implicit enclosure of *Genesis* is made explicit in the *Apocalypse of Moses* 17.1; *bKetubbot* 77b; *bShabbath* 119b; *Vita Adam* 31.2, 40.2.

[2] See especially J. Delumeau, *Une histoire du paradis*, 2 vls. (Paris, 1992–1995); Ch. Auffarth, *Mittelalterliche Eschatologie* (Göttingen, 1999) Ch. 2.

[3] J. Jeremias, "*paradeisos*", *ThWNT* 5 (Stuttgart, 1954) 763–71.

and **daeza* "wall".[4] As more often, the Greeks took their words from the Medes rather than from the Persians, just as, e.g., Greek *satrapes* is the Median form of this Iranian title.[5] Like its Old Persian equivalent **paridaida*,[6] the Median form is not attested in the few surviving Old Persian texts and it is unlikely that it will ever turn up in Median writings, since the Medes never seem to have developed a script;[7] however, the Median form does recur in the later Avestan *Videvdad* as *paridaeza* (3.18).

The occurrence of such a Median term as loanword in Greek, and, as we soon shall see, Akkadian, Hebrew and Aramaic, is one more testimony to the influence of the enigmatic Medians. The tribe itself has left very little traces and its early history is hard to reconstruct, but the fact that the Greeks called their formidable Eastern opponents first Medes and only later Persians, attests to their former importance; similarly, the Jews speak of Medes in *Isaiah* (13.17, 21.2) and *Jeremiah* (51.1, 28), but of Medes and Persians only in the post-exilic books of *Ezra, Nehemiah, Esther* and *Daniel*.[8] The increasing attention to linguistic derivations, which has become possible with the growing insight into the Median and Persian dialects, will perhaps shed more light on this problem in the future.[9]

If its linguistic and etymological background is clear, the precise semantics of the term are more problematic. Given the absence of early Iranian material we will have to take recourse to its use as loanword in more or less contemporary Akkadian and Elamite texts in order to reconstruct its meaning in the oldest period of the Persian, multicultural empire. We start with the Babylonian texts.

Virtually immediately after the Persian capture of Babylon in 539

---

[4] For other examples of Iranian *-ae-* into Greek *-ei-* see R. Schmitt, *Die Iranier-Namen bei Aischylos* (Vienna, 1978) 29.

[5] R. Schmitt, "Der Titel 'Satrap'," in A. Morpurgo-Davies and W. Meid (eds.), *Studies in Greek, Italic and Indo-European Linguistics offered to L.R. Palmer* (Innsbruck, 1976) 373–90; J. and L. Robert, *Fouilles d'Amyzon en Carie* (Paris, 1983) 98f.

[6] P. Lecoq, "Paradis en vieux-perse?", in F. Vallat (ed.), *Contribution à l'histoire de l'Iran. Mélanges offerts à Jean Perrot* (Paris, 1990) 209–11.

[7] R. Schmitt (ed.), *Compendium linguarum Iranicarum* (Wiesbaden, 1989) 87–90 ("Medisch"); M. Mayrhofer, *Ausgewählte kleine Schriften* II (Wiesbaden, 1996) 390–2.

[8] D.F. Graf, "Medism", *J. of Hell. Stud.* 104 (1984) 15–30; C. Tuplin, "Persians as Medes", in A. Kuhrt and M. Root (eds.), *Achaemenid History* 8 (1994) 235–256, who also discusses the occurrence of Medes in other languages (236–8).

[9] The short observations by Tuplin, "Persians as Medes", 252 n. 20 are insufficient, the more so since he does not call attention to the problem of the *Verschriftlichung* of the Median language.

we find three Babylonian documents of the last decades of the sixth century,[10] in which temple authorities are responsible for maintaining and establishing *pardesu*. One of these is a vineyard, another is associated with planting date-palms and making bricks, and a loan document of 465/4 BC mentions an "upper *pardesu*" (i.e. at the upper side).[11]

We find more information in only slightly later Elamite texts. After the fall of the Elamite empire in the seventh century, the Persians settled on its former territory and kept Elamite as the official language of their bureaucracy in Persis until about 460. In the thirties of this century excavators found hundreds of clay tablets in Elamite in Persepolis which, depending on their place of finding, were published as *Persepolis Treasury Tablets* (*PTT*) and *Persepolis Fortification Tablets* (*PFT*).[12] The former, 114 in all, can be dated to the period between 492 and 460 BC, when clay was probably given up in favour of parchment. From the latter more than 2000 have now been published, belonging to the years between 510 and 494 BC. It is especially in the *PFT*, which have been identified as tax-receipts,[13] that we regularly find mention of something called *partetas*, which the authoritative Elamite dictionary considers as corresponding to Old Persian **paridaida*.[14] From the texts there emerge the following meanings. *Partetas* figure as storage places for natural produce, such as

[10] For the Persian influence in Babylon see A. Kuhrt, "Achaemenid Babylonia: Sources and Problems", in H. Sancisi-Weerdenburg and Kuhrt (eds.), *Achaemenid History* 4 (Leiden, 1990) 177–94.

[11] *Cuneiform Texts from Babylonian Tablets in the British Museum* 22.198is (Sippar: early Cyrus), which is perhaps the same as that in J.N. Strassmaier, *Inschriften von Cyrus, König von Babylon* (Leipzig, 1890) 212 (Sippar: 534 BC); *Yale Oriental Series* 3.133 (Uruk: 539/526 BC), cf. Tuplin, *Achaemenid Studies*, 113; M.W. Stolper, *Entrepeneurs and Empire* (Istanbul, 1985) 283 no. 120 (= *CBS* 13039: Nippur: 465/4 BC). For these texts see M. Dandamayev, "Royal *paradeisoi* in Babylonia", *Acta Iranica* II 9 (Leiden, 1984) 113–7. It is interesting that a country *Pardesu* is mentioned in a late writing exercise (probably *ca.* 85 BC), cf. T.G. Pinches, "Assyriological gleanings", *Proc. Soc. Bibl. Arch.* 18 (1896) 250–7, after p. 256, Plate III, AH 83–1–18, 1866 Reverse Column V. 15–7.

[12] For the standard editions see G. Cameron, *Persepolis Treasury Tablets* (Chicago, 1948) and "New Tablets from the Persepolis Treasury", *JNES* 24 (1965) 167–92; R.T. Hallock, *Persepolis Fortification Tablets* (Chicago, 1969) and "Selected Fortification Texts", *Cahiers de la Délégation Française en Iran* 8 (1978) 106–36.

[13] H. Koch, "Steuern in der achämenidischen Persis?", *Zs. f. Assyriologie* 70 (1980) 105–37.

[14] W. Hinz and H. Koch, *Elamisches Wörterbuch* (Berlin, 1987) I.160; similarly already R.G. Kent, *Old Persian* (New Haven, 1953²) 195.

figs, dates, peaches, apricots, pomegranates and "royal grain", mostly fairly close to Persepolis. It could also be the place in which a food-product, *kar*, was made. Although the size of a *partetas* was rather modest, it was large enough to contain sheep for a celebration of a religious ceremony, perhaps a sacrifice to Ahuramazda. Finally, there is a clear connection with trees. One tablet inventories 6,166 seedlings at five places, including three *partetas*, in which there are also 4931 trees.[15] The prominence of trees may be surprising, but the Persians attached great value to trees. This is already illustrated by a letter from Darius I to Gadatas, probably the overseer of a local "paradise", the *paradeisarios*, a term which recurs in Syrian as *pardayspana*, in the oldest Armenian texts as *partizpan*, and in the New Persian epic *Shanameh* as *palezban*.[16] In the letter the king praises Gadatas for cultivating in Western Asia Minor the fruit trees of Syria and berates him for taxing the sacred gardeners of Apollo and ordering them to till profane soil.[17] A certain Pythios, perhaps the grandson of Croesus, gave Darius a golden vine and plane-tree, which remained very famous until they were melted down by Antigonus in 316 BC.[18] When finding a fine plane tree a day east of Sardis, Xerxes decorated it with gold and appointed a perpetual guardian (Herodotus 7.31; Aelian, *Varia historia* 2.14). Cyrus the Younger showed Lysander the *paradeisos* at Sardis and claimed to have personally planted some trees (§ 2). Strabo, who probably goes back to fourth-century sources, even mentions that during their education the Persian boys "late in the afternoon are trained in the planting of trees" (15.3.18). It is surely this great concern with trees which made Plutarch relate that Artaxerxes II once gave permission to his soldiers, when they were very cold, to fell trees in *paradeisoi* (§ 2) "without saving pines or cypresses", while

---

[15] I summarize here the detailed discussions by Tuplin, *Achaemenid Studies*, 93–96, 178–82; P. Briant, *Histoire de l'empire perse de Cyrus à Alexandre* I (Paris, 1996 = Leiden, 1997) 456–8; A. Uchitel, "Persian Paradise: agricultural texts in the fortification tablets", *Iranica Antiqua* 32 (1997) 137–44.

[16] *Paradeisarios*: Hesychius, s.v. *hernokomon*. Syrian: R. Payne Smith, *Thesaurus Syriacus* II (Oxford, 1901) c. 3240 (*horti custos*); K. Brockelman, *Lexicon Syriacum* (Halle, 1928) 593b (*horticultor*). Armenian: H. Hübschmann, *Armenische Grammatik* I (Leipzig, 1897) 229. New Persian: *Shanameh* 3.1504.

[17] R. Meiggs and D. Lewis, *A Selection of Greek Historical Inscriptions to the End of the Fifth Century BC* (Oxford, 1980[2]) no. 12; *SEG* 36.1042; Briant, *Histoire*, 507–9 (function of Gadatas).

[18] Herodotus 7.27; Xenophon, *Hellenica* 7.1.38; Chares *FGrH* 125 F 2; Amyntas *FGrH* 122 F 6; Phylarchus *FGrH* 81 F 41; Diodorus Siculus 19.48.7; Pliny, *Natural History* 33.137; Himerius, *Eclogae* 31.8; Photius, *Bibliotheke* 612.

he himself felled the largest and most attractive tree (*Artaxerxes* 25).[19]

We can now draw our first conclusions. In the early Persian Empire two closely related words were current for "paradise": Median **paridaeza* and Old Persian **paridaida*. The latter was adopted in the Elamite *Kanzleisprache*, the former by Babylonians, Greeks and Jews (§ 2). Secondly, early Iranian "paradise" had no fixed meaning. It could be a storage-place, vineyard, orchard, stable, forest or nursery of trees. Evidently, it was a kind of *vox media* of which the most prominent element was the enclosure. Thirdly, none of these descriptions closely fits the Garden of Eden yet.

2. *The later Achaemenid period*

Having looked at the earliest occurrences of the word, let us now turn to its examples in the later Achaemenid era. The connection between trees and "paradise", which we noted in the Elamite *partetas*, recurs in the *Old Testament*, where in *Nehemiah* the homonymous protagonist requests building wood "to make beams for gates of the palace" (2.8) from the overseer of the king's *pardes*. The passage seems to derive from Nehemiah's original memoir, which dates from the second half of the fifth century, and thus is a valuable testimony to the presence of Persian "paradises" not only in Anatolia but also elsewhere in the Persian empire. Nehemiah does not mention the location of his "paradise", but it may have been situated in Lebanon.[20] King Solomon imported cedars from Lebanon for the building of the temple (1 *Kings* 5); carpenters from the region are already well attested in Babylon in the early sixth century, and in 538 BC the royal administration ordered the Sidonians and Tyrians to bring cedars from Lebanon.[21] Trees also figure in the *Song of Songs*, which

---

[19] On trees and the Persian king see Briant, *Histoire* II, 244–50 (with interesting illustrations from Persian seals), who also points to the Vulgate version of *Esther* 1.5 where the feast is celebrated in the court of the *horti et nemoris quod regio cultu et manu consitum erat*. For comparable medieval connections between kings and gardens see Th. Finkenstaedt, "Der Garten des Königs", in H. Bauer *et al.* (eds.), *Wandlungen des Paradiesischen und Utopischen* (Berlin, 1966) 183–209.

[20] Thus Briant, *Histoire*, 433 and many commentaries. However, other possibilities, such as the forests near Jericho, cannot be excluded.

[21] Ph. Gauthier, *Nouvelles inscriptions de Sardes* (Geneva, 1989) 22–32; R. Zadok, "Foreigners and Foreign Linguistic Material in Mesopotamia and Egypt", in K. van Lerberghe and A. Schoors (eds.), *Immigration and Emigration within the Ancient Near East* (Louvain, 1995) 431–47 at 432f.

was perhaps written in Jerusalem around 400 BC.[22] Here we find a "*pardes* of pomegranates, with pleasant fruits; camphire with spikenard, spikenard and saffron; calamus and cinnamon, with all trees of frankincense" (4.13–14).

There is a chance that *paradeisos* already appeared in Greek literature in the later fifth century. According to the Aristotelian pupil Clearchus, the sixth-century Samian tyrant Polycrates of Samos used to imitate the luxury of the Lydians and even had "constructed in the city the famous '(Red-light) Quarter' of Samos to rival the park at Sardis called Sweet Embrace".[23] The passage probably derives from Clearchus' *Lives* where he relates: "The Lydians in their luxury laid out *paradeisoi*, making them like parks and so lived in the shade . . . they would gather the wives and maiden daughters of other men into the place called, because of this action, Place of Chastity, and there outrage them".[24] As Clearchus elsewhere in this passage must have used the Lydian historian Xanthus,[25] an older contemporary of Herodotus, it seems not unlikely that Clearchus also derived his information about Polycrates from Xanthus. If this is true, it means that Xanthus was perhaps the first Greek to use the term *paradeisos* in writing. This would not be unlikely, since being a Lydian he may well have known the Sardian *paradeisoi* (below) personally.

Unfortunately, the passage is not crystal clear. The most likely interpretation seems to be that in order to enjoy the shade the Sardians laid out *paradeisoi*. As befitted *paradeisoi* (§ 1 and below), they consisted of trees, but the Sardians apparently had transformed them into a more cultivated environment than the normal Persian ones (below), with perhaps pavilions to receive their "guests". In any case, there was a house and a place with a canopied bed in the Babylonian *paradeisos* where Alexander the Great died,[26] and pavilions long

[22] For the date see A. Robert *et al.*, *Le Cantique des Cantiques* (Paris, 1963) 20–22. Admittedly, this is only a reasonable guess, but in any case more persuasive than M.H. Pope, *Song of Songs* (New York, 1977) 22–33.

[23] Clearchus, fr. 44 Wehrli = Athenaeus 12.540, translated by C.B. Gulick, Loeb, cf. P. Briant, "Chasses royales macédoniennes et chasses royales perses: le thème de la chasse au lion sur la *Chasse de Vergina*", *Dialogues d'histoire ancienne* 17 (1991) 211–55 at 235 n. 45.

[24] Clearchus, fr. 43a = Athenaeus 12.515e, translated by C.B. Gulick, Loeb.

[25] As is observed by Wehrli *ad loc.* who compares Eusthatius on *Iliad* 16.702 = Xanthus *FGrH* 765 F 4c.

[26] The Macedonian royal Diaries in *FGrH* 117 F 3; Ephippos *FGrH* F 4; Arrian, *Anabasis*, 7.25; for more examples of buildings in *paradeisoi* see Tuplin, *Achaemenid Studies*, 107.

remained a characteristic feature of Persian parks.[27] At first sight it may be surprising that Clearchus speaks of *paradeisoi* in the plural, but the texts frequently speak of multiple *paradeisoi*. Some earlier examples are, presumably, the *paradeisoi* in Susa (Aelian, *Natura animalium* 7.1), the wild parks (below) of Pharnabazus (Xenophon, *Hellenica* 4.1.15, 33), the hunting *paradeisoi* given to Demetrius Poliorcetes in his place of exile (Plutarch, *Demetrius* 50) and the Syrian cypress-*paradeisoi* mentioned by Theophrastus (*Historia Plantarum* 5.8.1).

We move on firmer ground in the fourth century when we find the first certain occurrences of the term *paradeisos* in the works of Xenophon.[28] Unfortunately, the chronology of his works is not very clear, but it seems reasonable to start with the *Cyropaedia*, a novel-like book in which Xenophon displays much of his knowledge of the Persian empire. Here he lets Astyages tell his grandson, the future Cyrus the Great: "I will give you all the game present in the *paradeisos* and collect many more, which you, as soon as you have learnt to ride, may pursue" (1.3.14). In fact, Cyrus proved to be such an enthousiastic hunter in the *paradeisos* that his grandfather was unable to collect enough animals for him (1.4.5): not surprisingly, since it was only a small one (1.4.11). Astyages' insistence on the hunt had evidently left a big impression on Cyrus, for he ordered his satraps to "lay out *paradeisoi* and breed game" (8.6.12), and when he had acceded to the throne "he would lead those nobles, whom he thought in need of it, out to the hunt in order to train them in the art of war, since he considered the hunt by far the best preparation for war . . . and whenever he was bound to stay at home, he would hunt game reared in the *paradeisoi*" (8.1.34–8).

We receive a more detailed picture of a specific *paradeisos* in the *Oeconomicus* through an anecdote which goes back to Lysander's own report according to Xenophon. When Cyrus the Younger showed the Spartan Lysander his *paradeisoi* in Sardis, Lysander admired "the

---

[27] D. Wilber, *Persian Gardens & Garden Pavilions* (Rutland and Tokyo, 1962); W.L. Hanaway, "Paradise on Earth: The Terrestrial Garden in Persian Literature" and R. Pinder-Wilson, "The Persian Garden: *Bagh* and *Chahar Bagh*", in R. Ettinghausen *et al.*, *The Islamic Garden* (Washington DC, 1976) 41–67 and 69–85, respectively; S. Bianca, *Hofhaus und Paradiesgarten. Architektur und Lebensformen in der islamischen Welt* (Munich, 1991) 108–23; T.S. Kawami, "Antike persische Gärten", in M. Carroll-Spillecke (ed.), *Der Garten von der Antike bis zum Mittelalter* (Mainz, 1992) 81–99; A.R. Littlewood, "Gardens of the Palaces", in H. Maguire (ed.), *Byzantine Court Culture from 829 to 1204* (Washington DC, 1997) 13–38.

[28] C. Schuler, *Ländliche Siedlungen und Gemeinden im hellenischen und römischen Kleinasien* (Munich, 1998) 123–5, does not offer anything new.

grandeur of the trees, the uniform distances at which they were planted, the straightness of the rows of the trees, the beautiful regularity of all the angles and the number and sweetness of the odours that accompanied them as they walked around".[29] Cyrus was not the only one to have *paradeisoi* in Sardis. Tissaphernes, the satrap of Sardis during Xenophon's Persian service, had a *paradeisos* in the same region, which he called Alcibiades because of the latter's charm.[30] His *paradeisos* contained a river and had been laid out at great expense with plants, meadows and "all other things that contribute to luxury and peaceful pleasure".[31] A Sardian third-century tax inscription also mentions the gift of two *paradeisoi*, which had once been given by King Antioch, to a temple.[32] Tissaphernes had another house in Tralles and recently published evidence suggests that he there also owned a *paradeisos*—in any case, epigraphical evidence attests to a place called Paradeisos there in the third century BC.[33]

Xenophon supplies additional information about specific *paradeisoi* in the *Anabasis*, the report of his wanderings as a mercenary in the Anatolian part of the Achaemenid Empire, which dates from the first decades of the fourth century. In Kelainai, the capital of Greater Phrygia, he saw the palace of Cyrus the Younger and "a large *paradeisos* full of wild animals, which he (Cyrus) hunted on horseback whenever he wanted to exercise himself and his horses.[34] The Maeander River flows through the middle of the *paradeisos*" (1.2.7). Further to the west Cyrus' army found the "very large and fine *paradeisos* with everything which the seasons produce" of Belesys, the satrap of Syria, which Cyrus had "chopped down"; the term clearly suggests the

---

[29] Xenophon, *Oeconomicus* 4.20–5 (quoted by Cicero, *De senectute* 17.59), translated by J. Thompson and B.J. Hayes. For Persian presence and influence in Lydia see N.V. Sekunda, "Achaemenid colonization in Lydia", *R. Et. Anc.* 87 (1985) 7–29; Briant, *Histoire*, 721–5.

[30] See also T. Petit, "Alcibiade et Tissapherne", *Les Études Classiques* 65 (1997) 137–51.

[31] Plutarch, *Alcibiades* 24; Diodorus Siculus 14.80.2 (quote).

[32] W.H. Buckler and D.M. Robinson, *Sardis* VII.1 (Leiden, 1932) no. I.1, 15, 16, cf. K. Atkinson, "A Hellenistic Land-conveyance", *Historia* 21 (1972) 45–74.

[33] Xenophon, *Hellenica* 3.2.12; *I. Tralles* 250.19, cf. R. Descat, "Le paradis de Tissapherne", *DATA. Achaemenid History Newsletter* 1, April (1992) Note 6. For other toponyms called *Paradeisos* see Tuplin, *Achaemenid Studies*, 99f.; add W. Günther, "Inschriften von Didyma", *Istanbuler Mitteilungen* 21 (1971) 97–108, no. 1.

[34] For Persian presence in Greater Phrygia see N.V. Sekunda, "Achaemenid settlement in Caria, Lycia and Greater Phrygia", in H. Sancisi-Weerdenburg and A. Kuhrt (eds.), *Achaemenid History* 6 (1991) 83–143; Briant, *Histoire*, 725–7.

presence of trees (1.4.10).[35] A similar type of *paradeisos*, "large, fine, and thick with all kind of trees", was situated in Babylon near the Tigris (2.4.14, 16).

Finally, in the work of his old age, the *Hellenica*, Xenophon lets us meet Pharnabazus, the hereditary satrap of Hellespontine Phrygia, in his capital Daskyleion.[36] Here the Persian had his palace and "very fine wild animals, some in enclosed *paradeisoi*, some in the open country. A river full of all kinds of fish ran past the place" (4.1.15–6). However, this idyllic area had not escaped the ravages of war, but, as Pharnabazus complains, "my father left me fine buildings and *paradeisoi* full with trees and wild animals, in which I delighted, but I see all of that cut down and burned down" (4.1.33).[37]

Our last example comes from the Roman antiquarian Gellius. When discussing the word *vivarium* he quotes Varro, the most learned Roman of the Late Republic, that "*vivaria*, the term now used for certain enclosures in which wild animals are kept alive and fed, were once called *leporaria*".[38] Of these *vivaria* Gellius adds that the Greeks call them *paradeisoi* (2.20.1, 4). We have no idea as to how Gellius acquired this knowledge, but given the paucity of references to wild animals in *paradeisoi* in the post-Achaemenid period he will have derived his information, directly or indirectly, from a Hellenistic, perhaps historiographical source.

What have we learned so far about these "paradises"? First, the passages in *Nehemiah* and the *Songs of Songs* seem to suggest that, in addition to the hunting *paradeisoi* attested by Xenophon, other meanings

---

[35] For Belesys see now M. Stolper, "The Babylonian Enterprise of Belesys", *Pallas* 43 (1995) 217–38.

[36] For recent excavations see D. Kaptan-Bayburthuoìglu, "A group of seal-impressions on the bullae from Ergili/Daskyleion", *Epigraphica Anatolica* 16 (1990) 15–26; T. Bakir, "Archäologische Beobachtungen über die Residenz in Daskyleion", *Pallas* 43 (1995) 268–85. For Persians in the region see N.V. Sekunda, "Persian settlement in Hellespontine Phrygia", in A. Kuhrt and H. Sancisi-Weerdenburg (eds.), *Achaemenid History* 3 (1988) 175–96; Briant, *Histoire*, 718–20; for Persian elements in adjacent Mysia see M. Cremer, *Hellenistisch-Römische Grabstelen im nordwestlichen Kleinasien* I (Bonn, 1991); N.V. Sekunda, "Itabelis and the Satrapy of Mysia", *Am. J. of Anc. Hist.* 14 (1989 [1998!]) 73–102.

[37] For the possible location of the *paradeisos* see L. Robert, *Les noms indigènes*, 348–9 and *A travers l'Asie Mineure* (Paris, 1980) 269; V. Manfredi, *La strade dei diecimila* (Milano, 1986) 37.

[38] For these Roman wild parks see F. Olck, "Gartenbau", *RE* 7 (Stuttgart, 1912) 768–841 at 838. Note also that Cicero uses the term *viridarium*, a "pleasure-garden", in the context of the *Cyropaedia* (*Att.* 2.3.2).

of Persian "paradise", such as orchard and place to grow trees, remained alive. Secondly, the early Greek *paradeisoi* are related to the Iranian ones only to a limited extent. They are not orchards, vineyards or storage-places—phenomena for which the Greeks of course had words of their own. On the other hand, as is stated explicitly in *Hellenica* 4.1.15, they were enclosed and in this respect they reflect their Iranian origin. Thirdly, they seem to be a relatively unknown phenomenon to the Greeks, since in his *Oeconomicus* Xenophon effectively glosses the term by saying that "there are parks, the so-called *paradeisoi*" wherever the king goes; in other passages the description sufficiently indicates the meaning of *paradeisos*.[39] Fourthly, these particular "paradises" were characterised by a modest size, vicinity to other ones,[40] the presence of animals, water (be it a river or a lake), the prominence of trees and, in general, by lush vegetation. Although such "paradises" have not yet turned up in Babylonian and Elamite texts, they were not absent from the Persian heartland, since the *paradeisos* in Susa was irrigated (Ctesias *FGrH* 688 F 34), and Cyrus' tomb in Pasargadae was situated in a *paradeisos* with a grove "with all sorts of trees and irrigated, and deep grass had grown in the meadow".[41] Fifthly, these *paradeisoi* were the possession of the highest Persian aristocracy.[42] Although he does not mention the term, Curtius Rufus clearly alludes to the *paradeisoi* when he calls the *magnos recessus amoenosque nemoribus manu consitis* of Media the *praecipua regum satraparumque voluptas* (7.2.22). They may therefore have become emblematic of Persian authority, as the choice by the Phoenicians in their revolt of 351 BC of the "royal *paradeisos*" for their first target seems to suggest.[43] Sixthly and finally, unlike the "paradise" in *Genesis*, the hunting *paradeisoi* were filled with wild animals and served the Persians to keep themselves into condition for war via hunting.

[39] As is observed by Tuplin, *Achaemenid Studies*, 120.

[40] So rightly Tuplin, *Achaemenid Studies*, 111, with more examples.

[41] Arrian, *Anabasis* 6.29.4 = Aristobulus *FGrH* 135 F 51, translated by P. Brunt, Loeb; D. Stronach, *Pasargadae* (Oxford, 1978) 108–12; *idem*, "The Royal Garden at Pasargadae: evolution and legacy", in L. de Meyer and E. Haerinck (eds.), *Archeologia Iranica et orientalis* (Ghent, 1989) 475–502; *idem*, "The garden as a political statement: some case studies from the Near East in the first millennium BC", *Bull. Asia Inst.* NS 4 (1990) 171–82; H. Koch, *Es kündet Dareios der König . . .* (Mainz, 1992) 265–6; Briant, *Histoire*, 98f.

[42] Tuplin, *Achaemenid Studies*, 110; add Suda, *S* 1681.

[43] Fauth, "Der königliche Gärtner", 7, overlooked by M. Miller, *Athens and Persia in the fifth century BC* (Cambridge, 1997) 124.

3. *The post-Achaemenid times*

After the fall of the Achaemenid empire the hunting *paradeisoi* quickly disappeared, since the hunt did not play the same role in the life of Alexander the Great and his successors as it did among the Persian magnates. Only the already quoted *paradeisoi* of Demetrius Poliorcetes in the immediate post-Achaemenid era still remind us of the traditional hunting *paradeisoi*. However, other *paradeisoi* continued to exist, but without the wild animals. We can note this change already fairly early in the third century, since in 246 BC the small Cretan polis of Itanos dedicated a "holy *temenos*" near the gate, presumably a kind of public garden, as *paradeisos* to Ptolemy III (246–221).[44] This surely was not a hunting park. Neither, presumably, were the *paradeisoi* attached to royal residences, which are mentioned in a late third-century papyrus from Tebtunis;[45] other combinations of palaces and parks, as listed below, clearly suggest that these *paradeisoi* were parks as well. In the third- and second-century *Septuagint*,[46] *paradeisos* is connected with water (*Numeri* 24.6; *Isaiah* 1.30) and trees (*Ezekiel* 31.8,9), strongly contrasted with the desert (*Isaiah* 51.3) and other desolate places (*Joel* 2.3),[47] and a sign of great wealth (*Ezekiel* 28.13), but nowhere do we hear about animals. In *Ecclesiastes*, which seems to date from the third century BC, Solomon says: "I have made me gardens and *pardesim*, and I planted trees in them of all kind of fruits" (2.5). As in the already mentioned case of the *Song of Songs*, modern translations use "orchard", and indeed, in modern Hebrew the word for "orchard" is *pardes*.

Early examples of "paradisiac" orchards probably occur in a demotic Egyptian text, which is a translation of a lost Greek original.

---

[44] *I. Creticae* III.IV.4.8. For this and similar donations see Ch. Habicht, *Gottmenschentum und griechische Städte* (Munich, 1970²) 121f, 146 n. 29; Gauthier, *Nouvelles inscriptions*, 61f. For such *temenê* see M. Carroll-Spillecke, *Kepos: Der antike griechische Garten* (Munich, 1989) 34–8; V. Karageorghis and M. Carroll-Spillecke, "Die heiligen Haine und Gärten Zyperns", in Carroll-Spillecke, *Der Garten*, 141–52.

[45] *P. Tebt.* 3.1.703.211f.: *tôn basilikôn oikêseôn kai tôn pros tautais paradeisôn.* Note also the *basilikos kêpos* in *PSI* V.488.12 (257 BC) and the gift of the Sardian *paradeisoi* by King Antioch (§ 2).

[46] For the date of the translation of the individual books of the *Septuagint* see M. Hengel, "Die Septuaginta als 'christliche Schriftensammlung', ihre Vorgeschichte und das Problem ihres Kanons", in M. Hengel and A.M. Schwemer (eds.), *Die Septuaginta zwischen Judentum und Christentum* (Tübingen, 1994) 182–284 at 236–51.

[47] The contrast of *paradeisos* and desert recurs in *P. Lond.* 2043; *UPZ* 114 I 10, II 10, 33, 37.

In this comprehensive survey of Egypt under Ptolemy II (308–246) in 258 BC a census was ordered of ". . . the embankments that are ploughed and cultivated, specifying orchard by orchard the trees with their fruits", that is, presumably, the various *paradeisoi*.[48] More orchards can be found in later documentary papyri from Egypt, which contain numerous references to *paradeisoi*.[49] These "paradises" will have been utilitarian gardens, since their avarage size is extremely small, mostly less than a hectare. It is therefore not surprising that we occasionally hear about them being sold or bought, such as the *paradeisoi* bought "from the state" (*P. Tebt.* I.5.99: 118 BC) or the "royal *paradeisos*" bought by an Apollonius in 235 BC (*P. Tebt.* III.1.701.175f.). Although these *paradeisoi* can supply a considerable amount of bricks,[50] they often contain various kinds of trees, from fig-trees to conifers, in addition to the fruit-trees. Olives and palms must have been common, since we regularly find an *elaiônoparadeisos*, a *phoinikoparadeisos* and, perhaps inevitably, an *elaiônophoinikoparadeisos*. These Egyptian *paradeisoi* normally also have basins and wells. The *Wisdom of Ben-Sira*, which was written in Egypt in the early second century BC and translated into Greek towards the end of the same century, well illustrates their irrigation by actually mentioning "a water channel into a *paradeisos*" (24.30). Although these smaller Egyptian *paradeisoi* do not contain rivers or possibilities for walking, they must have been attractive enough for *Ben-Sira* to state that "kindness" and "fear of the Lord" are "like a *paradeisos*" (40.17, 27).[51]

The connection of Solomon with *paradeisoi* in the *Song of Songs* and *Ecclesiastes* may have helped later generations to identify certain *paradeisoi* with those of famous kings. In any case, Josephus mentions that Solomon's *paradeisos* at Etan contained flowing streams (*AJ* 8.186)

---

[48] I quote from the English translation of a provisional Italian version in S. Burstein, *The Hellenistic Age from the battle of Ipsos to the death of Kleopatra VII* (Cambridge, 1985) 97f. The original text has now been published by E. Bresciani, *Egitto e Vicino Oriente* 6 (1983) 15ff., to be read with the important corrections by K.-Th. Zauzich, "Von Elephantine bis Sambehdet", *Enchoria* 12 (1984) 193f.

[49] These orchards may continue older Egyptian gardens, cf. C.J. Eyre, "The Water Regime for Orchards and Plantations in Pharaonic Egypt", *J. Egypt. Arch.* 80 (1994) 57–80. Add to his bibliography of Egyptian gardens (p. 58 n. 7): J.-C. Hugonot, "Ägyptische Gärten", in Carroll-Spillecke, *Der Garten*, 9–44, who stresses the erotic aspect of the "Lustgarten".

[50] *PCZ* 59825.14 mentions a consignment of 10,000 bricks.

[51] Tuplin, *Achaemenid Studies*, 97–99 (small size), 102 n. 79 (water), 104–5 (trees, word coinages).

and near Jerusalem there was a spring in King David's *paradeisos* (*AJ* 7.347), which was perhaps different from the royal "paradise" four stades from Jerusalem (*AJ* 9.225). Hyrcanus (135–104 BC) followed his royal "predecessors" or Ptolemaic contemporaries by constructing a *paradeisos* 17 km west of Amman, the present Araq el Emir (*AJ* 12.233).[52] Near Jericho there were also "very dense and beautiful *paradeisoi*" spread throughout an area of some 45 square kilometers with many nice trees, palms, cypresses and, especially, balsam.[53] And just as Xenophon enhanced the beauty of Pharnabazus' *paradeisos* by letting him bewail its loss, so Josephus illustrates the desolation of Judaea after the Jewish revolt by mentioning the Roman destruction of the *paradeisoi* (*BJ* 6.6).

Pardes also recurs in some Aramaic fragments of the Dead Sea scrolls. In an early second-century fragment of 1 Enoch we read about the *Pardes* of Justice, a place with many trees (4Q206 3 21 = 1 Enoch 32.3, also mentioned in 4Q209 23 9), including the Tree of Wisdom as we can read in the more fuller preserved Ethiopian version. And in a very fragmentary text from the *Book of Giants*, which dates of the time of the beginning of the first century,[54] there survives only a reference to "this *pardes*, all of it, and . . .", shortly before preceded by "its three roots" (6Q8 2 3), presumably of the one tree that survived the angelic cutting down of all the others.[55] However, none of these texts suggests the picture of a park with water, pavilions and walking amenities.

The latter possibility must have been a feature of at least some *paradeisoi* in the Hellenistic era, since the learned Byzantine bishop Photius defines *paradeisos* as: "a place for walking (*peripatos*) with trees and water" (*Lexicon* 383.2), which comes very close to the description of *Genesis*. As we have seen (§) Lysander walked with Cyrus the Younger in his *paradeisos*; in the book *Susanna*, which is perhaps to be dated to the later second century BC,[56] Susanna also walks in her

[52] P. Gentelle, "Un 'paradis' hellénistique en Jordanie, étude de géo-archéologie", *Hérodote* 4 (1990: *non vidi*); N. and P. Lapp, "Iraq el-Amir", in E. Stern (ed.), *New Encyclopaedia of Archaeological Excavations in the Holy Land* (New York, 1993) 646–9; Tuplin, *Achaemenid Studies*, 111f.

[53] Posidonius *FGrH* 87 F 70; Josephus, *BJ* 1.361, 4.467 and *AJ* 15.96.

[54] F. García Martínez, *Qumran & Apocalyptic* (Leiden, 1992) 114f.

[55] L.T. Stuckenbruck, *The Book of Giants from Qumran* (Leiden, 1997) 200–3.

[56] For *Susanna* see H. Engel, *Die Susanna-Erzählung* (Freiburg and Göttingen, 1985); A. de Halleux, "Une version syriaque révisée du commentaire d'Hippolyte sur

husband's *paradeisos* (7, 36), which was enclosed (17, 20) and even contained a place to bathe (15, 17). The presence of walking possibilities probably explains why Lucian called the Platonic Academy a *paradeisos* (*Vera Historia* 2.23) and why the Rhegion *paradeisos*, which had been planted by the tyrant Dionysius I of Syracuse, was turned into a gymnasium.[57] Photius adds that comic authors (*PCG* Adespota 523 Kassel-Austin) even used the term *paradeisos* for highly insensible individuals—people one could trample on. Unfortunately, he does not specify them, but we probably have to think of New Comedy, that is of post-Achaemenid times, since such walking possibilities are mentioned only once regarding the Xenophontic wild parks. Trees, as we have seen, were already an outstanding feature of the Persian *paradeisoi* and they would remain so all through ancient history, from Xenophon to the *Historia monachorum in Aegypto* and Procopius.[58] Even the talking trees met by Alexander in India were situated, naturally, in a *paradeisos*.[59]

In Roman times the *paradeisoi* became even more cultivated, as appears from the *paradeisoi* in the second-century Greek novels of Longus and Achilles Tatius. There are still springs and trees, both barren and fertile ones, but the landscape has become much more artificial. We now notice the presence of meadows and flowers planted in beds: roses, daffodils and hyacinths; instead of the wild animals of earlier times the "paradise" is now inhabited by swans, parrots and peacocks.[60] However attractive these parks had become, in Roman times the word remained a loanword for the Greeks and it was avoided by fanatic purists.[61]

Susanne" and "Hippolyte en version syriaque", *Le Muséon* 101 (1988) 33–40 and 102 (1989) 19–42, respectively.

[57] Theophrastus, *Historia plantarum* 4.5.6; Pliny, *Natural History* 12.71.

[58] Tuplin, *Achaemenid Studies* 104. Trees are also an outstanding feature of Greek utopian gardens: *Odyssey* 1.51; Hesiod, *Theogony* 216; Simonides 22.7 West^2; Pherecydes *FGrH* 3 F 16.

[59] *Historia Alexandri Magni* (L, ed. Von Thiel) 3.6.17, which is translated *paradisus* in Iulius Valerius, *Res gestae Alexandri Macedonii* 3.17.526 Rosellini, one of the very few Latin passages where *paradisus* means a profane park.

[60] Longus 4.2–4; Achilles Tatius 1.15, whose horticultural description is used in Byzantine times, cf. O. Schissel, *Der byzantinische Garten* (Vienna, 1942) 11–21; see also Aristaenetus 1.3.

[61] Scholion on Lucian, *Vera Historia* 2.23. For the practise of purism in Roman times see now C. Charalambakis, "Zum Sprachverfall in der griechischen Antike", in G.W. Most *et al.* (eds.), *Philanthropia kai Eusebeia. Festschrift für Albrecht Dihle zum 70. Geburtstag* (Göttingen, 1993) 36–45; S. Swain, *Hellenism and Empire* (Oxford, 1996) 17–64.

Admittedly, in the Roman period the Persian royal hunts were still remembered, but, interestingly, they were now quoted in a negative way. Apollonius of Tyana declined to join the Persian king in hunting in his *paradeisoi*, since it gave him no pleasure "to attack animals that have been ill-treated and enslaved against their nature" (1.37). Dio Chrysostom even lets the good king abhor the "Persian hunt", although he considers hunting an excellent preparation for war: "those people (the Persians) would enclose the game in *paradeisoi* and then, whenever they wanted to, killed the game as if it were in a pen, showing that they neither sought physical exercise or danger, since their game was weak and broken in spirit" (3.135–7). The thought is perhaps far-fetched, but is it totally impossible that in these protests against killing enslaved animals there is something of a hint at contemporary Roman *venationes*?

It cannot even be excluded that the detractors of the "Persian hunt" had heard about contemporary hunting *paradeisoi* further to the East, since an event in the Persian expedition of Julian the Apostate demonstrates that these had continued to exist. The historian Zosimus relates that in the neighbourhood of Meinas Sabatha, a city near the Naarmalcha canal which runs between the Euphrates and the Tigris, the Roman army came "to an enclosure which they called the 'King's Chase'. This was a large area enclosed by a small wall and planted with all kinds of trees, in which all sorts of wild animals were locked up. These received more than plenty of food and offered the king very easy opportunities for hunting whenever he wanted" (3.23.1–4). From the parallel notice in Libanius (18.243) we gather that the "*paradeisos*" was situated close by the palace. In fact, this is perhaps the best description of what a hunting *paradeisos* will have looked like with the obligatory elements of the enclosure, trees and wild animals, which Ammianus specifies as lions, bears and boars (24.5.1f.). The vicinity of the palace is already well attested in Xenophon (§ 2), in *Chronicles* (the case of Manasseh: § 4), in Ptolemaic Tebtunis (above), and in *Susanna* (Susanna's very wealthy husband's *paradeisos* is adjacent to his house: 4). The vicinity remained a feature of Persian grandees in the novel, where the combination of palace and *paradeisos* already points to the courtly parks of later Persian, Islamic and Byzantine magnates (note 27).[62]

---

[62] Tuplin, *Achaemenid Studies*, 110 compares Chariton 4.2.8 and Heliodorus 7.23.

Let us conclude our observations on Persian hunting with a few more observations. When the Persians started to conquer Greece, they occupied the islands of Chios, Lesbos and Tenedos, one after the other, and caught the people as with drag-nets in the following manner according to Herodotus: "having joined hands, the men stretch right across the island from north to south and then move over the whole of the island, hunting everybody out".[63] In this case the prey were people, but the great Swiss scholar Karl Meuli adduced a number of examples from early to early modern Chinese and medieval Mongolian sources to show that indeed Oriental rulers used their armies as enormous battues in order to surround large animals and kill them. By analogy we may presuppose similar battues for the Persians, since in a source neglected by Meuli, the *Sayings of the Desert Fathers*, we are told that Abba Milesius met two sons of the Persian king who had gone hunting "according to their custom. They spread nets around a wide area; at least forty miles, so as to be able to hunt and shoot everything that was found inside the nets".[64] The story has no need for beaters, but surely behind the two royal princes there must have been an army of Persians to chase the game into the nets. Herodotus uses the verb *sagêneuo* for the Persian tactic and indeed, the word *sagênê* is also used for the Greek hunt on the tuna-fish, again a tactic to catch as large a group of prey in the nets as possible.[65] In fact, hunting with nets was so important for the Persian aristocracy that the art of net (*sagênê*) making was part of their education (Strabo 15.3.18).

Meuli also observed that some of these Oriental rulers also made wild parks in order to hunt more at ease—understandably, since their "army hunts" could last up to four months. Consequently, he suggests that the Persians, too, had constructed their *paradeisoi* in connection with their battues. This conclusion is attractive but probably goes too far. The Oriental wild parks are only attested for the Middle Ages and were very large (the one of the son of Dzengish Khan, Ögädäi, had a circumference of two day-journeys), whereas the evidence we have strongly suggests that the average Persian *paradeisos*

[63] Herodotus 6.31. For the method see also *ibidem* 3.149; Plato, *Menexenos* 240b, *Laws* 3.698d; Appian, *Mithradates* 285; Herodian 6.5.9ff., cf. K. Meuli, *Gesammelte Schriften* II (Basel and Stuttgart, 1975) 699–729; Briant, *Histoire*, 310–11.
[64] *Apophthegmata Patrum*, in *Patrologia Graeca* 65, 298.
[65] Meuli, *Gesammelte Schriften* II, 725.

was much smaller and, at least to some degree, landscaped (§ 2).

It may be sufficient to draw only a few conclusions from this section. First, *paradeisoi* occurred mainly in areas once dominated by the Persian empire. Secondly, the variety of usage of the Iranian "paradise" survived the fall of the Achaemenid empire. Thirdly, with the disappearance of the Persian elite their hunting *paradeisoi* had vanished as well, except for the more eastern parts of the former empire. Fourthly, in the course of time the Graeco-Roman *paradeisos* became more and more artificial.

4. *Conclusion*

Before answering the question as to why the translator(s) of the *Septuagint*, in the third century BC, chose *paradeisos* to render the Hebrew *Gan Eden*, we have to solve one other problem. Why did the translators not prefer the equally possible Greek term *kêpos*, "garden"? Like the *paradeisos*, the *kêpos* is connected with water (*Isaiah* 1.29), but it is clearly simpler than the majestic *paradeisos* and only the place of "herbs" (*Deuteronomium* 11.10; 1 *Kings* 20.2). This is perhaps the reason that in 2 *Kings* (21.18) King Manasseh was buried in his *kêpos*, as apparently David (*Nehemiah* 3.16LXX), but in the third-century *Chronicles* (33.20) in his *paradeisos*, a version followed by Josephus (*AJ* 10.46).

This impression of greater simplicity is confirmed by what we know about the *kêpos* from other sources. Admittedly, Greek gardens have long been neglected, but recent investigations have considerably clarified their picture.[66] These gardens were primarily wanted for their productivity and closely connected with residential housing. They were small, walled, intensely cultivated and loved for their vegetables and flowers; moreover, their luxuriant growth often evoked sexual associations.[67] In other words, for the Jewish translators the word *kêpos* will have hardly conjured up the image of a royal park

---

[66] See Olck, "Gartenbau", 783–7; Carroll-Spillecke, *Kepos*, and "Griechische Gärten", in *eadem, Der Garten*, 153–75; R. Osborne, "Greek Gardens", in J.D. Hunt (ed.), *Garden History: Issues, Approaches, Methods* (Washington, 1992) 373–91.

[67] This is especially true for the meadow, cf. J.M. Bremer, "The meadow of love and two passages in Euripides" "*Hippolytus*", *Mnemosyne* IV 28 (1975) 268–80; S.R. Slings, in J.M. Bremer *et al., Some recently found Greek poems* (Leiden, 1987) 45; D.L. Cairns, "The Meadow of Artemis and the Character of the Euripidean *Hippolytus*", *Quad. Urb. Cult. Class.* 57 (1997) 51–75.

worthy of Jahweh.[68] That is probably also the reason that Alcinoos" Utopian garden in the *Odyssey* (7.114–31) is compared with paradise only once in the whole of early Christian literature.[69] Still, in some places the difference between *kêpos* and *paradeisos* may have been relatively small, and in first-century Tebtunis we actually find a *kêpoparadeisos*.[70]

But if the translators preferred *paradeisos*, which "paradise" did they have in mind: the Persian one (§ 1), the early Greek one (§ 2), or those in Ptolemaic and Roman Egypt or contemporary Palestine (§ 3)? We can most certainly discard the old Persian meanings of storage room or vineyard and the usage attested in Xenophon, since neither God nor Adam display any interest in hunting nor do they drink alcohol. We can almost certainly also neglect the *paradeisoi* of later Hellenistic and Roman Egypt, since they were too small, too simple and too utilitarian to be worthy of Jahweh. This leaves us the contemporary royal *paradeisoi* in Hellenistic times, as they are somewhat dimly visible in various descriptions: royal parks with many trees, suitable for walking, less wild than their Persian predecessors but more foresty than their later Roman descendants.

Such parks of course fit the time of the *Septuagint*, which started to be translated in Alexandria in the second quarter of the third century BC.[71] Unfortunately, our knowledge of early Alexandria is too sketchy to point with any certainty to a royal *paradeisos* in the time of Ptolemy II.[72] Yet there is a clear indication for an association of Jahweh's *paradeisos* with the world of the Ptolemies. A decade ago the papyrologist Geneviève Husson drew attention to the translation of *Gan Eden* in *Genesis* (3.23) as *paradeisos tês tryphês*.[73] As she

---

[68] For the kingly aspects of Jahweh see now A.M. Schwemer and M. Hengel (eds.), *Königsherrschaft Gottes und himmlischer Kult im Judentum, Urchristentum und in der Hellenistischen Welt* (Tübingen, 1991).

[69] As is observed by C. Riedweg, *Ps.-Justin (Markell von Ankyra?), Ad Graecos de vera religione (bisher "Cohortatio ad Graecos")* II (Basel and Berlin, 1994) 440.

[70] *PSI* VIII 917.5; *P. Mich.* V 282.3 (the same garden!).

[71] See most recently P.M. Fraser, *Ptolemaic Alexandria* I (Oxford, 1972) 689–94; E. Bickerman, *Studies in Jewish and Christian History* I (Leiden, 1976) 167–75; J. Mélèze Modrzejewski, *The Jews of Egypt: from Rameses II to Emperor Hadrian* (Princeton, 1997²) 99–106.

[72] G. Grimm, "City Planning?", in P. Green *et al.*, *Alexandria and Alexandrianism* (Malibu, 1996) 55–74.

[73] G. Husson, "Le paradis de délices (*Genèse* 3, 23–24)", *R. Et. Grecques* 101 (1988) 64–73. For the meaning of *'eden* see now J.C. Greenfield, "A Touch of Eden", *Acta Iranica* II 9 (Leiden, 1984) 219–34.

pointed out, *tryphê* was a term much used by the Ptolemaic monarchy to characterise its leisurely life with its prosperity and magnificence. Three kings were surnamed Tryphon and various princesses Tryphaena; in Roman times, *tryphê* even became synonymous with the "good life".[74] Clearly, the time of the Ptolemies was no longer the era of Cyrus with its physical hardship and sweat, but the world of wealth, leisure and luxury. Behind the *paradeisos* of the heavenly king in the *Septuagint* version of *Genesis*, there loom the cultivated *paradeisoi* of the all too earthly rulers of contemporary Egypt.

Appendix: "Paradise" in Cyprus

According to the *Etymologicum Magnum*, the Cypriots had their own term for a "paradise": *ganos: paradeisos hypo de Kypriôn* (223.47). The lemma (223.42ff.) derives from the *Etymologicum Gudianum* (300.16–20 De Stefani), which in turn derives from the Middle Byzantine *Lexicon aimôdein* (gamma 3 b–8 Dyck), which explains Agathias, *Hist.* 2.28, although this passage does not contain the "Cypriot" information.[75] On Cyprus, the term perhaps occurs in *ICS* 309.12 (*ka-no-se*);[76] another possibility may be an inscription from Mytilene (*IG* XII.2.58.(a) 17). Traces of the same lemma occur in Hesychius, s.v. *ganos: paradeisos*, which Kurt Latte, its most recent editor, assigned to Diogenianus, on the basis of the occurrence of the same explanation in the *Etymologicum Magnum* (223.47) and the indication of the dialect. Although such a conclusion is valid for some cases, it is not correct in this particular one, since the lemma in the *Etymologicum Magnum* certainly derives from the *Etymologicum Gudianum* and the lemma in Hesychius must derive from Cyril's glossary.[77] We may also note Hesychius s.v.

[74] Cf. A. Passerini, "La *tryphe* nella storiografia ellenistica", *St. It. Filol. Class.* 11 (1934) 35–6; J. Tondriau, "La *tryphe*, philosophie royale ptolémaique", *R. Et. Anc.* 50 (1948) 49–54; H. Heinen, "Aspects et problèmes de la monarchie ptolemaïque", *Ktema* 3 (1978) 177–99 at 188–92; P. Briant, "Histoire et idéologie. Les Grecs et la 'décadence perse'," in M.-M. Mactoux and E. Geny (eds.), *Mélanges Pierre Lévêque* II (Paris, 1989) 33–47. "Good life": L. Robert, *Hellenica* 13 (1965) 187f.

[75] We now know that the lexicon was called *Etymologiai diaphoroi*, cf. A.R. Dyck, *Epimerismi Homerici* II (Berlin and New York, 1995) 846.

[76] Cf. O. Masson, *Les inscriptions chypriotes syllabiques* (Paris, 1983^2). Unfortunately, the text is mutilated and was destroyed during the Second World War.

[77] W. Bühler, *Gnomon* 42 (1970) 342, had already observed that Latte underestimated Cyril.

ganea: kêpous and *Etymologicum genuinum* s.v. *ganos*, where the term is paraphrased with *gê*, "earth" (= *Etymologicum Magnum* 221.18ff.).

The conclusion seems to be that the Cypriots had derived their term *ganos*, like some other words,[78] from their long Phoenician association.[79] Its meaning was evidently glossed by some lexicographers from a context (contexts?) which now escapes us.[80]

[78] Cf. E. Masson, *Recherches sur les plus anciens emprunts sémitiques en Grec* (Paris, 1967) 70–6.

[79] Cf. G. Markoe, *Phoenician Bronze and Silver Bowls from Cyprus and the Mediterranean* (Berkeley, Los Angeles, London, 1985) 7f. For Cyprus in Persian times see J. Wiesehöfer, "Zypern unter persischer Herrschaft", in Sancisi-Weerdenburg and Kuhrt, *Achaemenid History* 4, 239–52; Tuplin, *Achaemenid Studies*, 9–79.

[80] For information I am much indebted to my friends and colleagues Klaus Alpers, Stefan Radt, Gerrit Reinink, Marten Stol, Eibert Tigchelaar and Jos Weitenberg. Peter van Minnen helpfully commented on the penultimate version and Bob Fowler kindly corrected the English.

GAN-EDEN IN THE CONTEXT OF THE MYTHOLOGY OF THE HEBREW BIBLE

ED NOORT

1. *Introduction*

The loanword "paradise", from the Median[1] **pari-daeza*, "enclosure", finds its way with the same meaning into New Babylonian as *pardēsu*[2] and into Late Biblical Hebrew as *prds*.[3] There too it is used in a secular way.[4] The use of *prds* as an enclosed garden is represented by Qoh 2:4–5 where the king "did great things: I built myself palaces, planted vineyards, made myself gardens and *prdsym*, planting every kind of fruit tree in them". *Prdsym* is traditionally translated as "orchards", which fits with the last part of the sentence and represents the tradition of the Ancient Near Eastern "royal gardens". The LXX uses παράδεισος for Hebrew *gn*, *gnh*, *ʿdn*, and *prds*. The shift to a more religious meaning as the garden of the gods in the history of reception occurred when the LXX used παράδεισος as a translation for all the terms for *gan Eden*, the garden of primeval times in Gen 2–3[5] and the garden of God in Ez 28 and 31.[6] παράδεισος took on the connotation of the garden of God.

The Hebrew expression *gn-ʿdn* has its own difficulties. Probably the root *ʿdn* is connected with *ʿdn* I "delight",[7] here used in a geographical way as a "land of delight". In this way the Vg translates *gn-ʿdn* with "paradisus voluptatis". The popular derivation from Akkadian *edinu* "desert"[8] must be discarded.

---

[1] For a discussion of the linguistic, etymological and semantic background and the history of reception of the term, see J.N. Bremmer, "Paradise: From Persia, via Greece, to Israel" in this volume.

[2] *AHW* II, Wiesbaden 1972, 833a; III, Wiesbaden 1981, 1582a.

[3] *HAL* III, Leiden 1983, 907a.

[4] Cant 4:13; Neh 2:8; Qoh 2:5 (plural). For an overview of the connection of the late secular *paradeisoi* with the mythological motives of Ancient Mesopotamia see: W. Fauth, "Der königliche Gärtner und Jäger im Paradeisos: Beobachtungen zur Rolle des Herrschers in der Vorderasiatischen Hortikultur", *Persica* 8 (1979) 19–31.

[5] Gen 2:8.9.10.15.16; 3:1.2.3.8 (2x).10.23.24.

[6] Ezek 28:13; 31:8 (2x).9.

[7] Ps 36:9.

[8] *HAL* III, Leiden 1983, 749 in a correction of *KBL*, Leiden 1958, 684.

In the Hebrew Bible *ʿdn* is used in different combinations.[9] It appears as *gn-bʿdn mqdm* (Gen 2:8), "a garden in Eden, in the east". When *qdm* is taken here not only in a spatial sense of "far away, but in a temporal sense too, the garden in Eden is planted both 'far away' and 'in the pre-time'".[10] The second combination is *gn-ʿdn*[11] and is especially connected with the story of the expulsion from the garden. Only *ʿdn* is used several times.[12] *ʿdn* with the appositional *gn-ʾlhym*, "(in) Eden, the garden of God, . . ." appears in Ezek 28:13. Ezek 31:9 mentions *kl-ʿṣy-ʿdn ʾšr bgn hʾlhym*, "[all] the Eden trees in the garden of God". What is meant in Gen 3:7 (JHWH Elohim walks in his garden) is said expressively in Ezekiel. The garden is the garden of God. From here the question of a possible relationship between Gen and Ezek grows important.

2. *Ezekiel 28*

In this chapter, which is important regarding the garden of God, two interpretations for this divine garden have played an important role. The oracle of the King of Tyre in Ezek 28 has been understood "either as a description of the fall of a heavenly *k^erûb*, Satan or Lucifer, or as a variant of the story of Gen 2–3".[13] The crux is the interpretation of *ʾt-krwb mmšḥ hswkk*[14] *wnttyk*[15] from v. 14.

In one interpretation, MT is read. *ʾt* as a feminine singular[16] should be taken as an (unusual, but possible)[17] form of the masculine sec-

---

[9] Cl. Westermann, *Genesis* (BKAT I/1), Neukirchen 1974, 284–287.

[10] E.J. van Wolde, *A Semiotic Analysis of Genesis 2–3: A Semiotic Theory and Method of Analysis Applied to the Story of the Garden of Eden* (SSN 25), Assen/Maastricht 1989, 146–147, n. 28.

[11] Gen 2:10(?).15; 3:23.24; Ezek 36:35; Joel 2:3.

[12] Gen 4:16; Isa 51:3; Ezek 31:9.16.18 (2x).

[13] J.E. Miller, "The Maelaek of Tyre (Ezekiel 28:11–19)", *ZAW* 105 (1993) 497–501.

[14] *hswkk* is used as the technical terminus for the cherubim covering, protecting the *kprt* (Ex 25:20) in the *ʾhl mwʿd*, stretching their wings. The priestly theology makes a distinction between *yšb hkrwbym* of the temple in Jerusalem, where the cherubim, not the ark, function as a throneseat for YHWH, and YHWH "meeting" (*yʿd* nif.) and "speaking to" (*dbr*) Moses, as B. Janowski, *Sühne als Heilsgeschehen: Studien zur Sühnetheologie der Priesterschrift und zur Wurzel KPR im Alten Orient und im Alten Testament* (WMANT 55), Neukirchen-Vluyn 1982, 345 correctly states.

[15] Postposition of the verb after emphatic *waw* in the sense of "to appoint" (Jer 1:5; Ezek 33:7). *waw* should not be deleted (BHS app.).

[16] The continuation is masculine.

[17] Num 11:15; Deut 5:27 etc.

ond person pronoun or be vocalized as *ʾattā*:[18] "*You* are the wing-spread[19] *krwb*. I appointed you as the 'guardian'". The king of Tyre is described as the primeval *krwb*, who functioned as a "guardian" in the garden of God. After his sin (v. 16) he is cast out into Sheol. This *krwb* is the only living being in the garden of God and in this way a myth of a fallen cherub is reconstructed.

In the second interpretation, the shorter and different reading of the LXX: μετὰ τοῦ χερουβ ἔθηκά[20] σε ἐν ὄρει ἁγίῳ θεοῦ, "*With* the cherub I positioned you on the holy mountain of God" is (partly) taken as the original text. The LXX has *ʾatt* understood as *ʾet*. In this way the king of Tyre is not compared with the cherub, but with a companion who was *with* the cherub. This companion could be the prototypical human being and these two together in the Garden of God, in *gn-ʿdn*, bring the paradise stories of Gen 2–3 and Ezek 28 close together.

The decision as to which line should be preferred must be taken after the interpretation of v. 16. The first interpretation is defended by van Dijk and others: "By the abundance of your trade you have filled yourself with injustice and you have sinned. And I shall strike you down, away from the mountain of God, and I shall destroy you, O Guardian Cherub, out of the stones of fire".[21] The second position is put forward by Zimmerli, who translates: "Through the abundance of your trade <you filled> your heart with violence and sinned. Then I thrust you away from the mountain of God into uncleanness, and the guardian cherub <drove you into destruction> out of the midst of the stones of fire".[22] The main difference is clear. In the first view the guardian cherub is the sinner and God drives him out of his garden. In the second part of the verse the cherub is taken

---

[18] H.J. van Dijk, *Ezekiel's Prophecy on Tyre (Ez. 26:1–28:19): A New Approach* (BibOr 20), Rome 1968, 119–120.

[19] The problem of *mmšḥ* is unsolved. The root is either *mšḥ* II which fits the Vg "extentus" and is supported by Ugaritic: "Your wings of strength, O Lady Anat, your wings of strength Baal will spread out (*ymšḥ*), Baal will spread them out (*ymšḥ*) for flight". See M. Dahood, "Ugaritic Lexicography", *Mélanges E. Tisserant* I, Rome 1964, 95; van Dijk, *Prophecy*, 119 reading *mamšuḥ*. The second possibility is *mšḥ* III "to shine" (*HAL* II, 564).

[20] τίθημι for *ntn*. So: Ezek 4:1.3.6; 5:14; 6:14; 14:3; 16:18.19.38; 19:9; 25:13; 30:24; 32:27; 35:9; 43:8.

[21] Van Dijk, *Prophecy*, 93.121.

[22] Zimmerli, *Ezekiel* 2:86.

as a vocative. The second view sees the "companion" as the sinner and the guardian cherub is the executioner of the punishment.

Though there are some textual difficulties it seems clear that the MT has indeed the first position in mind. V. 16b reads: *wʾbdk krwb hskk mtwk ʾbny-ʾš*. The Pi. *wʾbdk* comes from the original *wʾʾbdk*[23] and "according to this, the king of Tyre, as in v. 14, is himself addressed as a cherub. This is how the MT takes it".[24] Again the difference is made by the LXX which reads: ἐτραυματίσθης ἀπὸ ὄρους τοῦ θεοῦ, καὶ ἤγαγέν σε τὸ χερουβ ἐκ μέσου λίθων πυρίνων, "You (the King of Tyre) were wounded, away from the mountain of God and the cherub drove you out of the midst of the stones of fire". There is no doubt that the MT sees the cherub as the object of being driven out of the mountain of God in the last part of the sentence, while the LXX sees the cherub as the subject of this action. In this way there is no "better" reading. The MT and the LXX have clearly different concepts. Both versions work with certain motifs of a paradise myth. Some of these motifs have a relation with Gen 2–3, others are more general. By and large it can be stated that it is the LXX and not the MT which suggests a direct relationship with Gen 2–3. The paradise myth of the MT of Ezekiel has its own background.

2.1 *The motif in Ezekiel 28: Being like a god*

To demonstrate some of the motifs, we start with Ezek 28:2: "Son of man, say to the Prince (*ngyd*) of Tyre: Thus has [the Lord] YHWH said: Because your heart has been presumptuous and you have said: "God I am (*ʾl ʾny*), I sit on the seat of the gods in the midst of the sea", whereas you are a man and not a god, but in your mind you have thought that you were like a god". The basic attitude of the Prince of Tyre is pride, to be like a god. It is repeated in v. 6 and 9. The same motif, but in a different way, is used in Gen 3:5. There, at the end of the dialogue between the woman and the snake, the snake promises: "You will be like God (*whyytm kʾlhym*), knowing good and evil". Most commentators see here "man's basic falsehood and his original sin".[25] But the myth of Gen 3 touches another point.

[23] H. Bauer, P. Leander, *Historische Grammatik der hebräischen Sprache*, Halle 1922 (Reprint: Hildesheim 1965), § 53m.

[24] Zimmerli, *Ezekiel* 2:86.

[25] Zimmerli, *Ezekiel* 2:77.

After having eaten from the fruit of the tree of knowledge of good and evil, YHWH Elohim himself states: "See, man has become one of us (*hyh kʾḥd mmnw*), knowing good and evil" (3:22). Here, it is not man himself who tries to be like a god—that motif is only present in the eating—but the statement is made twice from outside: one time from the snake, the second time by YHWH Elohim. So the snake was right!

2.2 *The priestly language*

After "You were in Eden, the garden of God" at the beginning of v. 13 and the middle part with the precious stones, either as a hedge, c.q. fence[26] around the wonderful garden or more likely as a part of the garment[27] of the mythical being, the expression *bwm hbrʾk*, "on the day you were created", is used. It is repeated in v. 15, specified with *tmym ʾth bdrkyk*, "blameless (were) you on your way". The verb

[26] Van Dijk, *Prophecy*, 116 argues that the pointing of *msktk* (without dagesh forte) makes it likely that the root is *swk*, not *skk*. The former can signify "to hedge about". Van Dijk refers to an article by W.E. Barnes, "Ezekiel's Denunciation of Tyre (Ez 26–28)", *JTS* 25 (1934) 50–54, who finds the same usage in Gen 33:17 and Job 1:10. He adds Mic 7:4: *mswkh*, "hedge, fence", Prov 15:19 and Isa 5:5. Barnes, "Denunciation", 51–52, quoted by van Dijk, *Prophecy*, 117 explains the equation: "The connection between temple and garden is quite obvious to the Eastern mind. A temple in the Ancient East was not a building but a sacred enclosure round a (small) shrine. The earliest Semitic sanctuaries were gardens planted in oases where the unexpected fertility of the soil suggested to the Semite the presence of a beneficent deity. The Solomonic temple preserved the meaning of Eden, the garden-sanctuary, for its walls were adorned with figures of guardian cherubim (Gen 3:24), palm trees and flowers (1 Kgs 6:29.32)". Van Dijks refers for the connection of temple and garden to Pss 116:19; 135:2; 92:14. The problem of this equation is the view on the oldest forms of sanctuaries and the role of nomads. This does not mean that Eden can only be understood from the secular tree- and hunting garden from Persian and Greek times. Even the hunting of the kings in Egypt and Mesopotamia has deep mythological, religious roots. Wild beasts represent chaos. The hunting king demonstrates his power over this chaos. Only in this way can one explain the reliefs of Egyptian and Assyrian kings where battle and hunting scenes are shown together (E. Noort, *Die Seevölker in Palästina*, Kampen 1994, 62–66). Therefore the religious, mythological background of the garden and mountain of God in the Ancient Near East is too strong to understand them in a purely secular way. There is indeed a relationship between creation-garden-temple, but only in this triangle.

[27] That the first interpreters of the Ezekiel text understood the precious stones of the *mskh* as a part of a garment is sustained by the additions of the stones. They add the first two and fourth rows of jewels from the *ḥšn* of the high priest of Ex 28:17–20 to connect them with the row of the stones of Ezek 28. All the versions, with a minor exception, pay heed to this parallelism between Ex 28 en Ezek 28. See Zimmerli, *Ezekiel* 2:82.

used for "to create" (*br'*) belongs to the cultic, priestly language, where it occurs in the story of creation in Gen 1 and in Second-Isaiah.[28] Moreover to be *tmym* returns in the beginning of the Priestly Codex of the Flood with the characterization of Noah (Gen 6:9). In that version his being *tmym*, "blameless" is the reason for his being rescued from the waters of the flood.

In Ezekiel *tmym* marks the state of the mythical being until his "fall". It has always been noticed that the Priestly Codex does not know a story of the fall of man. Man is created and blessed and the blessing is demonstrated by the continuation of the story of creation in the genealogy of Gen 5. Without a narrative of guilt and sin the Priestly account starts in Gen 6:9, the Story of the Flood. The question remains whether the Yahwistic account of Gen 2–3 in the final redaction of the primeval history replaced a priestly version of man, who becomes guilty. Now it is remarkable that Ezekiel knows such a narrative and uses it in his own judgement oracle against the Prince of Tyre. Not only the signal words *br'* and *tmym* for the positive aspect are used, but in v. 16 *mlw*[29] *twkk ḥms*, "'your midst' was full of violence" appears. In the Priestly account of the Flood, the being *tmym* was the reason for the rescue of Noah, and in Gen 6:11 *wtml' h'rṣ ḥms*, "the earth was filled of violence" is the reason for the coming of the flood. In both narratives, the story of the Flood and Ezek 28, the same keywords *tmym* and *ḥms* are used.[30]

This brings us to an interesting phenomenon. The LXX tries to connect the judgement oracle against the king of Tyre with the existing story of the Yahwistic account of Gen 2–3. But the priest-prophet Ezekiel uses the same language as the later priestly version of the story of the flood does. Maybe he demonstrates the background of a narrative story which fills the gap of the "fall" of man in the primeval priestly story.

---

[28] *br'* in Second-Isaiah demonstrates influence from the cultic use in the Psalms.

[29] See app. BHS. The MT has been vocalized as a plural: "they filled", which does not fit. After ἔπλησας of the LXX, *millē'tā* could be read. The better solution is to repoint *mlw* as inf.abs. used as a finite verb. See L.C. Allen, *Ezekiel 20–48* (WBC 29), Dallas 1990, 91.

[30] After Zimmerli, *Ezekiel*, 86:93 it is a later hand which adds the formula-like "full of violence" after Ezek 7:23; 8:17; 12:19. There is no imperative need for this judgement.

2.3 *The mountain of God and the geography of Paradise*

Following v. 14. and again v. 16, Paradise in Ezek 28 is associated with the common Ancient Near Eastern motif of the "the holy[31] mountain of God". Here, the background of the Mesopotamian and Canaanite mythology becomes visible. In the related text Isa 14:13–14, the foreign king states: "I will ascend to heaven, higher than the stars of El I will set my throne. I will sit on the Mount of Assembly on the crests of Safon. I will ascend above the heights of the clouds and make myself like the Most High".[32] In this text an interesting mixture appears of the heights of Safon (Ug. *mrym ṣpn*) as the residence of Baal and the mountain of assembly of the gods, connected with El, the head of the pantheon.[33] The intermingling of the dwelling places of Baal and El is not a specific point of the Isaiah-text, but it mirrors the different conceptions in the Ugaritic texts. Though a development in the myths of Ugarit can be noticed, it is more probable that the motifs could be mixed than that the text mirrors the ascent of Baal and the descent of El.

In the specific Israelite traditions the mountain of God was Sinai (Ex 3:1; 18:5; 24:13). With the growing importance of Jerusalem, Zion took over the function of the mountain of God. It was here that Canaanite traditions were used to express the seat of YHWH in Jerusalem. Ps 48:3 reads *hr ṣywn yrkty ṣfwn qryt mlk rb*, "the mountain of Zion, crests of the North (Safon), city of the Great King". Here Safon appears and Ps 46:5 even states that "there is a river, whose streams refresh the city of God, it sanctifies the dwelling of the Most High". Again the conceptions of the holy mountain and the dwelling of the Most High at the primeval river are mixed. Only in this intermingling of Canaanite mythological concepts with Jerusalem

[31] The only reason to see *qdš* as an addition, is that it is metrically superfluous and appears redundant alongside v. 16 (Zimmerli, *Ezekiel* 2:85). But *qdš* is well attested from a text critical point of view. The metrical point is uncertain because of the character of the reconstruction of the original poem. The language of Ezekiel offers many variations in the same expressions.

[32] See K. Spronk, *Beatific Afterlife in Ancient Israel and in the Ancient Near East* (AOAT 219), Neukirchen-Vluyn 1986, 213–227; *id.* "Down with Hêlēl! The Assumed Mythological Background of Isa. 14:12", in: M. Dietrich, I. Kottsieper (Hrg.), *"Und Mose schrieb dieses Lied auf". Studien zum Alten Testament und zum Alten Orient. Festschrift für Oswald Loretz*, Münster 1998, 717–726.

[33] Spronk, *Afterlife*, 215, n. 2.

can the expressions of "Zion, on the crests of the North" and the not present river[34] in Jerusalem be explained.

This last concept, the connection of the mythological river with Paradise, can be found in Gen 2:10–14 too. The text reads: (10) "And a river flows out (*yṣ᾽ m*) of Eden to water the garden and from there it divides (*mšm yprd*) to make four streams. (11) The first is named the Pishon, it is the one which flows around the whole land of Havilah where there is gold. 12) The gold of this land is pure. Bdellium and onyx stones are found there. (13) The second river is named Gihon and this encircles the whole land of Cush. (14) The third river is named Tigris, it flows to the east of Assur. And the fourth river is the Euphrates".

In the stories of Gen 2–3 Paradise is not located; it is far away. But in this mythic-geographical fragment, probably a learned addition to the original text, a (partial) localization is tried. Localization[35] however, is not the only intention. The text offers a graduation in the reverse direction, from "well known" to "unknown", from geography to myth, from the short communication of the familiar Euphrates to a broad description of the land of gold. The well known river Euphrates gets only one half verse, only four words: *whnhr hrbyʿy hw᾽ prt*. So does the river Tigris (*ḥdql*) further east. The Tigris has one half verse too, but there is an apposition: *hw᾽ hhlk qdmt ᾽šwr*, "it flows to the east of Assur". The next river, Gihon, has one verse of its own. And the river Pishon gets two verses.

The discussion about v. 14, whether the capital of Assyria, Assur, or the land of Assur is meant, can be decided in favour of the city. The land of Assur is situated east and west of the river and does not fit the *qdmt* of the text. The critical remark that countries, not cities are mentioned in 2:10–14, is not a strong argument. The other regions are vaguely described. The expression *qdmt* fits the best if the city is meant, for the river flows east (or "in front of") the city. The capital had lost its main function by the first millennium and from the 9th century on other Assyrian capitals came into being: Nimrūd (Kalchu); Dūr Šarrukîn (Chorsabad) and Ninivé. In spite of

---

[34] The identification of the Gihon spring as the river from Ps 46 does not make sense.

[35] For a summing up and evaluation of the older exegetical positions, see: W.H. Gispen, "Genesis 2:10–14", in: *Studia biblica et semitica Theodoro Christiano Vriezen qui munere professoris theologiae per XXV annos functus est, ab amicis, collegis, discipulis dedicata*, Wageningen 1966, 115–124.

these political facts, the famous name of Assur was maintained in the first millennium too. Sennacherib rebuilt the temple of Assur, Salmanassar III did the same with the Ištar temple. The Sîn-Šamaš temple was renewed by Assurnaṣirpal and Sennacherib. Tiglat-Pileser I built a new Anu-Adad temple. The Assyrian kings Assurbelkala, Assurnaṣirpal II, and Šamši Adad V were buried here. In the first millennium the name Assur was still a famous one; it might be used here as *pars pro toto*.

The real problems start with the Gihon from v. 13. Normally, Gihon is the main spring in Jerusalem,[36] but because of the description "it encircles the whole land of Cush", this cannot be meant. "Gihon" is rendered Γηων by the LXX. This brings us to Jer 2:18, where the MT reads *mh-lk ldrk mṣrym lštwt my šḥwr wmh lk ldrk ʾšwr lštwt my nhr*, "What is the good of going to Egypt now, to drink the water of Šiḥor and what is the good of going to Assur, to drink the water of the Euphrates?"[37] In an unpublished article A. Alt points out that "to drink the water of X" is a political expression, meaning a relationship of dependence.[38] In this case, it aims at the situation of the dying Assyrian Empire before 612 BC and the renewed claims of Egypt for political hegemony in the Levante. From here the *my šḥwr* stands *pars pro toto* for Egypt. The Hebrew expression *šiḥōr* is derived from Egyptian *š(j)-ḥr*, "pond of Horus" and means waters in the eastern part of the delta of Egypt. Because it is used in descriptions of boundaries, together with the *mn-ʿd* formula,[39] the change to a more general meaning, in later times as an expression for the Nile, was possible.[40] So the LXX translates Γηων, the expression of Gen 2:13 for Jer 2:18 *šḥwr*. The LXX did not see a difference between Gihon and Šihor. In Sir 24:25–27 wisdom brims over like famous rivers and here Pishon, Tigris, Euphrates, Jordan and Γηων are mentioned. Most probably the Nile is meant again.[41] That the Nile was favoured by later exegesis can be demonstrated by Josephus:

[36] 1 Kgs 1:33.38.45; 2 Chr 32:30; 33:14. Probably the name *gḥn* is derived from *gyḥ* or *gwḥ*, "to break loose".

[37] *nhr* without article in the OT means generally the Euphrates.

[38] A. Alt, Ägyptologische Lesefrüchte zum Alten Testament: Zu Jer 2,18 (Manuskript), in: S. Herrmann, *Jeremia* (BK XII/2), Neukirchen-Vluyn 1990, 132–134.

[39] Jos 13:3.

[40] See Isa 23:3 with its parallelism of *šḥr//yʾwr* (Nile) and the excursus of S. Herrmann, *Jeremia*, 136.

[41] W.H. Gispen, *Genesis* I (COT), Kampen 1974, 117.

Γηὼν δὲ διὰ τῆς Αἰγύπτου ῥέων. . . . ὃν δὴ νεῖλον ἕλληνες προσαγορεύουσιν. . . .[42] "Γηων flows through Egypt . . . the Greeks call him the Nile".

There are two arguments in favour of the Nile as the Gihon of Gen 2:13. First, when the big rivers of antiquity are mentioned, the Nile cannot be missed. Second, the land of Cush means in the great majority of the Old Testament texts the land south of Egypt:[43] Nubia and Ethiopia (LXX: Αἰθιοπία). But in spite of this, there is a strong, decisive argument against it too. If the Nile was meant, it is strange that the usual name, *(h)y'r*, does not appear here in opposition to the other famous rivers of antiquity, Euphrates and Tigris. In the table of nations in Gen 10:8 an interpolation in the main text reads: "Now Cush fathered Nimrod". Cush stands here for the Cassites from western Iran.[44] This opens the possibility of understanding the Gihon in connection with Cush as one of the rivers or canals of East Mesopotamia. Later interpreters, influenced by the political map of their time, relocated Gihon and gave it a place in Egypt.

The unknown Pishon[45] of v. 11 encircles the land of Havilah.[46] The other OT texts point in the direction of Arabia.[47] Traditionally Havilah is associated with the large tribal federation of *Haulān* in South-West Arabia, but Knauf has suggested that the name could have survived in the North Arabian town *ḥā'il*.[48] The geographical terminology is not complete enough for an exact localization, so most explanations combine biblical and classical literary dates with historical and legendary places, which yield gold. So Pishon stands here either for the Red Sea and the Persian Gulf, "which encircle the land of Havilah" or an unknown river in Arabia. This Havilah is the land where good gold is found as well as bdellium and onyx stones. Bdellium is an aromatic substance, but the LXX translates ἄνθραξ, a precious stone, making a correspondence again with the

---

[42] Fl. Josephus, *Ant.* I 3 39.

[43] Isa 11:11; 20:3.5; Jer 13:23; 46:9 etc.

[44] E.A. Speiser, *Genesis* (AB), New York 1969, 20.

[45] From *pwš*, "to leap", see *HAL* III, Leiden 1983, 870.

[46] *ḥwylh* as a personal name is either a son of Cush (Gen 10:7//1 Chr 1:9) or a son of Joktan (Gen 10:29//1 Chr 1:23). As a place it is used as a border point for the Ishmaelites (Gen 25:18), 1 Sam 15:7 transfers it to the Amelekites.

[47] J. Simons, *The Geographical and Topographical Texts of the Old Testament: A concise commentary in XXXII Chapters* (Studia Francisci Scholten Memoriae dicata 2) Leiden 1959, 40–41.

[48] E.A. Knauf, *Ismael* (ADPV), Wiesbaden 1985, 64.

gold and jewels of Ex 28 and Ezek 28. "They were widely used in decorating the tabernacle and temple . . . and in the high-priestly vestments . . . Paradise in Eden and the tabernacle/temple share a common symbolism".[49] Moreover, the four streams going out from Eden share a common background in the iconography of the Ancient Near East. The oldest proof is a wallpainting in the palace of Mari from the 18th century BC. In a panel flanked by two trees and cherubs, two goddesses each hold a vase with a tree or plant from which four water streams with fishes rush out.[50] From the new palace in Assur (13th century BC?) comes an ivory with the mountain god holding a vase where four water streams are poured out, probably flanked by trees and a winged lion.[51] And even later in the 8/7th century BC we find the same motif of the four water streams combined with priests drawing water on a relief, again in Assur.[52]

Summing up, Gen 2:10–14 presupposes the primeval river rising in Eden and splitting up into four branches. The last two are well known: Euphrates and Tigris.[53] Using these rivers, familiar to every reader, the text suggests that "Eden is somewhere in Armenia near the sources of the Euphrates and Tigris".[54] However, if Havilah is understood as (a part of) Arabia, and the Gihon and Cush as a part of Egypt, this first impression cannot persist. There are two solutions.

The first solution suggests that the rivers do not split up after Eden, but converged in Eden before entering the garden.[55] In this

---

[49] G.J. Wenham, *Genesis*, 65.

[50] M.Th. Barrelet, "Une peinture de la cour 106 du palais de Mari", *Studia Mariana*, Paris 1950, 9–35.

[51] W. Andrae, *Das wiederauferstandene Assur*, zweite, durchgesehene und erweiterte Auflage heruasggeben von B. Hrouda, München 1977, 163–164, Pl. 143.

[52] A. Parrot, *Assur*, Paris 1969, 74, Pl. 82–83.

[53] These main rivers of Mesopotamia are associated with creation in Akkadian mythology too. When in Atrahasīs the Annunaki make the Igigi to bear the workload, the Igigi "had to dig out canals, had to clear channels, the lifelines of the land. The gods dug out the Tigris river (bed) and the gods dug out the Euphrates" (I 21–25). So both rivers are dug out by the gods, not by man, who is created later. In the Creation Myth *Enūma eliš* Marduk defeats Tiamat. Using the corpse of Tiamat for creating heaven and earth the text continues: "He placed her head, heaped up [. . . .], opened up springs: water gushed out. From her eyes he opened Euphrates and Tigris" (V 53–55).

[54] Wenham, *Genesis*, 66.

[55] E.A. Speiser, *Genesis* (AB), New York 1969, 14 translates v. 10: "A river rises in Eden to water the garden; outside, it forms four separate branch streams" and comments: "*rises in*. Not the traditional 'went out of', nor even 'comes out of, issues from', since the garden itself is in Eden. *outside*, Heb literally 'from there' . . . What

way Eden can be connected with a location in the neighbourhood of the Persian Gulf. Wenham has even suggested that with this location the ancient Mesopotamian tradition of the paradise of Dilmun comes in.[56]

The Sumerian myth of Dilmun is a composition with different stories about Enki and Ninsikila and Enki and Ninchursaga. Dilmun is described both as a "city" and as a "land": "The land Dilmun is pure, the land Dilmun is clean, the land Dilmun is most bright" (5–6).[57] In Dilmun there is peace between the animals: "In Dilmun the raven utters no cries, the *ittidu*-bird utters not the cry of the *ittidu*-bird. The lion does not kill, the wolf snatches no lamb, unknown is the kid-devouring wild dog(?)" (13–17).[58] Death and illness are unknown: "The sick-eyed do not say: 'I am sick-eyed' . . . its old woman does not say: 'I am an old woman', its old man does not say: 'I am an old man'" (22–25).[59] After a command of the water-god Enki the city and the land are full of sweet water. We do not need to follow the whole story, but it is clear that in primeval times dynamic fails. There is neither death nor life as reality knows them. In the second story, life starts with an abundance of fertility, but that unbroken fertility is reduced and at the end of the myth life and death are balanced.[60] Nevertheless Dilmun continues to be the land where eternal life is possible. In the Sumerian myth of the Flood, the king and high-priest Ziusudra, who survives the Flood, is rewarded with god-like eternal life in Dilmun, because "he protected the human seed".[61]

All the Mesopotamian texts refer to the Persian Gulf for a location of Dilmun. Most probably Dilmun can be identified as Bahrein, maybe in combination with the Saudi-Arabian coast or the island of Failaka.[62] Because of the praise of the trade in the texts on Dilmun and the excavations in Bahrein, where proof of trade connections

---

this means is that, before reaching Eden, the river consists of four separate branches" (16–17).

[56] Wenham, *Genesis*, 66.

[57] TUAT III/3:365.

[58] TUAT III/3:366.

[59] TUAT III/3:366f.

[60] F. Stolz, "Paradies I", *TRE* XXV/5, Berlin/New York 1995, 706.

[61] The Sumerian Floodmyth vi 9–11; *TUAT* III/3:457–458.

[62] B. Alster, "Dilmun, Bahrein, and the Alleged Paradise in Sumerian Myth and Literature", in: D.T. Potts (ed.), *New Studies in the Archaeology and Early History of Bahrein*, Berlin 1983, 39–74.

could be discovered, Bahrein is indeed the best candidate. Between India and Mesopotamia there was reciprocal trade exchange between 2500–1500 BC.[63]

It cannot be denied that the Sumerian, Mesopotamian paradise myths did have a wide range in the texts and that the land of Dilmun was known far beyond the boundaries of Sumer. But in this case, however attractive it may be, the text of Gen 2:10–14 is clear. The universal river rises in Eden and splits up after Eden. Therefore, apart from the difficulties with Cush and Gihon, Speiser's interpretation does not work. A geographical connection between Dilmun and Eden is not at the background of Gen 2:10–14.

The second solution tries to locate Gihon somewhere in the east of Mesopotamia towards present-day Iran. Gen 2:10–14 is understood as a move from the (unknown) far (south-)east to the west, ending up with the westernmost river: the Euphrates. Eden is inaccessible and unlocatable for the reader of the MT. For as understanding the Hebrew text this seems indeed the best solution.

Later interpretations drew other conclusions about paradise and geography. Surely the LXX interprets Gihon as the Nile. For the Egyptian background of the LXX it is clear that Egypt should be included in the story of the rivers, which came from paradise. With the geography of paradise the LXX connects Gen 2–3, Ex 28 and Ezek 28. Again Flavius Josephus, in his day, enlarged the map. To him the four rivers and the regions they cover include India. Thus, the Pishon is identified as the Ganges. The other three are Euphrates, Tigris and Nile.[64]

The flood of literature trying to solve the geographical problems of Eden in Gen 2:10–14 demonstrates two things. First, the narrator wants to offer a mystified location for Paradise. Through geography he wants to demonstrate the reality of Paradise. Well- known, famous rivers derive from the universal river starting in Eden. Later versions and explanations go in the same direction, now covering the whole known world of their day. On the other hand, he does not want to locate paradise in an accessible and locatable place. He transforms Paradise into reality by ending with the well-known Mesopotamian rivers. But this paradise is inaccessible. Regions, rivers

[63] A.L. Oppenheim, "The Sea-Faring Merchants of Ur", *JAOS* (1954) 6–17.
[64] *Antiquitates*, I 3 38.39.

and names appear which cannot be located except in a very general way. In this way the legendary attraction of *gan Eden* and the countries reached by its waters can be upgraded. Only a land you cannot place on a map has plenty of gold, precious stones and jewels. Coming from the unknown land, the direction of vv. 10–14, you reach well-known cities and countries at last. Going from the well-known places and rivers, to there, the direction of 10–14 reversed, you will not reach *gan Eden.* It is in this geography of *gan Eden,* that the end of the narrative of Gen 3 and of all Paradise stories, the loss of Paradise by man, is already included.

3. *Ezekiel 31*

In Ezek 31 Ezekiel addresses the world power, Egypt, in bold mythical language. Egypt is compared to the world tree, "which reaches all three regions of the world, aims as *imago mundi* (Eliade) to represent the world as a whole in the totality of its life-force".[65] It is "a cedar on Lebanon with fine branches and of great height, whose top was up in the clouds" (v. 3). The tree (read Egypt) is fed by water from the deep, and grows higher than all the trees in the countryside. It offers protection to every bird nesting there and every animal gives birth to its young in its shade. It has access to abundant water. But again, with the same themes as in Ez 28, its pride becomes unbearable. Therefore judgement is announced: the tree is expelled and cut down.

The relation to Eden and the garden of God is expressed several times. The beauty of the tree overshadows the trees in the garden of God: "The cedars in the garden of God could not rival its boughs . . . no tree in God's garden was like it" (v. 8). In this way a clear distinction is made between the cosmic tree and the trees in *gan Eden.* The same comparison is repeated in v. 9: "It (the cosmic tree) was the envy of all Eden's trees, which were in God's garden". The motif brought in here, the jealousy of the Eden trees, is worked out in v. 16: "I (YHWH) have made the nations quake at the crash of its (the cosmic tree/Egypt) fall, when I made it go down to Sheol to be with all who descend to the Pit. In the land below, however all the trees of Eden were comforted, the choicest of Lebanon".

[65] Zimmerli, *Ezekiel 2,* 146.

When the cosmic tree, Egypt, falls down, all the nations are in uproar. Even the cosmic tree goes to Sheol, but here the trees of Eden are comforted. The use of the motif can be compared with the fall of the foreign king from Isa 14, who tried to ascend to heaven but found himself back in Sheol. The same incomparability of the Eden trees with the cosmic tree is repeated in v. 18.

In the oracle of Ezek 31 the Eden motifs are used only to demonstrate the splendour and beauty of the cosmic tree. They do not have an independent place. In Ezek 28 an independent narrative of the fall of man was present in the judgement oracle. In Ezek Eden motifs are only interwoven with the mythical cosmic tree.

4. *Conclusions*

Every myth of Paradise, garden of God, cosmic mountain and world tree referring to primeval times is used in the Old Testament either to describe the transformation from the golden age into the real world or to announce the fall of a mighty ruler. The mythical concepts used here are well known in the world of the Ancient Near East. There is no dependence in a literal sense as we have in some parts of the Flood narratives. But it are the same motifs about God and man in the primeval world which are worked out here. An abundant use of mythological language can be found with Ezekiel. This "Calvin among the prophets" (Zimmerli) does not hesitate to use the myths of Mesopotamia for his own judgement-oracles or for a song of lamentation. The same use of motifs can be discovered in the narratives of Gen 2–3. The tree of life and the tree of knowledge of good and evil are not the same as the cosmic tree, but the functions of the trees can belong to the same category as iconography shows.[66]

Against this common Ancient Eastern background, Gen 2–3 tells an independent story. Man has to die; eternal life cannot be reached. Not by pure accident as in the Gilgameš epic[67] or in the myth of Adapa,[68] but by his own choice. Man, even in primeval times, is

---

[66] O. Keel, *Die Welt der altorientalischen Bildsymbolik und das Alte Testament*, Neukirchen ^{2}1977, 100–105.164–167.

[67] *Gilgameš* XI 285–291.

[68] *Adapa* B 28–34.60–70.

responsible for his own deeds. He lives in a situation where the choice is up to him.

How does Paradise function against the background of the common Old Testament tradition?[69] Paradise is the world of contrast to the real world people live in. In this world of contrast everything is possible which is not possible in the experience of daily life. Paradise is the bridge between nature and culture, between primeval time and history. The function of the myth of Paradise and the world of contrast is transformation.[70] In Gen 2–3 a world without death[71] becomes a world in which death belongs to life, to be naked is changed into being dressed, collecting food is changed into the world of the shepherd, the hunter and the farmer. Sexuality is associated with shame.

There is still another function of these transformations. The result of the transformation is the real, experienced world. The world of the words of punishment in Gen 3:14–19 against snake, woman and man is the real world of Palestine and the circumstances of life in the first millennium. But the texts aim at the reverse too. There is criticism in the reversed transformation. When 3:16 states: "I will multiply your pains in childbearing, you shall give birth to your children in pain. Your yearning shall be for your husband, yet he will lord it over you", the text describes normal life in the eyes of the ancients. Nevertheless, the myth tells too that this is not life after the original will of YHWH Elohim. So the myth and its transformation must be read in a twofold direction, one which describes the transformation to the real world and one in which man dreams of the lost world.

---

[69] F. Stolz, "Paradiese und Gegenwelten", *Zeitschrift für Religionswissenschaft* 1 (1993) 5–24; F. Stolz, "Paradies", *TRE* XXV/5 (Berlin/New York 1995) 708–714.

[70] Stolz, "Paradies", 708.

[71] This is the scope of the narrative. But Gen 3:22 presupposes death.

EDEN AND PARADISE: THE GARDEN MOTIF IN SOME EARLY JEWISH TEXTS (1 ENOCH AND OTHER TEXTS FOUND AT QUMRAN)

Eibert J.C. Tigchelaar

1. *Introduction*

The narrative of Adam and Eve in the Garden of Eden receives no attention in the Hebrew Bible outside of Gen 2–3. The garden, which is called "the garden of Eden", "the garden of YHWH" or "the garden of God", is mentioned a few more times in the Hebrew Bible, though without any reference to Adam and Eve. Thus, the poetic account of Ezek 28:12–19, presented as an oracle against the king of Tyre, presents in a related, but much more mythological, mode the expulsion of a cherub from his primeval abode, the garden of God in Eden, the holy mount of the gods.[1] In a different manner the trees of the garden of Eden enter the scene in Ezek 31. On the other hand, "paradisal" imagery, without explicit mention of Eden, or of Adam and Eve, may be detected in several prophecies, e.g. Ezek 47 and Zech 14. Phenomenological approaches or metaphorical readings may suspect allusions to Eden or Paradise in many other passages, e.g. in the Psalms passages referring to trees or waters in relation to the Temple, but the correspondence of these well-known images need not indicate a direct relation to Gen 2–3.

The different descriptions of Gen 2–3 and Ezek 28:12–19 show that the image of Eden is not consistently developed in the Hebrew Bible. Gen 2–3 describes an orchard from which a river issues, and two trees in the middle of the orchard, whereas Ezek 28:12–19 places the garden of God in Eden on the mount of the gods. Ezekiel does not mention any trees, but instead stones of fire. Although the description of the location is quite different, the narrative themes of both texts correspond in a general way. Adam and Eve, as well as the cherub, have gained knowledge, but are expelled from the garden. Both texts refer to the end of the former dwellers of the garden,

[1] Cf. the contribution of E. Noort in this volume.

though in Genesis they will return to "dust" (עפר), and in Ezekiel to "ashes" (אפר).

In later interpretations the description of Gen 2–3 served as the model for "paradise", the word used by the Septuagint to render גן, "garden", even though some details of Ezek 28:12–19 sometimes influenced the image. Here we are primarily concerned with the interpretation of the Eden-motif, i.e. the use of the garden and trees motif, in Early Jewish Literature. In addition some texts from Qumran that refer to the Genesis narrative will be briefly discussed.

2. *Paradise in 1 Enoch*

A sizeable part of Early Jewish literature consisted of writings attributed to Enoch. Five of these compositions have been preserved in Classical Ethiopic where this collection of writings, called in Ethiopic the *Book of the Prophet Enoch* and in modern scholarship *1 Enoch*, became part of the Ethiopian Bible, whereas another Enochic work has been transmitted in a Slavonic version (*Book of the Secrets of Enoch* or *2 Enoch*). Also related to the Enochic literature is the *Book of Giants*, parts of which have been preserved in Manichaean texts. Among the texts of Qumran, fragments of four of the five parts of *1 Enoch*, as well as of the *Book of Giants* were discovered.[2] Not found at Qumran is the second part of *1 Enoch*, the *Book of Parables* or *Book of Similitudes* (*1 Enoch* 37–71).

Palaeographic evidence indicates that the first part of *1 Enoch*, the *Book of Watchers* (*1 Enoch* 1–36) already existed in the beginning of the 2nd century BCE, and that the other three discovered compositions of *1 Enoch* were copied in the 2nd and 1st century BCE.[3] The

---

[2] Cf. the editions of J.T. Milik, *The Books of Enoch; Aramaic Fragments of Qumrân Cave 4*, Oxford 1976, and L.T. Stuckenbruck, *The Book of Giants from Qumran; Texts, Translation and Commentary*, Tübingen 1997.

[3] The two oldest manuscripts are 4Q201 (4QEn[a] ar), dated to the first part of the 2nd century BCE, and containing remnants of *1 Enoch* 1–12, and the hitherto unpublished 4Q208 (4QEnastr[a] ar), which Milik, *The Books of Enoch*, 273, dates to the end of the 3rd century BCE or the beginning of the 2nd century BCE. However, 4Q208 contains only fragments of the so-called Synchronistic Calendar, and one may ask whether it contained the *Astronomical Book of Enoch* or only this Synchronistic Calendar. *1 Enoch* 33–36 seems to give a summary of the *Astronomical Book*, which would imply that the *Astronomical Book* existed in one form or another in the 3rd century BCE.

Parables of Enoch, which are conspicuously absent from Qumran, are generally considered to be younger than the other writings of *1 Enoch*. Most scholars argue that the *Parables* originated in the first century CE, or perhaps slightly earlier. Not only is the *Parables* younger than the other parts of *1 Enoch*, it also seems to represent a different strand of Enochic tradition than that represented by the other parts which were found at Qumran.[4]

This distinction between the Qumran Enochic texts, on the one hand, and the *Parables* on the other, should be taken into account in the interpretation of the Enochic writings. The *Book of Parables* is a composite work, and some of its parts or traditions may be considerably older than the present composition. Nonetheless, one should take extreme care in using the *Parables* to elucidate the older Enochic writings. Between the Qumran Enochic materials and the *Book of Parables* there lie at least two centuries in which Judaism was subject to considerable developments.

This *caveat* with regard to the use of the *Parables of Enoch* is relevant to the investigation of the function and location of "paradise". Wittingly or unwittingly the descriptions of "paradise" in the *Parables* and other younger compositions were used in the interpretation of the older Enochic writings, thereby creating, in my opinion, more problems than were solved. The present investigation will focus on the Qumran Enochic writings, and will briefly discuss the *Parables* afterwards.

2.1. *The Paradise of Righteousness in the Book of Watchers and the Astronomical Book*

The first composition of *1 Enoch*, the *Book of Watchers* (*1 Enoch* 1–36), is a composite work which reflects several stages of growth.[5] The fact that the oldest manuscript, 4Q201 (4QEn[a] ar), stemming from the first part of the 2nd century BCE, reflects the final form of the *Book of Watchers* indicates that the composition as a whole, or at least major parts of the work, originates from the 3rd century BCE, whereas some of the sources or traditions of the work might be even older.

---

[4] D.W. Suter, *Tradition and Composition in the Parables of Enoch*, Missoula, MT 1979, 15–16, 32–33.

[5] Cf., e.g., E.J.C. Tigchelaar, *Prophets of Old and The Day of the End; Zechariah, the Book of Watchers and Apocalyptic*, Leiden 1996, 152–164.

This goes for the oldest section of the work, *1 Enoch* 6–11, which incorporates traditions that are referred to by the text of Gen 6:1–4.[6]

The second part of the *Book of Watchers* consists of partially overlapping accounts of Enoch's journeys, in which he is taken on a guided tour visiting both the edges and the centre of the world.[7] The second travel account describes Enoch's journey from the West, via the Centre of the Earth, to the East. Almost at the end of this journey he comes to the "*Pardes* of Righteousness" (*1 Enoch* 32:3: פרדס קשטא; παράδεισος τῆς δικαιοσύνης; *gannata ṣedq*).[8] He sees there many kinds of large, beautiful, sweet-smelling trees, and "the tree of knowledge", high like a pine, with leaves like the carob tree, with fruits like bunches of grapes, and with a penetrating smell. Enoch comments on the tree, and the angel Raphael, who is with him, identifies the tree: "This is the tree of knowledge from which your old father and your aged mother who were before you ate and learnt knowledge; and their eyes were opened and they knew that they were naked, and were driven from the garden" (*1 Enoch* 32:6).[9] The phrases used here are more or less the same as those of Gen 3:

1 Enoch 32:6	*Gen 3*
This is the tree of knowledge from which your old father and your aged mother, who were before you, ate and learnt knowledge;	And she took from its fruit and ate, and she also gave of it to her husband who was with her, and he ate. (Gen. 3:6)
and their eyes were opened, and they knew that they were naked,	And the eyes of both of them were opened, and they knew that they were naked (Gen 3:7a)
and they were driven from the garden	And the Lord God drove him from the garden of Eden (Gen 3:23)

[6] The relationship between *Genesis* 6:1–4 and the *Book of Watchers* requires a nuanced approach. Though the text of *Genesis* is older than that of the *Book of Watchers*, the latter seems to have preserved traditions, although probably in a revised form, that are as old as *Genesis*.

[7] One may distinguish between two separate travel accounts, chs. 17–19 and chs. 21–36, but both sections are composite. *1 Enoch* 17:1–18:5 and 18:6–16 probably had a different origin, and chs. 33–36 are only loosely related to the preceding journey. Cf. E.J.C. Tigchelaar, *Prophets of Old*, 157–163.

[8] In this article I prefer a transliteration, *Pardes*, rather than a translation ("Garden"; "Orchard"; "Paradise") of Aramaic פרדס.

[9] Translations of some passages of *1 Enoch* are given in the appendices at the end of this article.

The travel accounts in the *Book of Watchers* have different forms and functions. Thus, the account of *1 Enoch* 17:1–18:5 is essentially a catalogue listing the things Enoch saw, whereas *1 Enoch* 18:6–16 is slightly more descriptive, and relates some of the locations to the judgment of the host of heaven. *1 Enoch* 21–32, which partially depicts the same locations as described in *1 Enoch* 18:6–16, elaborates on the eschatological function of many of the abodes he visits. He sees the place where the stars of heaven are bound (*1 Enoch* 21:1–6), the prison of the angels (*1 Enoch* 21:7–10), the location where the spirits, the souls of the dead, are gathered until the day of judgment (*1 Enoch* 22), the mountain where the tree of life is preserved until it will be given to the righteous after the day of judgment (*1 Enoch* 24–25), as well as the valley which will be the place of judgment (*1 Enoch* 26–27). However, neither *1 Enoch* 23, which depicts the fiery course of the luminaries, nor *1 Enoch* 28–32, which describe the East of the world, refer in any way to the judgment. *1 Enoch* 28:1–32:2 differs structurally from the preceding chapters. Whereas *1 Enoch* 21–27 all consist of a description of a place, a question regarding the meaning of this abode, and an angel's elucidation, *1 Enoch* 28:1–32:2 gives in a catalogue-like form short descriptions of the East, describing mountains, trees, fruits, and spices.[10] Thus, these travel accounts serve two functions. On the one hand they present a geographic catalogue of more or less mythic locations, establishing *en passant* Enoch's fame of knowing everything and having seen everything. On the other hand, some of these descriptions are used to call attention to the day of judgment, and thus, ultimately, serve to warn the sinners and to comfort the righteous.

The section on the *Pardes* of Righteousness in *1 Enoch* 32:3–6 stands between both types of descriptions. It uses the description-question-elucidation scheme which is utilized in *1 Enoch* 21–27, but like *1 Enoch* 28–31 it describes trees, their fruit and fragrance. The angel's explanation of the tree of knowledge does not refer to the

[10] J.T. Milik, "Hénoch au pays des aromates (ch. xxvii à xxxii). Fragments araméens de la grotte 4 de Qumran", *RB* 58 (1965) 70–77 argues that Enoch's journey in these chapters corresponds to two ancient perfume and spice trade itineraries. Milik in addition claims that the number of spices and perfumes (eleven) corresponds to the number of ingredients of the liturgical incense, and that the six mountains with aromates, together with the Paradise of Righteousness, result in seven mountains corresponding to the seven mountains of *1 Enoch* 18:6–8 and *1 Enoch* 25:3.

future day of judgment, but instead to the past. The only reference to a present or future function of the tree might perhaps be suggested in the Greek text of *1 Enoch* 32:3 which has the problematic wording οὗ ἐσθίουσιν ἁγίου τοῦ καρποῦ αὐτοῦ, with "holy" qualifying "its fruit". The awkward syntax of this clause may be resolved by emending ἁγίου to ἅγιοι, which results in a more understandable sentence.[11] If this emendation is correct (but the Ethiopic manuscripts do not have a corresponding word), it would mean that the holy ones eat from the tree, and have great knowledge. Yet, since in the *Book of Watchers* "holy ones" denotes exclusively the angels, this statement has no eschatological meaning for readers. It therefore seems that the short depiction of the *Pardes* of Righteousness was placed at the end of Enoch's journey to the East in order to complete the description of the East, and not because of some special importance of this location.

The Eastern location of the *Pardes* of Righteousness corresponds to Gen 2:8 which states that God planted a garden in Eden מקדם, "in the East", although a double entendre of מקדם, meaning also "aforetime", or "in primeval time", could have been intended. The reference in *1 Enoch* 33:6 to Adam and Eve, though not mentioned by their proper names, in phrases similar to those of Gen 3, suggests that the description is based upon Gen 2–3. There are, however, some major differences between the two descriptions. *1 Enoch* 32:3–6 elaborates on the appearance of the Tree of Knowledge,[12] but lacks the details of the much longer narrative of Gen 2–3. Thus, the description of the *Pardes* of Righteousness does not mention the streams issuing from the garden (Gen. 2:10–14) or the tree of life (Gen. 2:9 and 3:22). Apart from these differences, there is an impor-

---

[11] As observed by R.H. Charles, *The Book of Enoch or 1 Enoch*, Oxford 1912, 61, the clause is a literal translation of an Aramaic construction beginning with די.

[12] R.A. Argall, *1 Enoch and Sirach; A Comparative Literary and Conceptual Analysis of the Themes of Revelation, Creation and Judgment*, Atlanta, Georgia 1995, 93–94, argues that the descriptions of the Tree of Knowledge in *1 Enoch* 32 and the metaphor of the Tree of Wisdom in Sir 24 "draw upon a common tradition that describes four principle aspects of the Tree of Wisdom: its height, foliage, fruit and fragrance", and suggests that the similarities between the two descriptions "derive from an oral tradition antecedent to both accounts. The tradition likens the tree's height to a needleleafed conifer, its foliage to that of a broadleafed tree, its fruit to the fruit of the vine, and its fragrance to the bark of aromatic trees". But apart from these general correspondences, many of which are present in other texts describing trees, there are few correspondences of detail, and the suggestion of a common tradition seems unwarranted.

tant distinction between Genesis and *1 Enoch*. In Genesis the tree is called the Tree of Knowledge of Good and Bad, and eating the fruits of this tree results in death. In *1 Enoch* the tree is called the Tree of Knowledge, without the object "Good and Bad", and eating of the tree results in "great wisdom".

The lack of any reference to the Tree of Life in Enoch's *Pardes* of Righteousness is not coincidental; it is because this tree was located in another abode. In the short account of Enoch's journeys, Enoch visits seven mountains somewhere in the northwest, the middle of which is said to be "like the throne of God" (*1 Enoch* 18:6–8). This short account only describes the stones of the mountains, but the corresponding long travel account of *1 Enoch* 24–25 describes at length an extraordinary tree. Enoch comments on that tree, and in response the archangel Michael explains that no person is permitted to touch that tree until the great judgment, after which it shall be given to the righteous and holy. Its fruit shall be given to the elect, and it shall be transplanted to the holy place, the temple of God. The fragrance of the tree shall be in the bones of those who enter the holy place, who then shall live a long life on earth (*1 Enoch* 25:4–6).

The descriptions of *1 Enoch* 24–25 and 32 display several similarities. In both abodes there are many trees, but one special tree is singled out and described in detail. In both sections Enoch expresses his interest in the tree in very much the same words, after which the angel who is with him elaborates on the subject. But whereas in *1 Enoch* 32 the abode is identified as the *Pardes* of Righteousness, and the tree as the Tree of Wisdom, *1 Enoch* 24–25 is less explicit. Nevertheless, the description of the tree in *1 Enoch* 25 shows that it is a tree of life: its fruit will be for life, its fragrance will be in the bones of the elect, and the righteous will live a long life. Likewise, in this long description the angel identifies the mountain which is "like the seat of a throne" (24:3 and 25:3) with God's throne where he will sit when he will descend to visit the earth (25:3). This mountain with the tree of life has been generally identified as another "paradise" or "garden of Righteousness", as a result of which the *Book of Watchers* was believed to have two "paradises", an earthly one with the Tree of Knowledge, and a heavenly one with the Tree of Life.

The Eastern location of a "paradise" with the Tree of Knowledge is compatible with the Genesis narrative, but the location of the Tree of Life in the northwest conflicts with the biblical account. In a famous and much quoted article Grelot argued that the two "paradises" in Enoch's journey present an attempt to harmonise the differing biblical traditions of the Genesis location of Eden in the East, the location of *Isaiah* 14 and other passages of the Mountain of God in the North, and the identification in Ezek 28 of the Garden of Eden with the Mountain of God.[13] Grelot summarizes his view of the harmonisation as follows:

> God dwells in the paradise on the Mountain in the northwest. Before the creation of man he planted a garden of Righteousness in the northeast, being an exact replica of the Garden of Righteousness in the northwestern Paradise. Temporarily God transplanted the Tree of Life from the northwestern mountainous Paradise to its earthly counterpart in the northeast, but after the Fall of man he brought it back to the northwestern paradise. It is this paradise to which Enoch was elevated. On the day of judgment he will transplant the Tree of Life to the New Jerusalem where the righteous will dwell; then the holy city will be, like Eden was, the earthly replica of the divine heavenly abode.[14]

Milik concedes that there were different traditions concerning the location of paradise, but suggests that the author of *1 Enoch* might have attempted to unify these locations, by placing them both in the North, one in the northwest, and the other in the northeast.[15]

One should question, however, the identification of the northwestern mountain with a paradise. Though the text calls the mountain the "seat of God" and places the Tree of Life there, it does not call the mountain a *pardes* or paradise. Second, *1 Enoch* 77:3 (Ethiopic) locates the *Pardes* of Righteousness in the North, but the Aramaic fragments show that this Ethiopic text is corrupt, and that a description of the North (omitted in the Ethiopic text) was followed by a description of three concentric parts of the earth. Third, a northwestern location of paradise is clearly indicated in the *Parables of Enoch*, but "paradise" in this younger text is completely different from that of the *Book of Watchers*. Fourth, the use of the word "paradise" with all its later Jewish and Christian connotations, may be an anachronism, which rather complicates than solves the problem.[16]

---

[13] P. Grelot, "La géographie mythique d'Hénoch et ses sources orientales", *RB* 65 (1958) 33–69.

[14] P. Grelot, "La géographie", 43.

[15] J.T. Milik, "Hénoch au pays des aromates", 77; *The Books of Enoch*, 33.

[16] J. Tromp, "Literary and Exegetical Issues in the Story of Adam's Death and

It is clear that the Enochic accounts are not completely compatible with the divergent Biblical traditions about Eden. The *Pardes* of Righteousness corresponds with the Garden of Eden in Genesis, except for the absence of the Tree of Knowledge. On the other hand the mountainous abode with the Tree of Life in the West or northwest corresponds to some extent to the description of Ezek 28. One wonders whether the transplantation—from the point of view of Genesis—of the Tree of Life to the northwest, presents an attempt towards harmonization of the conflicting Biblical accounts, or whether there might be another explanation.

According to many biblical scholars the Genesis tradition of *two* trees in the garden of Eden presents a conflation of traditions. Though a century of literary critical analyses have not resulted in convincing reconstructions of original texts and additions, many scholars suspected that the references to the Tree of Life in Genesis 2–3 were added to a tradition in which only the Tree of Knowledge stood in the Garden of Eden.[17] One may then wonder whether the Enochic account of the Tree of Knowledge without the Tree of Life in the Garden of Eden witnesses this old tradition before the conflation, or whether the author had observed the same difficulties as modern scholars.

This question should be directly related to the more general issue regarding the relation between *1 Enoch* and Genesis, especially with regard to Enoch's story of the Watchers vis-à-vis the short account in Genesis 6:1–4. It has been argued that *1 Enoch*'s story of the Watchers is essentially a midrash or commentary on Genesis 6:1–4, but other scholars claim that the Enochic story is dependent on an old tradition which was only mentioned in passing in Genesis. In other words, Enoch does not interpret Genesis, but relies on the same traditions. Though the descriptions of Enoch's journeys may not be equated with the long stories on the Watchers, the same

---

Burial (*GLAE* 31–42)", in: J. Frishman & L. van Rompay (Eds.), *The Book of Genesis in Jewish and Oriental Christian Interpretation; A Collection of Essays*, Leuven 1997, 25–41, esp. 30–32 underlines that the location of paradise in the *Greek Life of Adam and Eve* (*Apocalypse of Moses*) is equivocal and that the anthropology and cosmography of this text are not developed consistently. One might add, in my opinion, that the term "paradise" itself is equivocal.

[17] C. Westermann, *Genesis 6–11*, Darmstadt 1972, 26–28, who also shortly discusses other attempts to solve the problem of the two trees. More recent research has endeavoured to understand the present text as a literary unity.

might be the case here: *1 Enoch*'s description with only the Tree of Knowledge in the *Pardes* may reflect an original tradition without the Tree of Life.

The hypothesis that the Enochic account represents a separate stream of tradition independent of Genesis 2–3 is reflected in the name of the Garden and several other details. First, eating from the Enochic Tree of Knowledge does not result in death, but in "great knowledge". This reminds one of Ezek 28:12, even if that text does not refer to a tree at all, because it attributes "fullness of wisdom" to the king of Tyre. The emendation οὗ ἐσθίουσιν ἅγιοι τοῦ καρποῦ αὐτοῦ, with the "holy ones" being angels, also reminds one of Ezekiel where the addressee is a cherub.

The reference to the location as the "*Pardes* of Righteousness" might also indicate a separate tradition. Apart from *1 Enoch* 33:3 and 77:3, this designation only occurs, to my knowledge, in the later texts *4 Ezra* 7:36 and 8:52 (Armenian version),[18] and *Adam and Eve* 25,[19] and it is plausible that those later texts derived the expression from *1 Enoch*. It is not clear, however, why the author of *1 Enoch* used this particular phrase. One may wonder whether the use of the word *pardes* was directly or indirectly dependent on the use of παράδεισος as a rendering of Hebrew *gan* in Genesis 2, i.e., was it already in use as a technical term. Our knowledge of 3rd century BCE Judaism is limited, and there is not enough evidence to answer this question. One might note, though, that *pardes* is used in a non-technical manner in 6Q8 (6QGiants) 2 3, where it simply means "orchard".[20] The meaning "orchard" also fits well in *1 Enoch* 33:3, but the qualification "of Righteousness" indicates that it does not denote an ordinary orchard. In *1 Enoch* 20:7 παράδεισος is clearly used in a technical

---

[18] M.E. Stone, "Paradise in 4 Ezra iv:8 and vii:36, viii:52", *JJS* 17 (1966) 85–87

[19] G.W.E. Nickelsburg, "Some Related Traditions in the Apocalypse of Adam, the Books of Adam and Eve, and 1 Enoch", in: B. Layton (Ed.), *The Rediscovery of Gnosticism; Proceedings of the International Conference on Gnosticism at Yale, New Haven, Conn., March 28–31, 1978. 2. Sethian Gnosticism*, Leiden 1981, 515–539 (esp. 526–533) argues that *Adam and Eve* 25–29 and 49–50 are closely related to and influenced by *1 Enoch*.

[20] For the meaning "orchard", rather than "garden", cf. the contribution of J. Bremmer in this volume. In the small fragment 6Q8 2 no trees are mentioned, but only, in line 1, "shoots". However, the Middle Persian Kawân frag. *j*, which possibly refers to the same dream, mentions a garden (*bwy[st'n*; cf. Hebrew בוסתן) and trees, as does the second dream vision of the *Midrash of Shemchazah and Aza'el*. Cf. J.T. Milik, *The Books of Enoch*, 325, and L.T. Stuckenbruck, *The Book of Giants*, 201–203.

sense, but since this chapter is often regarded as a late redactional addition,[21] the technical use in that chapter cannot be taken as evidence for its use in *1 Enoch* 33:3.

In conclusion, since the identification of the seventh mountain in the northwest with a garden or "paradise" is not explicit in the text, and cannot be based upon contemporaneous data, one must conclude that the *Book of Watchers* knows only one "paradise", corresponding more or less to the garden of Eden, be it without the Tree of Life. It is by no means impossible that this description is based upon a tradition in which the Tree of Life had not yet been added to the paradise story. This would imply that the description of *1 Enoch* is not merely a re-interpretation of biblical narrative, but an independent witness to the tradition used by the author of Genesis 2–3.

The mention of the "*Pardes* of Righteousness" in the Astronomical Book of Enoch (*1 Enoch* 77:3) is part of a description of the three parts of the world. Although the Ethiopic text is corrupt and the Aramaic fragmentary, it seems that the author describes three concentric circles. The first and inner part is the inhabited world. The second part, surrounding the first one, was probably described as consisting of water and darkness, whereas, according to the Aramaic fragment, the third and outer part consisted of deserts and the *Pardes* of Righteousness. In between "the deserts" (מדברין) and the "*Pardes* of Righteousness" one short word is lost except for some traces. Milik suggested reading ולשׂׄ[ב]עׄ, "and for the Seven", which he interprets as the seven ultraterrestrial regions.[22] The connection between "deserts" and the "*Pardes* of Righteousness" may be indicated in 4Q530 (4QGiants^{b} ar) 2 ii 5 which tells that Mahaway, on his way to Enoch, חלף לשהוין מדברא רבא], "crossed bare regions, 'the Great Desert' [". According to 1QapGen XXI 11–12, מדברא רבא, "the Great Desert", is the Syro-Arabian desert to the East, but it is not certain that one may identify the mythic with the geographic topography.[23]

2.2. *Paradise in the Parables of Enoch*

The phrase "*Pardes* of Righteousness" is not present in the *Parables of Enoch*, which has only been preserved in Ethiopic. The *Parables*

[21] The chapter was in all likelihood part of the lost bottom section of 4Q206 (4QEn^{e} ar) col. XX.

[22] J.T. Milik, *The Books of Enoch*, 289, 291, whereas in "Hénoch au pays des aromates", 76, Milik did not yet suggest a reading.

[23] Cf. the discussion in L.T. Stuckenbruck, *The Book of Giants*, 133–134.

do, however, mention a Garden of the Righteous (*1 Enoch* 60:23)[24] and a Garden of Life[25] (*1 Enoch* 61:12) where the first fathers, the chosen and righteous, dwell. In *1 Enoch* 70:3–4 this garden is explicitly located in the northwest, but *1 Enoch* 60:8 is more ambiguous. The verse refers to the desert Dundayn, which is said to be on the East of the garden where the chosen and righteous dwell. This name Dundayn might perhaps be related to that of the desert Doudael in *1 Enoch* 10:4, but no commonly accepted explanation of this name has been given.[26] In *1 Enoch* 60:8 the garden where the elect and righteous dwell is identified with the place where Enoch was taken up. One may compare this to *Jubilees* 4:23 which tells that Enoch was led into the Garden of Eden. The problems of comparing these texts are, however, manifold. First, it is clear that parts of *1 Enoch* 60 belonged to an Apocalypse of Noah, even though the preserved Ethiopic text attributes the text to Enoch. One cannot determine, however, to what extent this part of a Book of Noah was edited. It is therefore not certain whether the references to the Garden in this chapter belonged to a source used by the editor, whether the clause in *1 Enoch* 60:8 "where the elect and righteous dwell" is an addition or not,[27] and whether the northwestern location indicated by *1 Enoch* 70:3–4 was also the location meant in the possible original source of this text. A possible original text might simply have referred to the garden in which Enoch was taken up. According to the pre-

[24] M.A. Knibb, *The Ethiopic Book of Enoch*, Oxford 1978, mistakenly translates "Garden of Righteousness", this most likely being a *lapsus calami*.

[25] The "garden of life" is also mentioned in 4Q365 (4QSecond Ezekiel[a]) 6 ii 3 (frags. 6 + 9 + 24 + 34; cf. PAM 44.194), ימי חייהם \ . . . מו ב֯נן החיים, though D. Dimant, "A Citation of Nahum 3:8–10 in 4Q385 6 from Qumran" [Hebrew], in: S. Japhet (Ed.), *The Bible in the Light of Its Interpreters; Sarah Kamin Memorial Volume* [Hebrew], Jerusalem 1994, 31–37 reads ע֯ץ֯ החיים "tree of life", instead of ב֯נן החיים, which I prefer to read. The phrase is followed by a *vacat*, after which the text continues with the citation of Nahum 3:8–10.

[26] J.T. Milik, *The Books of Enoch*, 29–30, regards Dadouel as a transliteration of *Daddu'el*, "the (two) breasts of El", which would be the exact replica of the Akkadian *Mašu*, "twin mountains" (cf. Gilgamesh IX ii 9). This explanation is adopted by H.S. Kvanvig, *Roots of Apocalyptic; The Mesopotamian Background of the Enoch Figure and of the Son of Man*, Neukirchen-Vluyn 1988, 247, but dismissed by M. Black, *The Book of Enoch or 1 Enoch; A New English Edition*, Leiden 1985, 134. Departing from Milik's suggestion Kvanvig argues for a (North-)Western location of this paradise.

[27] The Ethiopic has two relative clauses determining the garden, "where the elect and righteous dwell, where my great-grandfather was taken up". The first clause mentioning the "elect and righteous" is reminiscent of *1 Enoch* 61:12 and 70:3–4, and may be an addition.

sent text of the *Parables*, the northwestern Garden of the Righteous is identical to the Garden of Eden, but one cannot be sure whether this was the original intention of the text.

Whichever is the case, the Garden of the *Parables* is different from that of the other Enochic writings, where the forefathers and the elect and righteous do not dwell in the "*Pardes* of Righteousness", nor in another paradise-like abode. Instead, the *Book of Watchers* states that the spirits of the dead are separated in different hollows in a mountain towards the West (*1 Enoch* 22), not identical to the Mountain with the Tree of Life, with one hollow being prepared for the spirits of the righteous until the day of judgment.

3. *Jubilees*

Contrary to the description of the "Pardes of Righteousness" in *1 Enoch*, the narrative of *Jub.* 3:1–35 should be regarded as a reinterpretation or re-writing of Gen 2–3.[28] The synopsis of the texts of Gen 2–3 and *Jub.* 3:1–35 shows clearly that the authors of *Jubilees* had little interest in the description of the garden of Eden. Thus, as in *1 Enoch* 33, there is no description of the streams issuing from the garden. Also, *Jubilees* mentions only the Tree of Knowledge and omits the references to the Tree of Life.[29] On the one hand this omission might be explained by the revisionary techniques and the theological interests of the authors. On the other hand, however, one wonders whether the authors of *Jubilees* were aware of the older tradition in which the Tree of Life was not located in the garden of Eden.

4. *Adam and Eden in some texts from the Judaean Desert*

Both the *Book of Jubilees* and other previously unknown compositions found in the caves of the Judaean Desert witness the popularity of compositions which are called in modern scholarship "re-written" or "re-worked Bible", i.e. texts which are based upon biblical texts, but

[28] Cf. J.T.A.G.M. van Ruiten in this volume for a discussion of the relation between Gen 2–3 and *Jub.* 3.

[29] *Jub.* 3 does not identify this tree, but *Jub.* 4:30 refers to it as "the Tree of Knowledge" (cf. 11Q12 5 3 [11QJub] [ע]ץ̊ הדעת).

have revised the text of what we now consider to be the Bible to a smaller ("re-worked") or larger ("re-written") extent. Thus, on the one hand, texts were found which correspond more than 95% to the "normative" biblical text such as the so-called *Reworked Pentateuch* (4Q365–4Q368). On the other hand some of the Pseudo- or Apocryphal works are reminiscent of biblical texts, often using portions of these, but clearly are new compositions.

Many of those re-written texts deal with Genesis, but in none of these texts has an interpretation or re-writing of the Paradise Story been preserved. This may be purely coincidental. Thus, the Jubilees fragments found in the Judaean Desert cover parts of both *Jub.* 2 and *Jub.* 4, but by chance no fragment belonging to *Jub.* 3, the section on the Garden of Eden, has been preserved.

In the case of the Genesis Apocryphon, the preserved sheets are sequentially numbered by the letters *pe, ṣade* and *qop*.[30] If the first sheet of the work was numbered with *alep*, then anything from 70 to 105 columns are missing from the beginning of the scroll. Of those seventy columns of text dealing with Genesis before the birth of Noah, some might have been devoted to the Paradise Story.

On the other hand, there are several indications that the story of Adam and Eve in Paradise was not very important or influential in the community which preserved the texts of the Judaean Desert. First, the discoveries in the Judaean Desert do not include apocryphal or pseudepigraphic writings with Adam as the prime figure.[31] More generally, apart from the Enochic literature, the *Genesis Apocryphon*, and a composition named *pars pro toto* the *Prayer of Enosh* (4Q369; 4Q499), the preserved texts display little interest in the forefathers before Noah. Thus, the composition named *4QAges of Creation* (4Q180) which claims to describe the sequence of the ages, "one age after another age" (4Q180 1 3), begins straight away with the ten generations of the sons of Noah, from Shem to Abraham until he sired Isaac, leaving aside (but perhaps by accident?) the ten generations from Adam to Noah. The same lack of interest in the generations before Noah is also witnessed in Ben Sira's praise of the fathers,

---

[30] M. Morgenstern, "A New Clue to the Original Length of the Genesis Apocryphon", *JJS* 47 (1996) 345–347.

[31] The provenance and date of the Adamic literature is not known, but G.W.E. Nickelsburg, "Some Related Traditions", 538, notes that *Adam and Eve* "circulated in circles for whom ritual immersion of one kind or another was an important rite".

which originally started with Noah. The Masada manuscript showed that the reference to Enoch (44:16) in the Greek and the medieval Ms B, but lacking in Syriac, is a later addition.

Second, the concern with the origin of sin, expressed so explicitly by Paul in his letter to the Romans, is remarkably absent from the scrolls. Instead of a concern with a historical moment in which sin had entered the world, the texts classify specific kinds of master-sins. Well known is the statement from the *Damascus Document* (IV 15–17) that the "three nets of Belial" are "fornication" (*zenut*), wealth (*hon*) and defilement of the Temple, and in the text called by the first editor *Wiles of the Wicked Woman* (4Q184 1 8), "she is the start of all ways of wickedness", where "she" could be interpreted both as *zenut*, "fornication", and as "folly". Revealing is the admonition in *Damascus Document* II–III where basic sins are illustrated by historical sinners in a chronological order. The list does not begin with Paradise or Adam and Eve, but with the Watchers of Gen 6.

Whereas no re-writings of the Eden narrative have been preserved, there are a few texts which in passing refer to the garden of Eden or the Tree of Knowledge.[32]

4.1. *4QMeditation on Creation A (4Q303)*

4Q303 (*4QMeditation on Creation A*)[33]

Hebrew		*translation*
]מבינים שמעו ו◦[	1	] understanding ones, listen; and [
חכ]מים [34]השביתו מעל כ֯[	2	*wise*] *men, desist from* . . .[
]נפלאות אל אש[ר	3	] the marvels of God *wh*[*ich*
]ל֯אור עולם ושמי טוה[ר	4	] *for* everlasting light and shining heavens [
]ר במקום תהו ובו[הו	5	] . . . in the place of voidness and emp[tiness
]כול מעשיהם עד קצ֯[	6	] all their *works/creatures* until *the period of* [
]ר בם מלך לכולם[	7	] . . . *among* them a king for all of them [
]ר ושכל טוב ורע ל[	8	] . . . and insight of good and bad *to* [
]לוקח ממנה אדם כיא֯[	9	] *Adam taking* from it, because [
]עשה לו עזר כ[נגדו	10	] made for him a [suitable] helper [
]לו לאשה כיא ממנו[	11	] for him as a wife, because from him [

---

[32] Those texts with a halakhic nature which refer to Adam and Eve are not discussed here, but in the contribution of F. García Martínez to this volume.

[33] Edited by T. Lim in *Discoveries in the Judaean Desert XX*, Oxford 1997, 151–153, pl. XIII.

[34] T. Lim reads וישביתו, but the letter read by him as *waw-yod* is clearly a *he* (cf. the identical *he* in line 10 עשה[).

The fragment called *4QMeditation on Creation A* might have belonged to the very beginning of a sapiential composition in which "understanding ones" are called upon to listen.[35] The meaning of the second line is obscure, but the broken text continues with a reference to the wonderful deeds of God, after which the following lines contain expressions taken from or reminiscent of Gen 1–3: מקום תהו ובו]הו, "place of emptiness and void" (cf. Gen 1:2), שכל טוב ורע, "understanding of good and bad" (Gen 2:17?), עשה לו עזר כ]נגדו[, "made for him a suitable helper" (Gen 2:18), and לו לאשה כיא ממנו][, "for him as a wife, because from him" (Gen 2:22–23). The meaning of several of the broken clauses is not clear, and it is difficult to grasp the development of ideas in the text. In view of the general correspondence of the remnants of lines 8 and 10–11 with Gen 2:16–23 one might hypothesize that "the understanding of good and bad" refers to the Tree of Knowledge, and that line 9 paraphrases Gen 2:17 where Adam is told not to eat from the Tree of Knowledge of Good and Bad. However, the syntax of the preserved words is ambiguous (is לוקח a *Qal* participle or a *Puʿal*?) and the feminine suffix in ממנה, "from it", does not correspond well with the masculine nouns עץ, "tree", or פרי, "fruit".

The reference to "insight of good and bad", however, need not of necessity be related to the Tree of Knowledge of Good and Bad. The left side of a small fragment called *4QMeditation on Creation C* (4Q305)[36] preserves the first words of three lines

4Q305 (*4QMeditation on Creation C*) col. ii

Hebrew		*translation*
ויברא בו חיות]	1	and He created animals in it [
נתן לאדם דע]ת	2	He gave to Adam knowled[ge
ורْעْ לדْעْתֹ כْ]	3	and evil to know . . . [

Most letters of the mutilated third line are uncertain,[37] but the second line seems to indicate that God gave knowledge to Adam (or

[35] T. Lim translates "having understood, they listened", probably because of his incorrect reading וישביתו in line 2, which suggests a narrative introduction. Vocatives followed or preceded by an imperative are quite common in sapiential literature. Cf. e.g., 4Q298 (4Qcrypt A Words of the Maskil to All Sons of Dawn) 1, and the formula ואתה מבין followed by an imperative in 4Q415ff (4QInstruction).

[36] T. Lim, *Discoveries in the Judaean Desert XX*, Oxford 1997, 156–157, pl. XIII.

[37] This goes especially for the two *ʿayins*, which are different from the *ʿayin* in line 2.

to man in general), whereas Gen 3 only mentions the knowledge acquired by man by eating from the Tree of Knowledge.

4.2. *4QParaphrase of Genesis and Exodus (4Q422) and 4QWords of the Luminaries*[a] *(4Q504)*

In a short article Esther Chazon[38] recently drew attention to the similarities between *Paraphrase of Genesis and Exodus* (4Q422)[39] and *Dibre Hamme'orot* or *Words of the Luminaries* (4Q504).[40] These two texts exhibit thematic parallels, and use similar language, especially in the Creation-Eden passages. The pertinent passages run as follows:

4Q422 (*4QParaphrase of Genesis and Exodus*) col. I (frag. 1)

Hebrew		*translation*
השמים והארץ וכול]צבאם עשה בד[	6	the heaven and the earth and all] their host he made by . . . [
מלאכתו אש]ר עשה ורוח קודש[ו	7	his work whi]ch he had done, and [his] holy spirit [
כול הנפ]ש החיה והרמש[ת על הארץ	8	every] living [creat]ure and what moves [on the earth
ע]ץ המשילו לאכול פר[י	9	*tr*]*ee*, he gave him dominion to eat the frui[t of
ל[ב]לתי אכול מעץ הד[עת	10	] with the [exce]ption of eating from the tree of *kn*[*owledge*
]יקום עליו וישכחו[	11	] he imposed upon him. And they forgot [
]ביוצר רע ולמען[	12	] with an evil inclination and *in order to* [
]שלום[	13	] peace [

4Q504 (*4QWords of the Luminaries*[a]) frg. 8 recto

Hebrew		*translation*
[תפלה ביום הראישון זכו]ר אד[ו]נ[י] כיא מע[	1	[Prayer for the first day. Remem]ber, Lord, that . . . [
]קתנו ואתה חי עול[מים	2	] . . . And you, who live for ev[er

[38] E. Glickler Chazon, "The Creation and Fall of Adam in the Dead Sea Scrolls", in: J. Frishman & L. van Rompay (Eds.), *The Book of Genesis in Jewish and Oriental Christian Interpretation; A Collection of Essays*, Leuven 1997, 13–24.

[39] T. Elgvin & E. Tov, *Discoveries in the Judaean Desert XIII*, Oxford 1994, 417–441, pls. XLII–XLIII.

[40] M. Baillet, *Discoveries in the Judaean Desert VII*, Oxford 1982, 137–168, pls. XLIX–LIII.

3	] נפלאות מקדם ונוראות[	] the marvels of old and the portents of [
4	אדם א]בינו יצרתה בדמות כבוד[כה	Adam,] our [fat]her, you fashioned in the image of [your] glory [
5	נשמת חיים נ]פחתה באפו ובינה ודעת [	the breath of life] you [b]lew into his nostril, and insight and knowledge [
6	בג]ן עדן אשר נטעתה המשלת[ו	over the gar]den of Eden, which you planted, you gave [him] dominion [
7	]ם ולתהלך בארץ כבוד א[	] and so that he would walk in a glorious land . . . [
8	]א שמר ותקם עליו לבלתי ס[ור	] . . . he kept. And you imposed upon him not to t[urn away
9	]בשר הואה ולעפר ה[	] he is flesh, and to dust . . . [

The so-called *Paraphrase of Genesis and Exodus* does not paraphrase the whole of Genesis and Exodus, but retells the Creation, the Eden story, the Flood narrative, and the Exodus account of the plagues which struck Egypt. The first section is not really a rewriting of Gen 1–3, but rather a very much abbreviated account of the creation and the fall of Adam. Chazon has shown that the first column of the liturgical work *Dibre Hamme'orot* also recounts the creation and fall of Adam, followed immediately by the Flood. Both texts use similar terms: the verbs המשיל, "to give dominion", and הקים על, "to impose upon", and the negative particle לבלתי, "that not", and seem to use the Creation-Eden and the Flood materials to demonstrate the sin-punishment theme.

The interest in these texts is not in the Garden of Eden or in the Tree of Knowledge, but in the Creation and Fall of Adam.[41] The few terms used with regard to the garden and the tree are derived from the Genesis narrative, except the peculiar term ארץ כבוד, "glorious land", in 4Q504 8 recto 7 which probably should be equated with עדן כבוד, "glorious Eden", in 1QH[a] XVI (Sukenik VIII) 20.

4.3. *4QInstruction (4Q423 2 1–4)*

An explicit reference to Eden with use of terminology derived from Gen 3 is found in the large sapiential composition, formerly called 4QSapiential Work A, and now referred to as *Instruction* or *Musar le-*

[41] For a more thorough discussion of these texts cf. E. Glickler Chazon, "Creation and Fall of Adam".

Mebin. One of the seven or more manuscripts of this work (1Q26, 4Q415–418, 4Q418a, 4Q423) preserves the following text:

4Q423 (4QInstruction[e]) frg. 2 1–4

1	]וֹכל פרי תנובה וכל עץ נעים נחמד להשכיל הלוא גן נ[עים	] and all the fruit of produce, and every fair tree, desirable to look at. Is it not a f[air] garden [
2	]לׄ[ה]שׂכיל מ[וא]דׄה ובו המשילכה לעבדו ולשמרו *vac* [	] to look at, very much. He set you in charge of it to till it and to guard it. *Blank* [
3	] קוץ ודׄרדר תצמיח לכה וכוחה לא תתן לכה [	] thorns and thistles it will bring forth for you, and its strength it will not give you [
4	]במועלכה *vacat* [	because of your unfaithfulness. *Blank* [

The editor of this manuscript, Elgvin,[42] argues for a distant join, placing frag. 1 to the left of frag. 2, but, even if this join is correct, it hardly adds anything to the text of lines 1–4. These lines use terminology derived from Gen 2–4, directed to a masculine singular addressee. Since the introduction of this section has been lost, one cannot determine the identity or status of this particular addressee,[43] nor is it clear in what sense or with what purpose the Genesis narrative was being paraphrased.[44] In view of some instructions in *4QInstruction* to farmers, one may consider the possibility that Eden and the paradise narrative is a metaphor for the earth (האדמה) in general, or the farmer's own land in particular, with, in the lost part between lines 2–3, the protasis of a conditional sentence. Alternatively, Elgvin argued that the following lines (6–8) refer to the end-time

[42] The *DJD* edition of *4QInstruction* is still due to be published, but cf. the preliminary edition in T. Elgvin, *An Analysis of 4QInstruction* (diss. Hebrew University 1998) 278–283. Elgvin also dealt shortly with this fragment in his "Admonition Texts from Qumran Cave 4", in: M.O. Wise *et al.* (Eds.), *Methods of Investigation of the Dead Sea Scrolls and the Khirbet Qumran Site; Present Realities and Future Prospects*, New York 1994, 179–194, esp. 187–188.

[43] In E.J.C. Tigchelaar, "The Addressees of 4QInstruction", forthcoming in D. Falk, F. García Martínez, E. Schuller (Eds.), *Proceedings of the Oslo IOQS Conference 2–4 August 1998*, I argue that in 4QInstruction the second person singular masculine is not one specific addressee, but is used more generally, to address wise men of different skills and social status. That is, the direct discourse with second person addressees is a literary form used to give instruction on a variety of topics.

[44] This sapiential composition also refers to Genesis 2 in the section dealing with family relations. 4Q416 2 iii 21–2 iv 1 refers to Genesis 2:18, 24, the latter verse possibly being completely quoted.

community, and that a paraphrase of Gen 2–3 was used as a background for a description of the inheritance of the elect.[45] Because of the lack of context one also cannot determine how the word השכיל was understood in this text. Is it merely taken from Gen 3:6, where it means "to look at", even though a word play on השכיל, "to make wise" seems likely? Or did the author interpret this word as derived from the root שכל, "to be wise"? One may observe that this text, like 4Q422 and 4Q504, uses the verb המשיל, and the use of this verb in the context of creation is possibly derived from Ps 8:7. Yet, on the other hand, המשיל is used disproportionately often in *Instruction* and denotes the tasks and the relationships ordained by God to the individual addressees.

5. *Conclusion*

The Genesis Eden narrative was wellknown, and is sometimes referred to or alluded to in the preserved texts. It is noteworthy, though, that neither Adam or Eve, nor Paradise itself evoked much interest, while most of the mythological aspects of the story of Gen 2–3 are neglected altogether. Apart from *Jub.* 3, which rewrites the narrative, the preserved texts do not interpret the narrative as a whole, but refer briefly to parts of the text. It appears that Gen 2–3 was used most to expound on the relation between male and female, and to express man's God-given authority over the earth. One or two texts do hint at Adam's disobedience, but there are no clear indications that this text was felt to be important because it deals with the origin of sin. Instead, it is remarkable that several texts referring to the Eden nar-

[45] T. Elgvin, *An Analysis of 4QInstruction*, 279. Elgvin dates the composition to the formative period of the Qumran Community, whereas e.g. the editors of the other 4QInstruction manuscripts, J. Strugnell and D.J. Harrington favour a pre-sectarian, possibly 3rd century BCE, dating of the work. A metaphorical use of Eden and other garden and arboreal images is applied to the Community in 1QH[a] XVI (Sukenik VIII) 4–26, in which the hymnist presents himself as the irrigator of the garden of trees of life, the eternal planting. This hymn draws upon many scriptural sections dealing with gardens and trees such as Gen 2–3; Isa 5:1–7; Ezek 31:2–14; Pss 36:9–10 and 80:9–15. J.R. Davila, "The Hodayot Hymnist and the Four Who Entered Paradise", *RevQ* 17/65–68 (1996) 457–78 argues that the scene is the garden of Eden which represents the heavenly temple, and the "shoot" or "eternal planting" the human community of faith residing spiritually in the heavenly temple. Davila may perhaps be correct, but one should note that the identification of the garden with Eden = heavenly temple is derived from other texts, not from the hymn itself.

rative state that God gave knowledge and insight to Adam (4Q305 2; 4Q504 8 recto 5).

Apart from *1 Enoch* there is no apparent concern with the location and present or future function of Eden. The later identification of Eden with the future Paradise, the transposition of Paradise to heaven, or the distinction between a heavenly Paradise or Eden and its earthly counterpart are not yet made in the Early Jewish texts.

Appendices

The Book of Enoch (*1 Enoch*) 32:2–6

Aramaic[46]	Greek (Panopolis)[47]	Ethiopic [± Tana 9][48]
[2]And from there I proceeded [to the Ea]st of all those mountains,	[2]And from there I proceeded over the summits of all those mountains,	[2]And from there I proceeded over the summits of those mountains,
far from them, to the East of the earth,	being far away, to the East of the earth,	far away to the East [+ of the earth]
and [I] passed on [ov]er the Red [Se]a, and went very far beyond it,	and I passed on over the Red Sea, and went <far>	and I went over the Red Sea, and I was far from it
and I crossed over the darkness, far from it.	and from there I went over Zotiel	and I went over [+ from it to] the angel Zotiel
[3]And I passed on to the Garden (*pardes*) of Righteousness, //	[3]And I came to the Garden (*paradeisos*) of Righteousness,	[3]And I came to the Garden (*gannat*) of Righteousness,
and I saw *m*[. . .]	and I saw beyond those trees many large trees <growing> there	and I saw beyond those trees many large trees growing there
differing [. . .] and [. . .]	very large, beautiful, glorious and magnificent	sweet-smelling, large, very beautiful and glorious,
not preserved	and the tree of knowledge (*phronesis*) from which the holy ones eat its fruit and know great knowledge.	and the tree of wisdom (*flebab*), those having eaten from it know great wisdom.
not preserved	[4]And that tree is like a pine in height,	[4](It is)
not preserved	and its leaves are like the carob tree	like the carob tree,

[46] 4Q206 = 4QEn^{e} ar 1 xxvi–xxvii. Cf. J.T. Milik, *The Books of Enoch*, 231–236. In F. García Martínez, E.J.C. Tigchelaar, *The Dead Sea Scrolls Study Edition Volume One. 1Q1–4Q273*, Leiden 1997, 424–427, there fragments are renumbered 4Q206 Frags. 3 + 4.

[47] Text between angled brackets presents emendations of the Greek text.

[48] The text in brackets renders unique additions to or omissions in the manuscript Tana 9, which, although corrupt in some places, often preserves original readings which are lost in the other Ethiopic manuscripts. Thus [+ xxx] means that only Tana 9 has this additional reading, whereas [- xxx] indicates that this reading, attested by other Ethiopic manuscripts, is lacking in Tana 9.

not preserved	and its fruit is like the bunches of grapes on a vine	and its fruit is like the bunches of grapes on a vine,
not preserved	and its smell penetrates afar from the tree.	and the smell of the tree spreads and penetrates afar.
not preserved	[5]Then I said: "How beautiful is the tree, and how pleasing its appearance!"	[5]And I said: "This tree is beautiful! How beautiful and pleasing is its appearance!"
not preserved	[6]Then Raphael, the holy angel who was with me, answered:	[6]And the holy angel Raphael who was with me, answered [- and said to me]:
[. . .] your mother of old and they [. . .]	This is the tree of knowledge from which your father ate *(Panopolis breaks off here)*	This is the tree of wisdom from which your old father and your aged mother, who were before you, ate and learnt wisdom;
[. . .] that they were naked *m*[	*not preserved*	and their eyes were opened, and they knew that they were naked,
not preserved	*not preserved*	and they were driven from the garden

The Book of Enoch (*1 Enoch*) 18:6–9a

Greek (Panopolis)	Ethiopic
[6]And I proceeded and saw a place which burns day and night where there are the seven mountains of magnificent stones, <three> towards the East, and three towards the South.	[6]And I proceeded to the South, and it burns day and night where there are seven mountains of magnificent stones, three towards the East, and three towards the South.
[7]And as for those towards the East <one> was of coloured stone, and one of pearl, and one of "antimony", and those towards the south of red stone.	[7]And as for those towards the East, one was of coloured stone, and one of pearl, and one of "healing stone", and those towards the south of red stone.
[8]But the middle one reached to heaven like the throne of God, of alabaster, and the summit of the throne was of sapphire.	[8]But the middle one reached to heaven like the throne of God, of alabaster, and the summit of the throne was of sapphire.
[9a]And I saw a burning fire.	[9a]And I saw a burning fire.

The Book of Enoch (*1 Enoch*) 24–25

Greek (Panopolis)

[24:1]And he showed me a mountain of fire which burnt at night.
[2]And I went beyond them and I saw seven magnificent mountains, all differing each from the other, the stones of which were magnificent in beauty, all (these mountains) magnificent and glorious and fair:
three towards the East, founded upon the other, and three towards the South, one upon the other, and deep rough ravines, no one of which joined with any other.
[3]And <. . .> the seventh mountain was in the midst of these, and it excelled (them) in height, like the seat of a throne, and fair trees encircled it.
[4]And amongst them was a tree such as I had never yet smelt, and no one else had enjoyed it, and nothing else was like it: it had a fragrance beyond all fragrance, and its leaves and the bloom and wood do not wither for ever; and the fruit is like the dates of a palm.

[5]Then I said: "How beautiful is this tree, and fragrant, and its leaves are fair, and its blooms fair in appearance."
[6]Then Michael answered me, one of the holy angels who was with me—and he was their leader:

[25:1]And he said to me: Enoch, what do you ask and wonder regarding the fragrance of the tree, and why do you wish to learn the truth?"
[2]Then I answered him: "I wish to

Ethiopic [± Tana 9]

[24:1]And from there I went to another place of the earth,
and he showed me a mountain of fire which burnt day and night.
[2]And I went beyond it and I saw seven magnificent mountains all differing each from the other, and the stones (thereof) were magnificent and beautiful, magnificent as a whole, of glorious appearance and fair exterior:
three towards the East, founded upon the other, and three towards the South, one upon the other, and deep rough ravines, no one of which joined with any other.
[3]And the seventh mountain was in the midst of these, and in height they were like the seat of a throne, and fragrant trees encircled it.

[4]And amongst them was a tree such as I had never yet smelt, neither was any amongst them nor were others like it: it had a fragrance beyond all fragrance, and its leaves and blooms and wood wither not for ever: and its fruit is beautiful, and its fruit is like the dates of a palm.
[5]Then I said: "Beautiful is this tree, and fragrant, and its leaves are fair, and its [- fruit; + leaves] are [- very] fair in appearance."
[6]And then Michael answered me, one of the holy and honoured angels who was with me—and he was their leader:
[25:1]And he said to me: Enoch what do you ask [- me] regarding the fragrance of this tree, and do you wish to know?"
[2]Then I [- Enoch,] answered him

know about everything, but
especially about this tree in
particular."
[3]And he answered saying: "This
high mountain, whose summit is
like the throne of God, is the
throne where the Great Lord, the
Glorious Holy One, the Eternal
King will sit, when he shall come
down to visit the earth in
goodness.

[4]And (as for) this fragrant tree, no
flesh is permitted to touch it till
the great judgment, in which is the
vengeance of all and the eternal
consummation. It then shall be
given to the righteous and holy.

[5]Its fruit shall be to the elect for
life, food: and it shall be
transplanted to the holy place, to
the temple of the Lord, the
Eternal King.
[6]Then they shall rejoice with joy
and gladness.
And into the holy place shall they
enter;
And its fragrance shall be in their
bones,
And they shall live a long life on
earth,
Where your fathers lived;
And in their days shall no sorrow
or plague
Or torment or calamity touch
them."
[7]Then I blessed the God of Glory,
the Eternal King, who prepared
such things for the righteous, and
created these and said to give
them.

saying: "I wish to know about
everything, but especially about this
tree."
[3]And he answered [- me] saying:
"This high mountain [- which you
have seen], whose summit is like
the throne of the Lord, is His
throne where the Holy (and) Great
One, the Lord of Glory, the
Eternal King will sit, when he shall
come down to visit the earth in
goodness.
[4]And (as for) this fragrant tree,
which no flesh is permitted to
touch it till the great judgment,
when He shall take vengeance on
all and bring everything to its
consummation for ever, it shall be
given to the righteous and holy.
[5]Its fruit shall be [- given] to the
elect for life: towards the north it
shall be transplanted to the holy
place, to the temple of the Lord,
the Eternal King.
[6]Then they shall rejoice with joy
and be glad.
[+ And] into the holy place shall
they enter;
And its fragrance shall be in their
bones,
And they shall live a long life on
earth,
Such as your fathers lived;
And in their days shall no tortures
or pains,
labours and blows touch them."

[7]Then I blessed the God of Glory,
the Eternal King, because he pre-
pared such things for the righteous
people, and created them and said
to give them.

The Astronomical Book of Enoch (*1 Enoch*) 77:3

Aramaic[49]	Ethiopic
3[And the north they call North] because in it all the bodies of the heavens hide and gather and revolve, and proceed to the east of heaven. [And the east Ea]st because from there arise the bodies of heaven. And also Orient because hundre[d]s arise. *vacat*	3And the fourth quarter, named the North
[And I saw three parts] of the earth:	is divided into three parts:
one of them for the dwelling of the sons of men in it;	one of them is the dwelling-place of men;
and one of them [. . .]	and another seas of water and the deeps, and forests, and darkness, and mist
[and one of them] for the deserts and for . . . [. . . and for the *parde*]*s* of righteousness. *vacat*	and another part the garden of righteousness.

[49] Combined text of 4Q209 (4QEnastr^b ar) 23 and 4Q210 (4QEnastr^c ar) 1 ii. Cf. J.T. Milik, *The Books of Enoch*, 287–291.

EDEN AND THE TEMPLE: THE REWRITING OF GENESIS 2:4–3:24 IN *THE BOOK OF JUBILEES*

J.T.A.G.M. van Ruiten

Introduction

As far as the final text is concerned, the narrative of Genesis 2 and 3 can be divided into two parts.[1] The first part (Gen 2:4b–25) is the creation story. It describes the creation of man, the garden, and the helpers of man (first the animals and then the woman). In this part the man acquires access to the Garden is prohibited from eating from the tree of the knowledge of good and evil. The second part of the story (Gen 3:1–24) describes the rejection from the Garden of Eden. The serpent tempts the woman to eat the forbidden fruit of the tree of the knowledge of good and evil. The woman seems to believe the words of the serpent, and eats the fruit. She then gives it to her husband, who also eats it. Thereafter, both man and woman become ashamed and make themselves aprons and hide from God, who accuses them and gives a judgement to the serpent, the woman, and the man. Finally, God dismisses the man from the Garden in order to prevent him from eating from the tree of life as well.

Although both parts of the story of the Garden of Eden are closely interwoven and can, to a certain extend, be read as one narrative, both the modern as well as the ancient reader have encountered some problems with the story. First, there is a duplication of the events included in another creation story in the bible: Genesis 1. Between the first and second creation narrative, however, there are many differences and even contradictory statements, which pose problems to the reader. Second, within the story of the Garden of Eden itself, there are also some elements that differ or even contradict one another. Modern readers, or at least modern exegetes, have tried to resolve the discrepancies by constructing different layers in the texts,

[1] For the structure of Gen 2:4–3:24, see G.W. Coats, *Genesis with an Introduction to Narrative Literature* (FOTL, 1), Grand Rapids, Mi 1983, 49–60; C. Westermann, *Genesis I.1* (BKAT I/1), Neukirchen-Vluyn, 1976², 259–269.

or by describing several traditions working within the text. Many of the ancient readers encountered the same sorts of problems with the biblical text. The way they try to harmonise the differences is, however, somewhat different from the harmonising method of modern exegetes.

In this article I discuss the story of the Garden of Eden in the Book of Jubilees, which was written in the middle of the second century BCE. It is presented as a revelation that Moses received at Mount Sinai, but it actually consists of a rewriting and interpretation of the biblical narrative from Genesis 1 to Exodus 16. Chapter 3 of the book concerns the story of the Garden of Eden, and in this article I will deal with this chapter. Firstly, I will give a short overview of the structure of Jubilees 3 in comparison with the story in Gen 2:4–3:24; secondly, I will look more closely at some of the differences between both texts.

1. *The structure of Jubilees 3 in comparison with Genesis 2:4–3:24*

The narrative of Jubilees 3, which runs parallel with Gen 2:4–3:24, can be divided into two parts. The first part (3:1–16) runs parallel with Genesis 2, which concerns the second account of the creation. The author of Jubilees, however, does not include a second account of creation. The events of Genesis 2 are the chronological continuation of the creation, which took place during the first week. The first part of Jubilees 3 can be characterised as a description of the first seven years of creation. The second part (3:17–35) runs parallel with the second part of the narrative of Genesis 2–3, which concerns the rejection from the Garden (Gen 3:1–24). The precise dating of the arrival of the serpent in 3:17 ("in the second month, on the seventeenth") and the departure of Adam and his wife from the Garden in 3:32 ("At the beginning of the fourth month") underlines the importance of chronology to the author of Jubilees. I have, therefore, named the second part of the story "The Last Forty-Five Days in the Garden." In the following table I give an overview of the general comparison of Gen 2:4–3:24 and Jub. 3:1–35.[2]

[2] In the table I put in "normal script" the corresponding elements between Gen 2:4–3:24 and *Jub.* 3:1–35 and in small caps the elements of Gen 2:4–3:24 which do not occur in *Jub.* 3:1–35, and vice versa. I underline those elements that show rearrangement; finally, I put in *italics* differences between Gen 2:4–4:1a and *Jub.* 3:1–35, other than addition and omission.

Part A. The creation story (Gen 2:4b–25)			Part A. The events in the first seven years of creation (*Jub.* 3:1–16)		
1.	2:4b–6	Time before the creation of man			
2.	2:7–15	Creation of man and garden			
		a. 2:7 creation of man			
		b. 2:8 creation of garden			
		c. 2:9–15: description of the garden (the trees [9], the rivers [10–14], the placing of man [15])			
3.	2:16–17	Prohibition against eating of the tree of he knowledge of good and evil			
4.	2:18–24	Creation of helper	1.	3:1–7	The events in the second week of creation
		a. 2:18 plan			a. 3:1–2 *presentation of the animals to Adam, naming*
		b. 2:19–20 creation of the animals, *presentation to the man and naming*			b. 3:3 experience of his loneliness
					c. 3:4 plan
		c. 2:21–24 *building of the woman*			d. 3:5–7 *building of the woman*
			2.	3:8–14	Postponement of the entrance into the Garden and *halakah* with regard to a woman who is giving birth
5.	2:25	*Time together in the garden before the temptation*	3.	3:15–16	*Time together in the garden before the temptation*

Part B. Rejection from the Garden (Gen 3:1–24)		Part B. The Last Forty-Five Days in the Garden (*Jub.* 3:17–35)	
1. 3:1–7	*Temptation and transgression*	1. 3:17–22	*Temptation and transgression*
2. 3:8–13	HIDING FROM God AND ACCUSATION		
3. 3:14–29	Judgement a. 3:14–15 *serpent* b. 3:16 *woman* c. 3:17–19 *man*	2. 3:23–25	Judgement a. 3:23ab *serpent* b. 3:23c–24 *woman* c. 3:25 *man*
4. 3:20–24	Conclusion a. 3:20 new name given to Eve b. 3:21 *second clothing* c. 3:22–24 *dismissal*	3. 3:26	Conclusion a. 3:26ab *second clothing* b. 3:26c *dismissal*
		4. 3:27–31	FINAL STATEMENTS a. 3:27 ADAM ACTING AS A PRIEST b. 3:28–29 ANIMALS STOP SPEAKING AND ARE DISMISSED FROM GARDEN c. 3:30–31 *HALAKAH* CONCERNING THE COVERING OF NAKEDNESS
		5. 3:32–35	DEPARTURE FROM THE GARDEN AND SETTLEMENT IN ELDA (among others new name given to Eve)

One of the most striking modifications to the story of Genesis 2–3 in the Book of Jubilees are the lengthy *omissions*. I point to the omission of Gen 2:4–17, which describes the creation of man and the Garden, and the prohibition against eating from the tree of the knowledge of good and evil; and to the omission of Gen 3:8–13, which describes the hiding of Adam from God after the transgression and the accusation. In addition to the omissions, there are also lengthy *additions* with regard to the text of Genesis. I point to the addition of *Jub.* 3:8–14, which stresses the postponement of the entrance of Adam and his wife into the Garden of Eden and relates this postponement to the *halakah* concerning the woman who is giving birth. There is also an *addition* to the end of the second part of the story. It is concerned with some final statements: Adam acting as a priest, the animals that are dismissed from the garden, and the *halakah* concerning the covering of nakedness. The differences between Genesis and Jubilees, however, are not only expressed in the omissions and additions, but also in passages that run parallel to each other. As can be seen in the synoptic overview of both passages in the appendix, there are extensive modifications.

2. *Some Differences between Jubilees 3 and Genesis 2–3*

A discussion of all the differences between Jubilees and Genesis is beyond the scope of this paper; therefore, only the most obvious differences will be covered. They mainly show the tendency to *harmonise*. The author of Jubilees first harmonises the two accounts of the creation; second, the contradictions within the story of the Garden of Eden itself; and third, the contradictions between the account in Genesis and other creation narratives related to the story in Genesis. The differences between both texts also show elements of interpretation, which I cannot attribute to the harmonising tendency.

2.1. *Harmonising the two accounts of creation*

The author of Jubilees harmonises both accounts of creation by applying the strategies of omission and rearrangement.

In the first place, there are some *contradictions* between Genesis 1 and 2. I point to Gen 2:5 ("when no plant of the field was yet in the earth, and no herb of the field had yet sprung up . . . there was no man to work the ground"). However, the plants and herbs had already been created at the third day of creation, whereas the man was created on the sixth day. Therefore, the text of Gen 2:5 is *omitted.*

In the second place, there is also some *duplication* of some elements included in the first account of creation in the second account. Genesis 2:9 describes the creation of the trees. They had already been created on the third day. Therefore the text of Gen 2:9 is omitted. Genesis 2:19 describes the creation of the animals; they had, however, already been created on the fifth and sixth days. Therefore, the author of Jubilees omits an account of their second creation. In *Jub.* 3:1–4, which is the rewriting of Gen 2:18–20, they are only brought to Adam in the second week of creation. Also, the creation of man in Gen 2:7 is a duplication of the creation in Genesis 1. There is also a contradiction related to the creation of man. In Genesis 1 man and woman are created at the same time; in Genesis 2, the man is created first, then the animals, and, finally, the woman. In Jubilees man is created in the first week of creation; he is not created again in the second. The woman is present within Adam, undeveloped, as one of his bones. Thus, the woman had already been created in the first week. However, in the second week she is actually taken out of man, she is completed, and she is presented to him. The formation of the woman in the second week is mainly a completion and a presentation of her to Adam.[3]

The author of Jubilees does not only harmonise the contradictions by omitting certain elements of the story of Genesis, but he also *rearranges* the text. I point to the description of the creation of the Garden of Eden on the third day in Jubilees (*Jub.* 2:5–7). The author has brought over several elements from Genesis 2. There may have been several reasons for the author to do so.[4] In the first place, the writer of Jubilees may have seen a link between the trees in Gen 1:11–12 ("... fruit trees bearing fruit in which is their seed..."), and the trees in Gen 2:9. According to Gen 2:16–17, all the trees in the Garden were fruit trees.

In the second place, the text of Gen 2:9a ("And out of the ground the Lord God made to grow every tree that is pleasant to the sight and good for food") and Gen 1:12 ("The earth brought forth vegetation, plants yielding seed according to their own kinds, and trees bearing fruit in which is their seed, each according to its kind") have several elements in common. It is striking that *Jub.* 2:7, which is a rewriting of Gen 1:12, has taken over some elements of Gen 2:9. In *Jub.* 2:7, as in Gen 2:9, it is God who made the trees grow out of the ground. In Gen 1:12 it is the earth which brings forth vegetation. Moreover, the words "for enjoyment and *for food*"[5] in *Jub.*

[3] See *Jub.* 3:8. For a discussion about the creation of Eve, see J.R. Levison, *Portraits of Adam in Early Judaism. From Sirach to 2 Baruch* (JSPSS 1), Sheffield 1988, 90–91, 214–215, note 10. Cf. note 16 below.

[4] J.C. VanderKam, "Genesis 1 in Jubilees 2", *Dead Sea Discoveries* 1 (1994) 311–312.

[5] The translation "for food" is defended by VanderKam. See J.C. VanderKam, *The Book of Jubilees* (Corpus Scriptorum Christianorum Orientalium 511; Scriptores Aethiopici, 88), Leuven 1989, 10.

2:7 have no equivalent in Gen 1:12. However, in Gen 2:9 the phrase "pleasant to the sight and good for food" is found.

In the third place, the transposition of the Garden of Eden to the context of Genesis 1 can also be brought about by the use of the expression מקדם in Gen 2:8. Usually, this expression in Gen 2:8 is translated as "in the east" (RSV: "And the Lord God planted a garden in Eden, in the east"). However, the meaning of קדם is not only "east," but also "in ancient time" or "aforetime." Therefore, מקדם can also be translated as "earlier" and "before."[6] Based on this translation Gen 2:8 can be interpreted as follows: the creation of Eden took place *before* the creation of man.[7]

2.2. *Harmonising contradictions within the story of the Garden of Eden*

In addition to the harmonising contradictions between the two accounts of creation, the author of Jubilees also harmonises discrepancies within the story of the Garden itself. Here also we see the application of the strategies of omission and rearrangement.

First, I point to the *omission* of Gen 2:16–17, where the tree with the forbidden fruit and the sanction associated with eating are mentioned. The omission of these verses can be due, of course, to the fact that, according to Jubilees, man has not yet entered the Garden of Eden. Thus there is no reason to speak about trees and the forbidden fruit in the Garden. But there are also some problems within the text of Genesis itself. First, in the temptation scene the woman appears to know about the prohibition of the forbidden fruit (Gen 3:2–3). However, at the point of the story where the prohibition is given, it is given to man only. Moreover, the woman is not yet created, or, according to Jubilees, she has not yet been presented to man and has not yet entered the Garden. By omitting the prohibition in the creation story, the author partly solves this problem. But, even more importantly, there are some contradictory statements in the text of Genesis with regard to the *sanction* associated with the

---

[6] Zie *Hebräisches und Aramäisches Lexikon zum Alten Testament, III*, 1000–1001; art. קדם (Kronholm), in: H.-J. Fabry – H. Ringgren (eds.), *Theologisches Wörterbuch zum Alten Testament, VI*, Stuttgart 1989, 1171–1175.

[7] The creation of Eden on the third day of creation can also be found in *Gen r* 15 and in 2 Enoch 30:1. Other texts put the creation of Eden even before the creation of the world (4 Ezra 3:6; the Palestinian Targums on Gen 2:8). In this opinion, מקדם is interpreted as "from the beginning." See R.H. Charles, *The Book of Jubilees or the Little Genesis*, London 1902, 14–15; VanderKam, *Genesis 1*, 312, note 32.

fruit, i.e., the death of Adam. First, it is said that *on the day* that Adam would eat of the tree of the knowledge of good and evil he would die (Gen 2:17). Second, after he ate from the tree God said to Adam that the ground was cursed and that in sadness he shall eat of the ground *all the days of his life until he would return to the dust* (3:17–19). Finally, in Gen 5:5 it is said that Adam died at the age of 930 years, and there is no mention of any curse.

All three statements come together in the statement about the death of Adam in *Jub.* 4:29–30:

29a At the end of the nineteenth jubilee, during the seventh week—in its sixth year—Adam died.
b All his children buried him in the land where he had been created.
c He was the first to be buried in the earth.
30a He lacked 70 years from 1000 years because 1000 years are one day in the testimony of heaven.
b For this reason it was written regarding the tree of knowledge:
c "On the day that you eat from it
d you will die."
e Therefore he did not complete the years of this day
f because he died during it.

In this final statement about Adam, the author of Jubilees refers to Gen 5:5 by mentioning the year of his death, which is implicitly his age.[8] Then the text describes that all the children of Adam buried him in the land, or in the earth, where he had been created. These words are an allusion to Gen 3:19: "Until you return to the *ground*, for out of it you were taken; you are *dust*, and to *dust* you shall

[8] Except for one word ("he died") the text of Gen 5:5 is changed completely. This is in line with the other entries in the genealogy of Jubilees 4. The rearrangement is caused by the fact that the mention of the death of Adam in 4:10, where the last time that Adam knew his wife is mentioned, would not have been the appropriate place in the sacred history. He died when he was 930 years old, and, in between, other things happened. The author prefers to put everything in its place. Cf. also, the death of Noah is delayed in the rewrite of Genesis (Gen 9:28–29; *Jub.* 10:15–17). The fact that he mentioned his death *after* the birth of Noah, which is in line with SamP (birth of Noah in 707), but not with MT (birth of Noah in 1056) or with LXX (birth of Noah in 1642), could be due to the fact that the birth of Noah and his name-giving (Gen 5:29c; *Jub.* 4:28e) are related to the curse of Adam (Gen 3:17–19; *Jub.* 3:25). In Gen 3:17 it is said that Adam shall eat in sadness *all the days of his life.* In the explanation of the name-giving of Noah it is said that he is the one who will give consolation from the sadness and from the earth that was cursed. If Adam had to suffer "all the days of his life," he could not enjoy the consolation of Noah. Moreover, the phrase "all the days of his life" evoke the death of the person involved. The relevance of Gen 3:17–19 (*Jub.* 3:25) for 4:29–30 is strengthened in the following lines.

return". *Jub.* 3:25 replaces the word dust (עפר) with *medr*, which can mean either land (or earth), or ground. The phrase "in the land (= earth) where he had been created" reflects "the earth from which you were taken," whereas "to be buried in the earth" reflects "to the earth you shall return."[9] The (natural) death of Adam is the execution of the sentence mentioned in Gen 3:19. It reveals a characteristic of the rewriting of the story of the Garden of Eden. The author of Jubilees removes the negative side of the Garden of Eden as much as possible.[10] Finally, *Jub.* 4:30 tries to reconcile the contradiction between Gen 5:5, which says that Adam lived 930 years, and Gen 2:17, where God says to Adam that on the day that he eats from the tree he would surely die, by way of an allusion to Ps 90:4 ("Because a thousand years in thy sight are but as yesterday"). By referring to this text, the author of Jubilees is able to say that

---

[9] Also according to *Apocalypse of Moses*, Adam's body was buried "in the place where God found the dust" (40:6). However, according to *Vitae Adae et Evae* 48:6, Adam was buried in parts of Paradise (48:6). According to Tg Ps-J Gen 2:7 and 2:15, the place where Adam was created was the place of the Temple ([2:7] "And he took dust from the site of the sanctuary"; [2:15] "Then God took Adam from the mountain of worship, the place where he had been created"). Tg Ps-J does not mention Adam's burial; however, according to Tg Ps-J Gen 3:23, Adam returns to "Mount Moriah from which he had been created." Also, according to rabbinic literature (e.g., *PT Nazir* 7, 56b; *Gen r* 14:8), the place where Adam was created was the place of the Temple. However, this is not the place of Adam's burial. The general opinion is that he was buried in the Cave of Machpelah, where not only Adam and Eve, but also Abraham, Isaac, and Jacob and their wives were thought to be buried (*BT Baba Bathra* 58a; *BT Erub* 53a). In *Pirqe de Rabbi Eliezer* 20 it is stated that Adam built a mausoleum beyond Mount Moriah for himself. This would seem to indicate a place in the neighbourhood of the temple. However, it is further stated that "therefore it is called Cave of Machpelah." See A.F.J. Klijn, *Seth in Jewish, Christian and Gnostic Literature* (NTS, 46), Leiden, 1977, 42–43.

[10] He also mentions that Adam is the *first* to be buried. This is in line with Enosh (*Jub.* 4:12), who is the *first* to call on the name of the Lord, and Enoch (*Jub.* 4:17–18), who is the *first* of mankind to learn the arts of writing, instruction, and wisdom. He does not reflect upon the residence of the body of Abel. Ginzberg states that the author of Jubilees alludes to the legend of Apocalypse of Moses and related sources, according to which the burial of Abel was delayed. See L. Ginzberg, *The Legends of the Jews, V*, Philadelphia, 1955[7], 125. Böttrich is more cautious: "*Jub.* 4,29 konstatierte noch schlicht, dass Adam als erster im Lande seiner Erschaffung begraben worden sei, ohne dabei über den Verbleib des zuvor erschlagenen Abels zu reflektieren." See Chr. Böttrich, *"Die Vögel des Himmels haben ihn begraben." Überlieferungen zu Abels Bestattung und zur Ätiologie des Grabes* (Schriften des Institutum Judaicum Delitzschianum, 3), Göttingen, 1995, 16. In later literature the delay of the burial of Abel until the death of Adam becomes an important theme. See, e.g., *Apocalypse of Moses* 40; *Vitae Adae et Evae* 48:1–2 ("And again the Lord said to the angels Michael and Uriel: "Bring me three linen cloths and spread them out over Adam, and other cloths over his son Abel, and bury Adam and his son"). For the delay of the burial of Abel, see Böttrich, *Vögel*, 15–28.

Adam did die on the day that he ate the fruit.[11] He introduces the reference to Gen 2:17 with the words "it was written." There are some modifications to the text of Gen 2:17. First, in the reference to the tree of knowledge, he omits the words "of good and evil." Second, in the speech of God, he omits the first phrase ("you shall not eat"), which is important because it shows again that the author of Jubilees tries to remove the negative side of the Garden of Eden as much as possible. Third, he uses the plural forms of "you eat" and "you will die", whereas MT uses the singular in both cases. By using the plural forms the prohibition and the sanction are also addressed to Adam's wife.[12]

Jubilees 3:1–7, which describes the events of the second week of creation, reflects a second example of the harmonising strategy that is applied to the rewriting of Gen 2:18–24, which describes the creation of a helper. As you can see in the synoptic overview in the appendix, this passage of Jubilees includes several verbatim quotations. Nevertheless, there are also omissions, additions, and variations. The author omits the creation of the animals, and brings over the presentation of the animals to Adam and the name-giving.

I would like to refer especially to the rewriting of Gen 2:18 in *Jub.* 3:4. It is again an example of *rearrangement.* In Genesis this statement is made by God *before* the creation of the animals and their presentation; in Jubilees it is made *after* their presentation. In the

[11] The reference to Ps 90:4 is unmistakable, although the verbal agreements are few. First, there is a verbal quotation ("because a thousand years"). Secondly, "but as yesterday" is replaced by "one day". This is also the case in 2 Peter 3:8 ("... with the Lord one day is as a thousand years, and a thousand years as one day") and rabbinic literature (cf. *Gen r* 8:2; *Lev r* 19:1; *Num r* 5:4; 14:12; *Songs r* 5:11,1). The comparative particle "as" is omitted. Nevertheless, many manuscripts (12 35[c] 39 42 44 47 48 58) add *kama* ("as"). They are probably influenced by Ps 90:4. Finally, "in the testimony of heaven" probably replaces "in thy sight," although it is also possible that with the words "in the testimony of heaven" the author indicates that he is referring to a biblical text. Also, in *Jub.* 23 the author of Jubilees is referring to Psalm 90. Cf. J.T.A.G.M. van Ruiten, "Van tekst tot tekst. Psalm 90 en Jubileeën 23:12–15", *NTT* 47 (1992) 177–185; J.C. Kugel, "The Jubilees Apocalypse", *DSD* 1 (1994) 322–337.

[12] MT, SamP, and Peshitta use the singular in both cases. The Septuagint, however, also reflects plural forms. Moreover, in MT Gen 3:1–3 (cf. *Jub.* 3:17–18) plural forms are also used with regard to the verbs "eating" and "dying." Finally, the use of the absolute infinitive ("you will *surely* die") in Gen 2:17 is not reflected in 4:30d. This seems to stress that, according to Jubilees, these words are not a punishment, but just the consequence of the action of eating.

text of Genesis it is God who observes that the man is alone, and He comes up with a plan. He creates the animals. However, He must admit that He has not created something that suits the man. Only then does He decide to build the woman. In Jubilees God's formation of the animals is not a mistaken attempt at finding a partner for Adam. The animals, which were just created in the first week are brought to Adam in the second week, and he gives them names. He observes the animals and sees that they are "male and female according to every kind," and he observes that he is alone,—that there is no one who is like himself, who will help him. It is the man himself who observes that he does not have anybody. Only after Adam discovers existential loneliness does God decide to make a helper.[13]

The modification of this part of the biblical story in Jubilees also shows that bringing the animals to Adam results in setting a new goal.[14] Not only do they get their names, but they reveal to Adam, while he is observing them, that he is alone and that he is, in fact,

[13] The quotation of Gen 2:18 in *Jub.* 3:4 shows some modifications. First, 3:4a includes one divine name, whereas Gen 3:18a includes two. Also, many MSS of LXX and EthGen 2:18 include one divine name. Second, 3:4a has the addition "to us" (the angels). See also 3:1a: "*we* brought to Adam, on the Lord's orders". One of the angels speaks to Moses. According to Jubilees, the angels had already been created on the first day of creation (*Jub.* 2:2). It is possible that "to us" is added because in 3:1a they had already been present and active. They presented the animals to Adam. With the addition of "to us," the author of Jubilees probably stresses the presence of the angels. It is also possible that the addition has something to do with the third modification, i.e., 3:4c reads "let us make" instead of "let me make." The plural form does occur also in LXX Gen 2:18: ποιήσωμεν. Also Vg and EthGen 2:18 include a plural form, whereas MT, SamP, and Peshitta include the singular. The reading of LXX does remind one of LXX Gen 1:26 ("Let us make man": ποιήσωμεν ἄνθρωπον). According to the Greek translator, the creation of the woman is at the same level as the creation of man. Cf. M. Harl, *La Genèse* (La Bible d'Alexandrie 1), Paris 1986, 105; M. Rösel, *Übersetzung als Vollendung der Auslegung. Studien zur Genesis-Septuaginta* (BZAW 223), Berlin & New York 1994, 68–69. The creation of man is formulated with a singular form in Jubilees (2:14: "He made"). The consequence of the addition of "to us" (3:4a) is that the plural form in 3:4c does not refer to God, but to God and the angels. It is possibly on account of a reaction against a textual tradition (attested in LXX, which includes a plural), that the author of Jubilees added "to us." It is possible that the *Vorlage* of Jubilees has the plural form ("Let us make"). The substantive "helper" (עזר) is rendered here with a substantive "helper" (*marde'a*), unlike 3:3e, where a verb "to help" (*rad'a*) is used to render the substantive. The Hebrew כנגדו, ("as his counterpart," "suiting him") is rendered here with "like him" as in 3:3e.

[14] For the following, compare G. Anderson, "Celibacy or Consummation in the Garden? Reflections on Early Jewish and Christian Interpretations of the Garden of Eden", *HTR* 82 (1989) 121–148 (esp. 128).

longing for a female. The addition and some of the modifications in 3:3 make clear that the bringing of the animals has a pedagogical function. It makes Adam aware of his incompleteness and his need for a partner.[15] Adam's recognition of his need and the provision of this need[16] leads to the sexual encounter of man and woman. The author emphasises their sexual encounter in his rewriting of Gen 2:22–24 with some additions and slight modifications in *Jub.* 3:6–7.

2.3. *Harmonising different traditions*

A third category of harmonising is not involved with harmonising contradictions between the first and the second accounts of creation, nor with contradictions within the story of the Garden of Eden itself, but with contradictions between the biblical story and traditions not documented in the bible—traditions that were authoritative for the author of Jubilees. One example of such a tradition is the *Book of Enoch.* In different places within the book of Jubilees, the author refers to several parts of 1 Enoch. See, for example, the material about Enoch himself in chapter 4.

In Jubilees 3 there might also be some influence of 1 Enoch, although it is less obvious than in chapter 4. First, I refer to the omission of the tree of life in Jubilees. In the story of Genesis, Adam is dismissed from the garden in order to prevent him from eating of the tree of life (Gen 3:22d–f, 24d). The omission of the reference to the tree of life might be because of the fact that it contradicts what God has said with regard to the sanction of eating from the tree of knowledge. However, the omission might also be because of the fact that when the *Book of Enoch* speaks about the Garden of Eden, it speaks about only one tree. It is the heavy smelling tree of wisdom from which Adam and his wife have eaten, and it will give life to the elect ones after the great judgement.[17] Second, according to 1 Enoch, the origin of evil in the world is attributed to the fall of the angels, who are also called the Watchers. The Book of Jubilees modifies this tradition in that the Watchers originally come with pos-

[15] Compare *Gen r* 17:4: "Then he paraded them again before him in pairs. Adam said: Every one has a partner, yet I have none."

[16] *Jub.* 3:5 (cf. Gen 2:21–22a) describes the completion of the woman, who was already created as one of the ribs of man. In Gen 3:8 this completion is interpreted as a presentation of the woman to Adam. Cf. note 3 above.

[17] See 1 Enoch 24–25; 32.

itive intentions (*Jub.* 4:15), but once they are on earth the positive intentions disappear (*Jub.* 4:22; 5:1–11). Although the author of Jubilees does not attribute the origin of sin to the fall of Adam and his wife in the Garden, he seems to feel bound to the biblical text.[18] Therefore, he cannot minimise the importance of the transgression in the Garden as much as in Enoch. However, one of the characteristics of the rewriting of Gen 2:4–3:24 in Jubilees is the fact that the author tries to minimise the negative side of Eden as much as possible. I point to the association of Eden with the Temple, to the portrayal of Adam as a priest, and to the softening of the expulsion scene.

2.4. *Eden as a Temple*

I now come to a last example of the differences between Genesis and Jubilees. I am not sure whether we can attribute this difference to the hermeneutic principle of harmonising or not. It is concerned mainly with the addition of 3:8–14.

The addition is connected with Gen 2:15, which was omitted in the beginning. This verse is quoted with some modifications in *Jub.* 3:9 ("we brought him into the Garden of Eden to work [it] and keep [it]),[19] and it is another example of *rearrangement.* The author stresses that not only the man, but also the animals and the woman are created outside the garden. This is in line with the first creation narrative in Genesis 1. In this respect, it is another example of harmonising. However, the rearrangement *delays* the entrance of Adam and Eve into the Garden of Eden—a delay that is related to the *halakah* of the woman who is giving birth.

The hermeneutic background of this modification of the creation story of Genesis is, in my view, the conception of Eden as a sanctuary. The Garden of Eden is a holy place, more holy than any

---

[18] Cf. VanderKam, *Enoch. A Man for All Generations* (Studies on Personalities of the Old Testament), Columbia, South Caroline 1995, 120.

[19] First, the subject of the action is not the Lord God, but "we", i.e., the angels. Also, in 3:1, 4a, and 15a the angels are the agents of the action. Second, the verb נוח ("to put") of Gen 2:15b is not used, nor the word שים ("to put") of Gen 2:8b. Instead 3:9b uses the verb *bo'a* ("to enter"; causative: "to bring"). Cf. also Josephus, *Ant.* 1:38. This verb is also used in 3:9d, 12b and is influenced by the verb בוא in Lev 12:4c (= *Jub.* 3:10f, 13c). By the use of this verb in connection with the entrance, the author of Jubilees facilitates the connection of the entrance of Adam and Eve into the Garden of Eden and the entrance of the woman who is giving birth into the Temple.

land (3:12); it is a place that belongs to the Lord (4:26), and is conceived as "the Holy of Holies and the residence of the Lord" (8:19). It means that the Garden of Eden is seen as a Temple, or, more precisely as a part of the Temple: the room which is in the rear of the Temple, where the ark of the covenant of the Lord is placed, and which is often called "Holy of Holies."[20] It is possible that the Garden of Eden is not seen as identical with the Temple, for sometimes Eden and the Temple are conceived as different entities. The author might see the relationship of the two as a sort of symbolic representation of one by the other.[21] In any event, the author of Jubilees subscribes to the conception that Eden is related to the Temple, and this has important consequences for the rewriting of Genesis in the Book of Jubilees.

First, the author has difficulties with the view that the consummation of the sexual relationship of Adam and Eve took place inside the Garden.[22] We know from the book of Exodus that before the descent and revelation of the Lord on Mount Sinai, the men of Israel should not go near to a woman for three days (Exod 19:15). And the book of Leviticus states that after having intercourse, the man is unclean until the evening, and he may not eat of the holy things unless he has bathed his body in water.[23] Some Qumran texts show a strict application of these laws: after having sex it is not permissible to enter the city of the Temple for three days.[24] This view

---

[20] Cf. Anderson, 129; J.M. Baumgarten, "Purification after Childbirth and the Sacred Garden in 4Q265 and Jubilees", in: G.J. Brooke – F. García Martínez (eds.), *New Qumran Texts and Studies. Proceedings of the First Meeting of the International Organization for Qumran Studies, Paris 1992* (STDJ, 15), Leiden 1994, 3–10; B. Ego, "Heilige Zeit—heiliger Raum—heiliger Mensch. Beobachtungen zur Struktur der Gesetzesbegründung in der Schöpfungs- und Paradiesgeschichte des Jubiläenbuches", in: M. Albani, J. Frey, A. Lange (eds.), *Studies in the Book of Jubilees* (TSAJ, 65), Tübingen 1997, 207–219, 211–215; C.T.R. Hayward, "The Figure of Adam in Pseudo-Philo's Biblical Antiquities", *JSJ* 23 (1992) 1–20 (esp. 6–7); J.T.A.G.M. van Ruiten, "The Garden of Eden and Jubilees 3:1–31", *Bijdragen* 57 (1996) 305–317 (esp. 311–312).

[21] See Ego, *Heilige Zeit*, 214.

[22] See Anderson, *Celibacy*, 128–131.

[23] Cf. Lev 15:18; 22:4–7.

[24] 11QT[a] 45:11–12 ("Anyone who lies with his wife and has an ejaculation, for three days shall not enter anywhere in the city of the temple in which I shall install my name . . ."); CD 11:21–12:2 (". . . And everyone who enters the house of prostration should not enter with impurity requiring washing . . . No man should sleep with his wife in the city of the temple, defiling the city of the temple with their impurity"); 4Q274 ("If a man has an emission of semen, his touch transmits impurity"); cf. Baumgarten, *Purification*, 7; J. Milgrom, "4QTohora[a]: an Unpublished

had a very important consequence for the rewriting of the biblical story of the Garden of Eden in the book of Jubilees, namely, that Adam and Eve are created not inside, but outside the Garden of Eden. This means that the first sexual relation between Adam and Eve does not take place in the garden of Eden, but *before* they enter. Only forty days after their first sexual relation is Adam permitted to enter the garden, and his wife must wait eighty days. The second sexual relation took place only in the second jubilee, a long time after they left the Garden of Eden (3:34). This means that laws concerning the Temple are applied to the Garden of Eden.

Second, in the Book of Jubilees the entrance of Adam and Eve into the Garden of Eden is explicitly related to the law concerning the woman who is giving birth, which is found in Leviticus 12. The mother observes seven days of impurity and thirty-three days of purification after the birth of a boy, and fourteen days of impurity and sixty-six days of purification after the birth of a girl. The reason for the disparity between the observation periods impurity and purification for the birth of a boy and the birth of a girl remains obscure. The author of Jubilees tries to give an explanation for this disparity by integrating Lev 12 into the story of the second week of creation. The author explains that the period of impurity following the delivery of a girl is double that of a boy because Eve was introduced to Adam in the second week of creation—seven days after he and the bone that became Eve had been created. Although the situation in Leviticus 12 does not completely fit the model of Jubilees, it is clear that the author tries to give an etiological reason for the disparity.[25] His radical changes to the text of Genesis 2–3 also reveal an exegetical effort to solve the problem of the lack of sufficient details in Leviticus 12.

Third, according to the author of Jubilees, Adam is acting as a prototype of a priest. He *burns incense* at the gate of the Garden of Eden (3:27: "On that day, as he was leaving the Garden of Eden, he burned incense as a pleasing fragrance—frankincense, galbanum, stacte, and aromatic spices—in the early morning when the sun rose at the time he covered his shame"). According to Exodus, the incense

Qumran Text on Purities", in: D. Dimant – L.H. Schiffman (eds.), *Time to Prepare the Way in the Wilderniss. Papers on the Qumran Scrolls* (STDJ 16), Leiden 1995, 59–68.

[25] See J. Milgrom, *Leviticus 1–16. A New Translation with Introduction and Commentary* (AB 3), New York 1991, 750; Baumgarten, *Purification*, 5.

is burned in front of the Holy of Holies. The burning of incense is a privilege given to the priests, namely the sons of Aaron.[26]

Related to the function of Adam as priest, is the covering of nakedness, which is a condition for offering. The priests are explicitly bidden to cover their nakedness.[27] The author of Jubilees lays emphasis on the covering of the nakedness. I point to 3:16, 21–22, 30–31. In 3:16, which is a modification of Gen 2:25, the statement refers to Adam alone ("*He* was naked . . . . . *he* was ashamed"). The addition of "but he neither knew it" stresses the innocence of Adam with regard to his nakedness. It refers to his own nakedness, but probably also to the nakedness of his wife. In 3:21–22 this is illustrated quite clearly. In this text, which is a quotation of Gen 3:6–7 with some modifications, it is stated that after eating the fruit, the woman first covered her shame and then gave the fruit to Adam. Only after that were his eyes opened, and "he saw that he was naked." The *halakah* concerning the covering of nakedness is even written in the heavenly tablets, as can be seen in 3:30–31. These last verses reveal that the emphasis on the covering of nakedness does not only result from the conception of Eden as a sanctuary. It also contains a protest against contemporary Hellenistic practices.[28]

Also, the fact that Enoch, who is led from among the children of men, is brought by the angels into the Garden of Eden for his greatness and honour illustrates this view of Eden as the Temple. In the Garden he is not only "writing down the judgement and condemnation of the world", but he is also burning incense, probably inside, maybe at the gate of the garden, or on the mountain of incense.[29]

---

[26] See Exod 30:7–8, 34–38; Num 16:39–40; 2 Chron 26:16–20.

[27] See Exod 20:26; 28:42. According to the author of Jubilees, the meaning of Gen 3:21 (cf. *Jub.* 3:26) is that God has clothed the man in *priestly* clothing. The use of כתנות עור, offers him the opportunity for this interpretation. Among the articles of clothing in which the priests are dressed are also the כתנות. See Ego, *Heilige Zeit*, 215; S.N. Lambden, From Fig Leaves to Fingernails. Some Notes on the Garments of Adam and Eve in the Hebrew Bible and Select Early Postbiblical Jewish Writings, in: P. Morris – D. Sawyer, *A Walk in the Garden. Biblical, Iconographical and Literary Images of Eden* (JSOTSS 136), Sheffield 1992, 74–90, esp. 82; Levison, *Portraits*, 93–95; Van Ruiten, *Garden*, 316.

[28] Cf. 1 Macc 1:13–14; 2 Macc 4:13–15.

[29] The Ethiopic reads *badabra qatr*: the mountain of the noon, or the mountain of the south. The word *qatr*, however, is probably a corrupted transcription of קטרה (= "incense"). So E. Tisserant, "Fragments syriaques du Livre des Jubilés", *RB* 30 (1921) 55–86, 206–232, esp. 77; J.C. VanderKam, *Enoch and the Growth of an Apocalyptic Tradition* (CBQMS 16), Washington 1984, 187.

Whereas Adam burned incense in the morning, Enoch burns the incense of the evening of the sanctuary.[30] The motif of Enoch as a priest is not documented prior to Jubilees.[31]

It can be defended that the stress on the conception of the Garden of Eden as a Temple is in line with traditions both inside and outside the Bible. If this is true, this element of the author's rewrite should also be attributed to the harmonising tendency. However, although there is a tradition-historical relationship between the Garden of Eden and the Temple, prior to the Book of Jubilees, as far as the Old Testament is concerned it is difficult to establish that certain texts, which could have influenced the author of Jubilees, *explicitly* relate Eden to the Temple. What can be said is that the Old Testament speaks about Eden in two ways. First, it is referred to in conjunction with the loss of former glory (Gen 13:10; Ezek 28:11–19; 31:6–9, 16–18; Joel 2:3), and second, it is referred to in conjunction with a restoration in the future (Isa 51:3; Ezek 36:35). Only with regard to the second reference is Eden explicitly related to Zion.

As far as the early Jewish literature other than the Book of Jubilees is concerned, there are passages in which Eden is related to Jerusalem. In all these passages Eden is always associated with the *future* temple. I point to 1 Enoch 24–27; the Testament of Levi 18:6 and Testament of Dan 5:12; Apocalypse of Moses 29:1–6; and some Qumran texts where the expression מקדש אדם is used (4Q174; 4Q265; 4Q421).[32] Although most of these texts are dated slightly later than the Book of Jubilees, it is possible, of course, that the author is referring to traditions within these texts.

Conclusions

I now come to some final conclusions. The rewriting of Genesis 2–3 in Jubilees 3 is characterised, in the first place, by the principle of

[30] The Syriac tradition reads "first" in stead of "sanctuary". This is most probably a corruption. See VanderKam, *The Book of Jubilees*, 28, n.

[31] It fits in with the tendency of Jubilees that makes all the important patriarchs in the line of Seth priests. Also Adam functions as a priest. Cf. VanderKam, *Enoch and the Growth*, 186.

[32] See J.T.A.G.M. van Ruiten, "Visions of the Temple in the Book of Jubilees", in: B. Ego, A. Lange, P. Pilhofer (eds.), *Community without Temple* (WUNT), Tübingen (forthcoming).

harmonisation. Many differences between Genesis and Jubilees can be attributed to this principle. The harmonisation in Jubilees 3 is concerned with conflicting statements between the two accounts of creation, conflicting statements within the story of the Garden of Eden itself, and conflicting statements between the biblical story and parallels and interpretations of the biblical story in early Jewish literature. In the second place, the rewriting is characterised by the fact that the Garden of Eden is conceived as a sanctuary. Many differences between Genesis and Jubilees can be reduced to this principle.

The author of Jubilees realises his hermeneutic principles in his rewriting of the biblical story by several exegetical strategies. In this paper I point to the omissions, additions, and other variations, and especially to the strategy of rearrangement. Also characteristic to Jubilees is the fact that the author inserts *halakot*, which are connected with the story-line. The *halakah* concerning the woman who is giving birth is related to the entrance in the Garden of Eden, and the *halakah* concerning the covering of nakedness is related to the departure from the Garden.

What was the ultimate purpose of the rewriting of Genesis in Jubilees? Did the author want to replace the book of Genesis by Jubilees in a canonical collection or did he want to relate the story of Genesis to a correct understanding of the Law, as a sort of *halakic midrash*? I have no clear answer to this question. We have to bear in mind that the boundaries of the canon were not yet fixed at the time Jubilees was written. Moreover, different groups within Judaism had different opinions about which books should be included in a canon of Holy Literature. The fact that the Book of Jubilees is attested quite well in the scrolls of Qumran suggests that at least one group within early Judaism was of the opinion that the Book of Jubilees should be included.

The method of rewriting Genesis in Jubilees has a parallel in the Bible. The books of Chronicles rewrites the story of Israel from the creation onwards, mainly focusing on the time of the kingdom. It can, therefore, be considered as a rewriting of the books of Kings. Both collections are presented in the canon of the Bible. The redactors received both written and oral traditions. They preserved at least part of them. But they also added their own interpretation of the older traditions. I refer to the way the primeval history is presented in the Bible. Both the older Yahwistic material and the priestly revision of it is recorded. It is puzzling, however, that the author of Jubilees cannot accept the diversity of the Yahwistic and priestly accounts of the primeval history. He tries to harmonise the accounts as much as possible by removing the contradictions and repetitions. It is, therefore, difficult to imagine that he would put his own account side by side with the biblical account(s) in a canonical collection of Holy Scriptures. Either it is meant to replace Genesis in a canonical collection—without contradictions and within a rigid chronological framework—or it is meant to be a form of Oral Torah *avant-la-date*. It the latter case it presents the correct interpretation of the *halakot*, adapting them to the changing situation of life.

APPENDIX: SYNOPSIS GENESIS 2:4–4:1A AND JUBILEES 3:1–35

In the synoptic overview I try to give a classification of the similarities and dissimilarities between Genesis and Jubilees. I put in SMALL CAPS the elements of Genesis which do not occur in Jubilees, and vice versa, i.e., the OMISSIONS and ADDITIONS. In "normal script" are the corresponding elements between both texts, i.e., the verbatim quotation of one or more words of the source text in Jubilees. I put in *italics* the *variations* between Genesis and Jubilees, other than addition or omission. The verbatim quotations and the modifications of them can occur in the same word-order or sentence-order in Jubilees as in Genesis. However, sometimes there is a rearrangement of words and sentences. I underline those elements.

Biblical verses are quoted according to the Revised Standard Version with slight modifications. Quotations from Jubilees are from J.C. VanderKam, *The Book of Jubilees* (CSCO 511, Scriptores Aethiopici 88), Leuven 1989, with slight modifications.

Genesis 2:4–17	
4a	THESE ARE THE GENERATIONS OF THE HEAVENS AND THE EARTH
4b	WHEN THEY WERE CREATED.
4c	IN THE DAY THAT THE LORD GOD MADE THE EARTH AND THE HEAVENS,
5a	WHEN NO PLANT OF THE FIELD WAS YET IN THE EARTH,
5b	AND NO HERB OF THE FIELD HAD YET SPRUNG UP,
5c	—FOR THE LORD GOD HAD NOT CAUSED IT TO RAIN UPON THE EARTH,
5d	AND THERE WAS NO MAN TO WORK THE GROUND;
6a	BUT A MIST WENT UP FROM THE EARTH
6b	AND WATERED THE WHOLE FACE OF THE GROUND—
7a	THEN THE LORD GOD FORMED MAN OF DUST FROM THE GROUND,
7b	AND BREATHED INTO HIS NOSTRILS THE BREATH OF LIFE;
7c	AND MAN BECAME A LIVING BEING.

(table cont.)

Genesis 2:4–17	
8a	AND THE LORD GOD PLANTED A GARDEN IN EDEN, IN THE EAST;
8b	AND THERE HE PUT THE MAN WHOM HE HAD FORMED.
9a	AND OUT OF THE GROUND THE LORD GOD MADE TO GROW EVERY TREE THAT IS PLEASANT TO THE SIGHT AND GOOD FOR FOOD,
9b	THE TREE OF LIFE ALSO IN THE MIDDLE OF THE GARDEN, AND THE TREE OF THE KNOWLEDGE OF GOOD AND EVIL.
10a	A RIVER FLOWED OUT OF EDEN TO WATER THE GARDEN,
10b	AND THERE IT DIVIDED AND BECAME FOUR RIVERS.
11a	THE NAME OF THE FIRST IS PISHON;
11b	IT IS THE ONE WHICH FLOWS AROUND THE WHOLE LAND OF HAV'ILAH,
11c	WHERE THERE IS GOLD;
12a	AND THE GOLD OF THAT LAND IS GOOD;
12b	BDELLIUM AND ONYX STONE ARE THERE.
13a	THE NAME OF THE SECOND RIVER IS GIHON;
13b	IT IS THE ONE WHICH FLOWS AROUND THE WHOLE LAND OF CUSH.
14a	AND THE NAME OF THE THIRD RIVER IS TIGRIS,
14b	WHICH FLOWS EAST OF ASSYRIA.
14c	AND THE FOURTH RIVER IS THE EUPHRATES.
15a	THE LORD GOD TOOK THE MAN
15b	*and put* him in the garden of Eden to work it and keep it.

(table cont.)

Genesis 2:4–17			
16a	AND THE LORD GOD COMMANDED THE MAN, SAYING:		
16b	YOU MAY FREELY EAT OF EVERY TREE OF THE GARDEN;		
17a	BUT OF the tree of the knowledge OF GOOD AND EVIL		
17b	YOU SHALL NOT EAT,		
17c	for on the day that you eat from it,		
17d	you will SURELY die."		(cf. Jub. 4:30)

Genesis 2:18–24		*Jubilees 3:1–7*	
18a	Then the Lord God said: "It is not good		
18b	that the man should be alone;		
18c	*Let me make* for him a helper like him."		
19a	SO OUT OF THE GROUND THE LORD GOD FORMED all animals OF THE FIELD AND all birds OF THE AIR,		[ ]
	[ ]	1a	ON THE SIXTH DAY OF THE SECOND WEEK
19b	and he brought them to the man		*we* brought *to Adam*, ON THE LORD'S ORDERS
	[ ]	b	all animals, ALL CATTLE, all birds, EVERYTHING THAT MOVES ABOUT ON THE EARTH, AND EVERYTHING THAT MOVES ABOUT IN THE WATER
		c	IN THEIR VARIOUS KINDS AND VARIOUS FORMS:
		d	THE ANIMALS ON THE FIRST DAY;
		e	THE CATTLE ON THE SECOND DAY;
		f	THE BIRDS ON THE THIRD DAY;
		g	EVERYTHING THAT MOVES ABOUT ON THE EARTH ON THE FOURTH DAY,

(table cont.)

Genesis 2:18–24		*Jubilees 3:1–7*	
		h	AND THE ONES THAT MOVE ABOUT IN THE WATER ON THE FIFTH DAY.
	TO SEE WHAT HE WOULD CALL THEM;		[ ]
19c	and whatever *the man* called *every living creature,* became *its* name.		
20a	And *the man* named *all cattle, the birds of the air, and all animals of the field;*	2a	*Adam* named *them all,* EACH WITH ITS OWN NAME.
		b	Whatever *he* called *them,* became *their* name.
	[ ]	3a	DURING THESE FIVE DAYS ADAM WAS LOOKING AT ALL OF THESE—
		b	MALE AND FEMALE AMONG EVERY KIND THAT WAS ON THE EARTH.
		c	BUT HE HIMSELF WAS ALONE;
20b	*but* for *the man he did not found* a *helper* like him.	d	*there was no one whom he found for himself*
		e	*who would help him who* was like him.
		4a	Then the Lord said TO US:
		b	"It is not good that the man should be alone.
		c	*Let us make* for him a helper *who* is like him".
21a	The Lord God imposed a sound slumber on *the man,*	5a	The Lord, *our* God, imposed a sound slumber on *him*
21b	and he fell asleep.	b	and he fell asleep.
21c	Then he took one *from* his bones [ ].	c	Then he took one BONE *from among* his bones FOR A WOMAN.
	[ ]	d	THAT RIB WAS THE ORIGIN OF THE WOMAN, FROM AMONG HIS BONES.
		e	*He built up* the flesh in its place,
21d	*He closed up* its place with flesh;	f	and *he* built [ ] the woman.
22a	and *the Lord God* built THE BONE, WHICH HE HAD TAKEN FROM THE MAN, INTO a woman		

(table cont.)

Genesis 2:18–24		*Jubilees 3:1–7*	
	[ ]	6a	THEN HE AWAKENED ADAM FROM HIS SLEEP.
		b	WHEN HE AWOKE, HE GOT UP ON THE SIXTH DAY.
22b	and he brought *her to the man.*	c	And he brought *(him) to her.*
	[ ]	d	HE KNEW HER
23a	And *the man* said [ ]:	e	and *he* said TO HER:
23b	"This is now bone of my *bones* and flesh from my flesh;	f	"This is now bone from my *bone* and flesh from my flesh.
23c	This one will be called *woman,*	g	This one will be called *my wife,*
23d	for she was taken out of *man.*"	h	for she was taken from *her husband.*"
24a	For this reason a man [ ]	7a	For this reason a man AND A WOMAN ARE TO BE ONE,
	leaves his father and his mother.	b	AND FOR THIS REASON HE leaves his father and his mother.
24b	He associates with his wife,	c	He associates with his wife,
24c	and they become one flesh.	d	and they become one flesh.

		Jubilees 3:8–14	
		8a	IN THE FIRST WEEK ADAM AND HIS WIFE—THE RIB—WERE CREATED,
		b	AND IN THE SECOND WEEK HE SHOWED HER TO HIM.
		c	THEREFORE, A COMMANDMENT WAS GIVEN TO KEEP SEVEN DAYS FOR A MALE (CHILD)
		d	AND FOR A FEMALE TWO (UNITS) OF SEVEN DAYS.
		9a	AFTER 40 DAYS HAD COME TO AN END FOR ADAM IN THE LAND WHERE HE HAD BEEN CREATED,
		b	*we brought* him into the Garden of Eden
		c	to work (it) and keep it.
		d	HIS WIFE WAS BROUGHT (THERE) ON THE EIGHTIETH DAY.
		e	AFTER THIS SHE ENTERED THE GARDEN OF EDEN.

(table cont.)

	Jubilees 3:8–14	
	10a	For this reason a commandment was written in the heavenly tablets for the one who give birth to a child:
	b	if she give birth to a male,
	c	she is to remain in her impurity for seven days like the first seven days;
	d	then for 33 days she is to remain in the blood of purification.
	e	She is not to touch any sacred thing
	f	nor to enter the sanctuary,
	g	until she completes these days for a male.
	11a	As for a female
	b	she is to remain in her impurity two weeks of days like the first two weeks
	c	and 66 days in the blood of purification.
	d	Their total will be 80 days.
	12a	After she had completed these 80 days,
	b	we brought her into the Garden of Eden,
	c	because it is the holiest in the entire earth.
	d	And every tree which is planted in it is holy.
	13a	For this reason the law of these days has been ordained for the one who give birth to a male or a female.
	b	She is not to touch any sacred thing
	c	nor to enter the sanctuary
	d	until the time when those days for male or female are completed.

(table cont.)

			Jubilees 3:8–14
		14a	THESE ARE THE LAW AND THE TESTIMONY THAT WERE WRITTEN FOR ISRAEL TO KEEP FOR ALL TIMES.

Genesis 2:25		*Jubilees 3:15–16*	
		15a	DURING THE FIRST WEEK OF THE FIRST JUBILEE ADAM AND HIS WIFE SPENT THE SEVEN YEARS IN THE GARDEN OF EDEN WORKING AND KEEPING IT.
		b	WE GAVE HIM WORK
	[ ]	c	AND WERE TEACHING HIM (HOW) TO DO EVERYTHING THAT WAS APPROPRIATE FOR WORKING (IT).
25a	*And the man and his wife* were both naked,	16a	WHILE HE WAS WORKING (IT)
		b	*he was* naked,
	[ ]	c	BUT HE DID NOT KNEW IT
25b	*and they were not* ashamed.	d	*nor was he* ashamed.
	[ ]	e	HE WOULD KEEP THE GARDEN AGAINST BIRDS, ANIMALS, AND CATTLE.
		f	HE WOULD GATHER ITS FRUIT
		g	AND EAT (IT)
		h	AND WOULD STORE ITS SURPLUS FOR HIMSELF AND HIS WIFE.
		i	HE WOULD STORE WHAT WAS BEING KEPT.

Genesis 3:1–7		*Jubilees 3:17–22*	
		17a	WHEN THE CONCLUSION OF THE SEVEN YEARS
		b	WHICH HE HAD COMPLETED THERE ARRIVED—
		c	SEVEN YEARS EXACTLY—

(table cont.)

	Genesis 3:1–7		*Jubilees 3:17–22*
		d	IN THE SECOND MONTH, ON THE SEVENTEENTH,
		e	THE SERPENT CAME
	[ ]	f	AND APPROACHED THE WOMAN.
3:1a	NOW THE SERPENT WAS MORE SUBTLE THAN ANY ANIMAL OF THE FIELD THAT THE LORD GOD HAD MADE.		[ ]
1b	*He* said to the woman:	g	*The serpent* said to the woman:
1c	"*Did God say:*	h	"*Is it* from all THE FRUIT OF the trees *in* the garden *(that) the Lord has commanded you, saying: Do* not eat *from it?*"
1d	*You shall* not eat from [ ] any tree *of* the garden?"		
2a	*The woman* said to *the serpent*:	18a	*She* said to *him*:
2b	"From [ ] the fruit of the trees *of* the garden *we may eat*;	b	"From ALL the fruit of the tree(s) *which are in* the garden THE LORD SAID TO US: *Eat.*
3a	but from the fruit of the tree which is in the middle of the garden *God* said [ ]:	c	But from the fruit of the tree which is in the middle of the garden *he* said TO US:
3b	You shall not eat from it	d	Do not eat from it
3c	and you shall not touch it,	e	and do not touch it
3d	so that you may not die."	f	so that you may not die".
4a	Then the serpent said to the woman:	19a	Then the serpent said to the woman:
4b	"You will not really die	b	"You will not really die
5a	because *God* knows that on the day you eat from it your eyes will be opened,	c	because the *Lord* knows that on the day you eat from it your eyes will be opened,
5b	and you will be like *God*, *knowing* good and evil."	d	and you will be like *gods*, AND *you will know* good and evil."
6a	And the woman saw	20a	The woman saw the tree,
6b	THAT the tree *was* good for food,	b	that it was delightful AND PLEASING to the *eye*
6c	that it was delightful to the *eyes*,	c	*and (that)* ITS FRUIT *was* good to eat.
6d	AND THAT THE TREE WAS TO BE DESIRED TO MAKE ONE WISE.		[ ]
6e	So she took of *its fruit*	d	So she took SOME *of it*
6f	and ate (it);	e	and ate (it).
	[ ]	21a	SHE FIRST COVERED HER SHAME WITH FIG LEAVES

(table cont.)

	Genesis 3:1–7		*Jubilees 3:17–22*
6g	and she ALSO gave it to *her husband*, WHO WAS WITH HER.	b	and then gave it to *Adam*,
6h	He ate (it),	c	He ate (it),
7a	the eyes *of both* were opened,	d	*his* eyes were opened,
7b	and *they knew* that *they* were naked;	e	and *he saw that he* was naked.
7c	*They* sewed fig leaves;	22a	*He* TOOK fig leaves
		b	and sewed (them);
7d	thus *they made themselves aprons.*	c	thus *he* made *himself an apron*
	[ ]	d	AND COVERED HIS SHAME.

	Genesis 3:8–13
8a	AND THEY HEARD THE SOUND OF THE LORD GOD
8b	WALKING IN THE GARDEN IN THE COOL OF THE DAY,
8c	AND THE MAN AND HIS WIFE HID THEMSELVES FROM THE PRESENCE OF THE LORD GOD AMONG THE TREES OF THE GARDEN.
9a	BUT THE LORD GOD CALLED TO THE MAN,
9b	AND SAID TO HIM:
9c	"WHERE ARE YOU?"
10a	AND HE SAID:
10b	"I HEARD THE SOUND OF THEE IN THE GARDEN,
10c	AND I WAS AFRAID,
10d	BECAUSE I WAS NAKED;
10e	AND I HID MYSELF".
11a	HE SAID:
11b	"WHO TOLD YOU
11c	THAT YOU WERE NAKED?
11d	HAVE YOU EATEN FROM THE TREE,
11e	OF WHICH I COMMANDED YOU NOT TO EAT?"
12a	THE MAN SAID:
12b	"THE WOMAN WHOM THOU GAVEST TO BE WITH ME, SHE GAVE ME FRUIT OF THE TREE.

(table cont.)

Genesis 3:8–13	
12c	AND I ATE."
13a	THEN THE LORD GOD SAID TO THE WOMAN,
13b	"WHAT IS THIS THAT YOU HAVE DONE?"
13c	THE WOMAN SAID:
13d	"THE SERPENT BEGUILED ME,
13e	AND I ATE."

VII. Gen 3:14–15		Jubilees 3:23ab	
14a	The LORD God SAID TO the serpent:	23a	The Lord *cursed* the serpent,
	[ ]	b	AND WAS ANGRY AT IT FOREVER.
14b	"BECAUSE YOU HAVE DONE THIS,		[ ]
14c	*cursed are you* ABOVE ALL CATTLE, AND ABOVE ALL ANIMALS OF THE FIELD;		
14d	UPON YOUR BELLY YOU SHALL GO,		
14e	AND DUST YOU SHALL EAT		
14f	ALL THE DAYS OF YOUR LIFE.		
15a	I WILL PUT ENMITY BETWEEN YOU AND THE WOMAN,		
15b	AND BETWEEN YOUR SEED AND HER SEED;		
15c	HE SHALL BRUISE YOUR HEAD,		
15d	AND YOU SHALL BRUISE HIS HEEL."		

Genesis 3:16–24		Jubilees 3:23–31	
		23c	AT THE WOMAN, TOO, HE WAS ANGRY
		d	BECAUSE SHE HAD LISTENED TO THE VOICE OF THE SERPENT
	[ ]	e	AND EATEN.
16a	To *the woman* he said:	f	He said to *her*:
16b	"I will indeed multiply your sadness and your childbearing;	24a	"I will indeed multiply your sadness and your pain.

(table cont.)

Genesis 3:16–24		Jubilees 3:23–31	
16c	in sadness *you shall bear* children,	b	*Bear* children in sadness.
16d	*yet your desire shall be for* your husband;	c	*Your place of refuge will be with* your husband;
16e	he will rule over you."	d	he will rule over you."
17a	Then he said to *the man*:	25a	Then he said to *Adam*:
17b	"Because you listened to THE VOICE OF your wife,	b	"Because you listened to [ ] your wife,
17c	and ate from the tree of which I commanded you: "*You shall not eat of it*,"	c	and ate from the tree from which I commanded you *not to eat*,
17d	*cursed is* the ground on account of you;	d	*may* the ground *be cursed* on account of you.
17e	IN SADNESS YOU SHALL EAT OF IT ALL THE DAYS OF YOUR LIFE;		[ ]
18a	thorns and thistles it shall bring forth for you;	e	May it grow thorns and thistles for you.
18b	AND YOU SHALL EAT THE PLANTS OF THE FIELD.		[ ]
19a	*You shall eat* [ ] bread in the sweat of your face	f	*Eat* YOUR bread in the sweat of your face
19b	until you return to *the ground,*	g	until you return to the *earth*
19c	*for* out of it you were taken;	h	*from which* you were taken;
19d	for *dust* your are	i	for *earth* you are
19e	and to *dust* you will return."	j	and to *the earth* you will return."
20a	<u>*The man* named his wife Eve,</u>		<u>(cf. Jub. 3:33)</u>
20b	BECAUSE SHE WAS THE MOTHER OF ALL LIVING.		[ ]
21a	*And the* LORD *God* made *for the man and for his wife garments* out of skins,	26a	*He* made *clothing* out of skins for *them*,
21b	and clothed them.	b	clothed them,
22a	THEN THE LORD GOD SAID:		[ ]
22b	"BEHOLD, THE MAN HAS BECOME LIKE ONE OF US,		
22c	KNOWING GOOD AND EVIL;		
22d	AND NOW, LEST HE PUT FORTH HIS HAND		
22e	AND TAKE ALSO OF THE TREE OF LIFE, AND EAT,		
22f	AND LIVE FOR EVER."		

(table cont.)

Genesis 3:16–24		Jubilees 3:23–31	
23a	—and THE LORD GOD dismissed *him* from the Garden of Eden, TO WORK THE GROUND, FROM WHERE HE WAS TAKEN.	c	and dismissed *them* from the Garden of Eden. [ ]
24a	HE DROVE OUT THE MAN;		
24b	AND AT THE EAST OF THE GARDEN OF EDEN HE PLACED THE CHERUBIM,		
24c	AND A FLAMING SWORD WHICH TURNED EVERY WAY,		
24d	TO GUARD THE WAY TO THE TREE OF LIFE.		

		Jubilees 3:27–31	
		27	ON THAT DAY, AS HE WAS LEAVING THE GARDEN OF EDEN, HE BURNED INCENSE AS A PLEASING FRAGRANCE—FRANKINCENSE, GALBANUM, STACTE, AND AROMATIC SPICES—IN THE EARLY MORNING WHEN THE SUN ROSE AT THE DAY WHEN HE COVERED HIS SHAME.
		28a	ON THAT DAY THE MOUTHS OF ALL THE ANIMALS, THE CATTLE, THE BIRDS, EVERYTHING THAT WALKS AND EVERYTHING THAT MOVES ABOUT WERE MADE INCAPABLE OF SPEAKING
		b	BECAUSE ALL OF THEM USED TO CONVERSE WITH ONE ANOTHER WITH ONE LANGUAGE AND ONE TONGUE.
		29a	AND HE DISMISSED FROM THE GARDEN OF EDEN ALL THE ANIMATE BEINGS THAT WERE IN THE GARDEN OF EDEN.

(table cont.)

		Jubilees 3:27–31	
		b	ALL ANIMATE BEINGS WERE DISPERSED—EACH BY ITS KIND AND EACH BY ITS NATURE—INTO THE PLACE(S) WHICH HAD BEEN CREATED FOR THEM.
		30a	BUT OF ALL THE ANIMALS AND CATTLE HE PERMITTED ADAM ALONE
		b	TO COVER HIS SHAME.
		31a	FOR THIS REASON IT HAS BEEN COMMANDED IN THE TABLETS REGARDING ALL THOSE WHO KNOW THE JUDGEMENT OF THE LAW
		b	THAT THEY COVER THEIR SHAME
		c	AND NOT UNCOVER THEMSELVES
		d	AS THE NATIONS UNCOVER THEMSELVES.

Genesis 4:1a		*Jubilees 3:32–35*	
	[ ]	3:32a	AT THE BEGINNING OF THE FOURTH MONTH ADAM AND HIS WIFE DEPARTED FROM THE GARDEN OF EDEN.
		b	THEY LIVED IN THE LAND OF ELDA,
		c	IN THE LAND WHERE THEY WERE CREATED.
	(cf. Gen 3:20)	3:33	Adam named his wife Eve [ ].
		3:34a	THEY WERE CHILDLESS THROUGHOUT THE FIRST JUBILEE;
4:1a	*Adam* knew *Eve his wife*	b	AFTERWARDS *he* knew *her*.
	[ ]	3:35a	HE HIMSELF WAS WORKING THE LAND
		b	AS HE HAD BEEN TAUGHT IN THE GARDEN OF EDEN.

MAN AND WOMAN: HALAKHAH BASED UPON EDEN IN THE DEAD SEA SCROLLS

Florentino García Martínez

1. *The Eden narrative in the Dead Sea Scrolls*

When we start reading the whole collection of manuscripts found at Qumran, looking for re-readings, interpretations or simply echoes or allusions to the Eden story as told in Gen 2–4, the biggest surprise is the small amount of material that this search brings to the fore. These chapters are scarcely represented in the biblical manuscripts preserved, and seem not to have had a strong influence in the non-biblical compositions found in the different caves.

In Qumran we have recovered twenty copies of the book of Genesis, but the remains of the Eden stories are extremely scarce; an isolated fragment (from 4Q7) with only the word ויצר י[הוה] could represent Gen 2:7 or Gen 2:19.[1] Another fragment (from 4Q8) has three incomplete words in two lines which could come from Gen 2:17–18.[2] We are on surer ground with the fragments 4 and 5 of 4Q10: the first, with remains of four lines but with only three complete words, has preserved parts of Gen 2:1–3 and presents no variants with MT; the second, with remains of three lines and eight complete words, contains part of Gen 3:1–2. Its only difference with MT is the specification of the *he* interrogative: האף, instead of אף of MT.[3] The only other biblical manuscript with traces of the Eden story is 1Q1.[4] 1Q1 2 is a fragment with remains of five lines in which almost 10 words are complete. Its identification with Gen 3:11–14 presents no problems, but the only difference with MT is (if *vera lectio*) the reading ער[ום] (as the Samaritan Pentateuch) instead of עירם of MT. This is

---

[1] 4Q7 (4QGen[g]) frg. 3, edited by J. Davila in DJD XII. See, Eugene Ulrich *et al.* (eds.), *Qumran Cave 4. VII: Genesis to Numbers* (DJD XII; Oxford 1994) 60.

[2] 4Q8 (4QGen[h2]), also edited by J. Davila, *ibid.* 62.

[3] 4Q10 (4QGen[k]), *ibid.* 78.

[4] 1Q1 frg. 2, edited by Dominique Barthélemy in D. Barthélemy and J.T. Milik, *Qumran Cave I* (DJD I; Oxford 1955) 49.

all we can find in the Biblical texts from Qumran concerning the Eden stories. However, in view of the fragmentary nature of most of the biblical manuscripts of Genesis, this could be purely accidental.

More surprising is the absence of non-biblical compositions which expand, comment or simply rewrite the Eden stories. In later Jewish and Christian literature these stories have led to the growth of a whole range of "Adamic" writings, and rewritings of the stories of the creation of Adam and Eve, the fall, the serpent, the garden itself and the four rivers (not to mention the stories about Cain and Abel), seem to have kept many generations of scribes and interpreters busy.[5] This absence contrasts strongly with the abundance of materials we find in the Scrolls dedicated to expanding or commenting on the stories of protagonists of other Genesis narratives, such as Noah.[6] Such an absence can hardly be accidental.

It is true that we cannot pretend to have recovered all the materials once present on the shelves of the library of Qumran, and that some of the compositions in which we would have expected to find a rewriting of these narratives are lacking precisely the sections in which this rewriting would have taken place. This is the case of *1QGenesis Apocryphon*.[7] The recovered sections (from column 1 to 22) are a rewriting of Gen 5 to 15, but Matthew Morgenstern recently noted that the surviving sheets containing columns 5 to 22 are marked with the consecutive letters of the Hebrew alphabet, *pe*, *tsade*, and *qop*.[8] Since *pe* is the seventeenth letter of the Hebrew alphabet, he has inferred that fifteen or sixteen sheets must have preceded the one in which the actual column one is preserved. If this assumption proves to be true, we have lost more than seventy columns at the beginning of the scroll in which there may have been a whole series of developments of Gen 1–5.[9] But this assumption is problematic,

[5] See, for example, M.E. Stone, *A History of the Literature of Adam and Eve* (SBL Early Judaism and Its Literature 3; Atlanta 1992).

[6] On the traditions about Noah see my contribution "Interpretation of the Flood in the Dead Sea Scrolls," in F. García Martínez and G.P. Luttikhuizen (eds.), *Interpretations of the Flood* (Themes in Biblical Narrative 1; Leiden 1998) 86–108.

[7] Edited by Nahman Avigad and Yigael Yadin, *A Genesis Apocryphon. A Scroll from the Wilderness of Judaea* (Jerusalem 1956).

[8] M. Morgenstern, "A New Clue to the Original Length of the Genesis Apocryphon", *JJS* 47 (1996) 345–347.

[9] One of the scrolls of Isaiah from cave 1 (1QIsa[a]), which has dimensions similar to those of *1QGenesis Apocryphon*, has only sixty four columns and contains the complete text of the Prophet.

because, among other things, the scroll would have had an enormous length not attested in any other found scroll (more than 15 meters), and would have been unmanageable.

On the length of *1QGenesis Apocryphon* we can only speculate, as we can only speculate on the reasons for the absence of specific compositions commenting on, expanding or rewriting the Eden narratives. That at Qumran these narratives were known is completely certain, not only because of their presence in the biblical text (of which, as already said, we have marginal remains) but also because they figure prominently in the book of *Jubilees*, which at Qumran had very high status,[10] and, albeit less prominently, in the *Books of Enoch*, also abundantly represented in the Qumran collection.[11]

One possible reason for the absence of commentaries on these stories could be the fact that the Qumran community adopted an explanation of the origin of evil different from the one these stories advocate (and the one advocated by *Jubilees*).[12]

Maybe it is not mere coincidence that the exposition of the history of salvation offered by the *Damascus Document* (2:14ff.) starts not with the fall of Adam but with the fall of the Watchers:

> For having walked in the stubbornness of their hearts the Watchers of the heavens fell; on account of it they were caught, for they did not heed the precepts of God. And their sons, whose height was like that of cedars and whose bodies were like mountains, fell. All flesh which there was on the dry earth expired and they became as if they had never been, because they had realized their desires and had failed to keep their creator's precepts, until his wrath flared up against them (CD2:17–21).[13]

In fact, 4Q180 ("An interpretation concerning the ages which God has made") also starts directly with "the sequence of the sons of Noah" followed by an "Interpretation concerning Azazel and the angels who came to the daughters of man and sired themselves giants."[14] But

---

[10] See the contribution of J. van Ruiten in this volume.

[11] See the contribution of E. Tigchelaar in this volume.

[12] See F. García Martínez, "The Origin of Evil and the Dualistic Thought of the Sect", in J.J. Collins *et al.* (eds.), *Encyclopaedia of Apocalypticism.* Vol. I (Cassel & Continuum: New York 1998) 166–172.

[13] Hebrew text and translation in F. García Martínez and E.J.C. Tigchelaar, *The Dead Sea Scrolls Study Edition. Volume One 1Q1–4Q273* (Leiden 1997) 552–553. All quotations of Qumran texts (until 4Q473) are taken from this edition, the most easily accessible, abbreviated in the following as *DSSS.*

[14] *DSSS*, 370–371.

as said, we can only speculate about the reasons for the absence. The fact is that the Eden narratives are far less prominent in Qumran than we would have expected.

There are, of course, some tantalizing allusions which may imply the knowledge of some of the traditions associated in later literature with the Eden stories. One such allusion is the mention of the לשון הקודש ("the holy tongue") in 4Q464 3 i 8,[15] a fragment which may reflect the tradition known by *Jubilees* 3:28 and 12:26 that Adam (and all the animals) spoke Hebrew before the fall.[16] Others are the reference of the *Astronomic Henoch* to the פרדס קשטא ("*Pardes* of Justice"), which also has a long development in later writings such as the *Slavonic Henoch*.[17] And, of course, the disputed מקדש אדם ("Temple of man/Adam") of *4QFlorilegium*.[18]

Even more tantalizing is a series of allusions which seems to indicate that a *Urzeit/Endzeit* typology of the Eden stories was already developed in the sectarian writings of Qumran. We have in CD 3:20 and in 1QH 4:15 the use of the expression כבוד אדם ("the glory of Adam") in an eschatological context:

> But God, in his wonderful mysteries, atoned for their iniquity and pardoned their sins. And he built for them a safe home in Israel, such as there has not been since ancient times, not even till now. Those who remained steadfast in it will acquire eternal life, and all the glory of Adam is for them (CD 3:18–20).[19]
>
> Even though you burn the foundations of mountains and fire sears the base of Sheol, those who . . . in your regulations. You protect the ones who serve you loyally, so that their posterity is before you all the days. You have raised an eternal name, forgiving offence, casting away all their iniquities, giving them as a legacy all the glory of Adam and abundance of days (1QH 4:13–15).[20]

The same happens with the expression נחלת אדם ("the inheritance of Adam") in 4Q171, a *pesher* on Psalms, which applies Ps 37:19 "They shall not be ashamed in the evil time" to:

---

[15] Published by E. Eshel and M. Stone in M. Broshi *et al.* (eds.), *Qumran Cave 4. XIV: Parabiblical Texts Part 2* (DJD XIX: Clarendon: Oxford 1995) 215–230.

[16] On this tradition, see DJD XIX, 219–221 and E. Eshel – M. Stone, "The Holy Language at the End of Days in Light of a New Fragment Found at Qumran", *Tarbiz* 62 (1993) 169–77 (Hebrew).

[17] See the contribution of E.J.C. Tigchelaar in this volume.

[18] 4Q174 1 i 6, see *DSSS* 352–353, where the most relevant literature on the topic is given.

[19] *DSSS*, 554–555.

[20] *DSSS*, 148–149.

> Those who have returned from the wilderness, who will live for a thousand generations, in salvation; for them there is all the inheritance of Adam, and for their descendants for ever (4Q171 iii 1–2).[21]

And, of course, we have (if *vera lectio*) the clearly eschatological use of the expression of יום הבריה ("day of creation")[22] in column 29 of the *Temple Scroll*:

> I shall sanctify my temple with my glory, for I shall make my glory reside over it until the day of creation, when I shall create my temple establishing it for my self for ever, in accordance with the covenant which I made with Jacob at Bethel (11Q19 29:8–9).[23]

But from these tantalizing expressions very little can be concluded as to the use, interpretation or transformation of the Eden stories in the Qumran writings. The Garden motif is also used as metaphor for the community in some poetical, liturgical and sapiential texts from Qumran, treated in the contribution of E. Tigchelaar to this volume. All that remains is the use of some elements of the Eden narrative in two halakhic texts, namely CD (*Damascus Document*) 4:20–21 and 4Q265 (*4QSerek Damesek*) 7 ii 11–17 which we will examine in some detail.

2. *CD 4:20–21*

This text is very well known and, because of its ambiguity and interest, has been discussed many times. The literature on the passage is therefore very extensive.[24] In what follows, I will limit myself to the essentials.

---

[21] *DSSS*, 344–345.

[22] This is the reading proposed by E. Qimron, "The Text of the Temple Scroll", *Lešonenu* 42 (1978) 142 (Hebrew); the editor of the text read יום הברכה, see Y. Yadin, *Meggilat ham-Miqdaš—The Temple Scroll*, Volume Two: Text and Commentary (Israel Exploration Society—The Hebrew University—Shrine of the Book: Jerusalem 1977) 91 (Hebrew).

[23] Text according to E. Qimron, *The Temple Scroll. A Critical Edition with Extensive Reconstructions* (Judean Desert Studies, Beer-Sheva—Jerusalem 1996) 44; translation from F. García Martínez, *The Dead Sea Scrolls Translated. The Qumran Texts in English* (Leiden 1994) 162.

[24] The most important studies are collected in F. García Martínez "Damascus Document: A Bibliography of Studies 1970–1989", in M. Broshi (ed.), *The Damascus Document Reconsidered* (Jerusalem 1992) 66. For a detailed bibliography from 1910 to 1956, see P. Winter, "Sadoquite Fragments IV 20, 21 and the Exegesis of Gen I 27 in Late Judaism", *ZAW* 68 (1956) 71–84. The latest published studies on the

The text reads in translation:

> The builders of the wall who go after Zaw—Zaw is the preacher of whom he said (Mic 2:6) "Assuredly they will preach"—are caught twice in fornication: by taking two wives in their lives, even though the principle of creation is (Gen 1:27) "male and female he created them"; and the ones who went into the ark (Gen 7:9) "went in two by two into the ark". And about the prince it is written (Deut 17:17) "He should not multiply wives for himself."[25]

Strictly speaking neither of the two references to Genesis belong to the Eden narratives. The last reference to Genesis is a quotation from Gen 7:9 and belongs to the narrative of Noah and the flood. The first is a quotation from Gen 1:27 and thus precedes the narrative of Eden. But its treatment here seems to be justified for the following reasons: a) because the same phrase is repeated in Genesis 5:2 (with the pronoun suffixed), which makes of this expression a sort of frame of the whole Eden narrative, b) because the general formula which introduces it, יסוד הבריאה ("the principle of creation") implies the creation of Eve not yet mentioned in Gen 1:27, and c) because the same quotation of Genesis 1:27 is followed by "therefore a man shall leave his father and mother and the two shall become as one; they are no longer two but one flesh" in the famous text of Marc 10:6–8, which shows that Gen 1:27 was already associated with Gen 2:24.

In order to understand the following discussion, both the immediate and the more general context of the passage of the *Damascus Document* need to be recalled, albeit summarily. Our passage is part of the so-called midrash on the three nets of Belial, with which the quotation of Isaiah 24:17 "Panic, pit and net against you, earth-dweller" is explained. As our text says: "They [the three expressions used by Isaiah] are Belial's three nets, about which Levi, son of Jacob spoke, by which he [Belial] catches Israel and makes them appear before them like three types of justice. The first is fornication; the second, wealth; the third, defilement of the temple. He who

topic are: J. Kampen, "A Fresh Look at the Masculine Plural Suffix in CD 4:21", *RevQ* 16/61 (1993) 91–97; G. Brin, "Divorce at Qumran", in M. Bernstein *et al.* (eds.), *Legal Texts and Legal Issues* (STDJ 23; Leiden 1997) 231–244; Tom Holmén, "Divorce in CD 4:20–5:2 and in 11QT 57:17–18: Some Remarks on the Pertinence of the Question", *RevQ* 18/71 (1998) 397–408.

[25] *DSSS*, 557.

eludes one is caught in another, and he who is freed from that, is caught in another."

The text goes on with the already quoted section, by which the first net of Belial, הזנות, is specified. The second of the nets ההון[26] ("wealth" or "riches") is passed over without any comment at all, and the third, טמאה מקדש ("defilement of the temple") is explained as not keeping separated according to the law, which is concretized as "lying with her who sees the blood of her menstrual flow", and as "taking as wife the daughter of his brother or the daughter of his sister", matters which apparently have very little relationship with the temple. It is certainly possible to interpret the first of these two sins in the light of *Psalms of Solomon* 8:12, which formulates the accusation in this way: "They walked on the place of the sacrifice of the Lord (coming) from all kinds of uncleanness; and (coming) with menstrual blood (on them), they defiled the sacrifices as if they were common flesh."[27] It is true that sexual intercourse during the period prohibited by the law would certainly render a man unclean, and the presence of such a man in the temple would consequently pollute it. But even so, it must to be concluded that the author selected rather weak examples of temple pollution.

For these (and other) reasons most of the authors think that the redactor of the *Damascus Document* is using here a source dealing with sexual halakhah, and that from this source he extracts the offenses he attributes to the others.[28] These accusations have a precise purpose. In its larger context, the whole midrash of the three nets of Belial is adduced to reinforce the central assertion of the first columns of the *Damascus Document* that God has abandoned Israel and now deals only with the community. As Philip Davies says: "The passage is a demonstration that those outside the community are misled, and consequently that their halakhah is demonstrably wrong; it is thought to be right by those who follow it only because they themselves are misled by Belial."[29] The justification of their own halakhah by means of proof texts taken from the Mosaic law, serves thus the purpose of proving that the halakhah followed by others is simply wrong. If

---

[26] The text apparently reads ההין, but there is no doubt that ההון is intended.

[27] In the translation of R.B. Wright in J.H. Charlesworth (ed.), *The Old Testament Pseudepigrapha*. Volume 2 (Garden City NY, 1985) 659.

[28] See, for example, P.R. Davies, *The Damascus Covenant. An Interpretation of the "Damascus Document"* (JSOTS 25; Sheffield 1982) 115–116.

[29] *The Damascus Covenant*, 129.

they have arrived at a different interpretation of the law than the one normative within the group, it is only because they have been misled by Belial.

With this larger and immediate context in mind, we can now look to our text in more detail in order to see what function it has in the reference to the assertion of Genesis that God זכר ונקבה ברא אותם "male and female created them". But first we need to elucidate the meaning of several problematic expressions in the text and give an answer to the following questions:

1) Who are the "builders of the wall" (בוני החיץ)?
2) At Qumran, what means זנות נות (which we have translated as "fornication")?
3) What does it precisely to be caught בשתים (which we have translated as "twice")?
4) How should we interpret the pronominal suffix "in their lives" בחייהם? In otherwords, does our text speak against polygamy or against divorce, or against both, or about something else?

1) The targets of the accusations of the group, the ones against whom the text is directed, are described rather cryptically as "the builders of the wall." The expression appears twice more in the *Damascus Document* (in CD 8:12 and 18), but also on these occasions its ambiguity remains. CD 12:12 makes clear that the biblical roots of the expression lie in Ezekiel 13:10 "and if anyone build a wall, these daub it with whitewash", where it is used against the false prophets who misled the people of Israel. In the *Damascus Document* the phrase has been interpreted in two ways: as a designation of the whole Israel outside the community, and as the designation of a specific rival group; and both interpretations have very good grounds.

For P. Davies, for example, the expression must refer to Israel as a whole; otherwise the argument would not make sense because in the *Damascus Document* it is Israel as a whole which is contrasted with the community: "One could not establish that Belial is leading Israel astray by pointing to the excesses of a group which the rest of Jewish society would oppose". He concludes: "The outcome of all the preceding discussionis as follows: the 'builders of the wall' are the whole of Israel outside the community."[30]

[30] *The Damascus Covenant*, 111 and 112.

For G. Jeremias,[31] on the other hand, the expression designates an enemy group: otherwise it would be impossible to understand why the author, after having asserted that all of Israel is ensnared by Belial in all three nets and each single individual is ensnared by one or another, the "builders of the wall" are ensnared specifically twice. And since the expression is qualified by the phrase taken from Hosea 5:11 "they go after Zaw" and Zaw is identified as מטיף ("preacher"), the group in question can be identified with the followers of the "Man of Lies," the מטיף הכזב which is mentioned not only in the *pesharim* but also at the beginning of the *Damascus Document* (CD 1:14).

In my opinion, the most likely understanding of the expression, especially in light of its use in CD 8:12, is as a designation for a rival group, but a group which is considered as representative of the whole of Israel outside the community. In CD 12:8 the same components appear, and the function of the one "who preaches lies" (מטיף כזב) is even more prominent and explicit. But in this case, the whole is situated in the context of the critique of the "Princes of Judah," and it seems to me clear that the expression does not refer to the whole of Israel outside the community. I conclude, therefore, that the target of the accusations of the group, "the builders of the wall" is one of the adversaries of the community, a very prominent group indeed, a group that, if we take into account the halakhah of MMT, could even be identified with the Pharisees.

2) On the meaning of זנות in the Dead Sea Scrolls we can be very brief. In classical Hebrew זנות means "prostitution", "fornication", and more generally "whoredom".[32] In Qumran the word, although remaining generally within the sexual sphere, is even more polyvalent:[33] generally it is employed in legislation concerning bigamy, divorce, incest, illegal sex with one's own wife, improper marriages between priests and laity, marriages with foreigners, etc., but it also appears to be related to temple defilement. It is even connected with

[31] G. Jeremias, *Der Lehrer der Gerechtigkeit* (SUNT 2; Göttingen 1963) 96–97.

[32] See, for example, D.J.A. Clines (ed.), *The Dictionary of Classical Hebrew*. Volume III (Sheffield 1996) 123–124.

[33] For an analysis of all the occurrences of the word in the texts of Qumran, see J. Kampen, "The Matthean Divorce Texts Reexamined", in G.J. Brooke with F. García Martínez (eds.), *New Qumran Texts and Studies* (STDJ 15; Leiden 1994) 149–167.

pure food, not to mention a whole series of texts in which it is employed metaphorically in conjunction with "heart", "eyes", "ways", etc. In short, from its semantic field we cannot expect any help in solving the problems of our text, because the word lacks the necessary precision (a conclusion which may surprise those who try to explain the exception clause of Matthew μὴ ἐπὶ πορνέιᾳ with the help of the use of זנות in Qumran).[34]

3) On the meaning of the בשתים the scholars are divided, depending on their general understanding of the text. For the ones who interpret the text as referring both to polygamy and divorce, it means that the transgressors are caught in two sorts of זנות: marrying two women and divorcing their wives. For others, such as Chaim Rabin,[35] it means that "they are caught in two respects in whoredom." This implies that, of the three nets, only זנות is discussed in the text: as taking two wives and as taking as wife a niece, although these two "respects" would have been separated by 5:5–7 (the third net of the text) which Rabin considers a parenthetical addition.

In my opinion the wording of the text "he who eludes one is caught in another" with מזה and בזה certainly suggests that בשתים indeed refers to the nets, and it can be translated "they are caught in two (of the three nets), namely in fornication . . . and in defiling the sanctuary." The objection of Rabin and Davies[36] that this understanding left unexplained the accusation of marrying one's niece does not hold if this accusation is seen as part of the defilement of the sanctuary. After all, marrying a niece is no more related to the sanctuary than lying with a menstruating women. Since our text is completely silent about the second of the three nets of Belial and only explains the first and the third, it does seem logical that the "builders of the wall" are indeed caught in the two which are mentioned.

4) The central problem posed by this text is the precise meaning of the pronominal suffix of בחייהם "in *their* lives".[37] In fact, the understanding of what the text is talking about, the accusation levelled against the enemies, depends primarily on the interpretation of the pronoun.

[34] See the studies listed by J. Kampen, 151–152.
[35] Ch. Rabin, *The Zadokite Fragments* (Oxford 1958²) 16–17.
[36] *The Damascus Covenant*, 114.
[37] On the different interpretations proposed, see J. Kampen, "A Fresh Look at the Masculine Plural Suffix in CD 4:21", *RevQ* 16/61 (1993) 91–97.

Vermes, in a famous article,[38] lists four main interpretations:—our text would prohibit both polygamy *and* a new marriage after divorce;—it would prohibit only polygamy (or, strictly speaking, bigamy) but not a new marriage after divorce;—it would only prohibit divorce;—it would prohibit every second marriage during one's whole life, even after the death of the first wife. Of these interpretations, only the last one interprets literally the masculine pronoun: every man who during his life takes two wives is caught in fornication, be it after divorce, after the death of the first wife or simultaneously. The other three interpretations (by far the more common) give the pronoun the value of a feminine pronoun, as if the text were talking of the wives' lives: the man would be caught in fornication if he marries two wives (simultaneously or successively) when they are alive. Either polygamy, divorce or both, would be forbidden in the text.

The Hebrew text is perfectly clear and employs a third person masculine pronominal suffix, בחייהם. But the resulting assertion seems to be so strange in a Jewish context that, to my knowledge, only two interpreters have dared to defend it until now. The first was J. Murphy-O'Connor,[39] who could not find any compelling reasons not to give the suffix its normal value, and postulated a literal translation of the sentence. The other was P.R. Davies,[40] who systematically dealt with all the arguments put forth by G. Vermes and adduced Josephus' description of the practices of the married Essenes as a plausible context for the legal norm of our text.[41] All the other interpreters, either assume a mistake in which the scribe wrote the masculine suffix instead of the feminine (in Hebrew a simple change

[38] G. Vermes, "Sectarian Matrimonial Halakhah in the Damascus Rule", *JJS* 25 (1974) 197–202, reprinted in *Idem, Post-Biblical Jewish Studies* (Leiden 1975) 50–56.

[39] J. Murphy-O'Connor, "An Essene Missionary Document? CD II,14–VI,1", *RB* 77 (1970) 201–229.

[40] In the chapter "Marriage and the Essenes" in his book *Behind the Essenes. History and Ideology in the Dead Sea Scrolls* (Brown Judaic Studies 94; Atlanta 1987) 73–85 and 141–143.

[41] L.H. Schiffman, "Laws Pertaining to Women in the *Temple Scroll*", in D. Dimant – U. Rappaport (eds.), *The Dead Sea Scrolls: Forty Years of Research* (STDJ 10; Leiden 1992) 210–228, explains the suffix in a different way, as referring to both parties in a divorce. After asserting that "This difficult passage indicates that it is considered fornication (*zenut*) to marry *two wives if they are both living*" [my emphasis], which apparently implies that he has read the suffix as feminine, Schiffman concludes: "The text seems to prohibit not only polygamy, but even remarriage after divorce. Neither party to the divorce may remarry as long as the other is alive. (This may be the reason for the difficult *be-hayyehem*, with a masculine suffix. It may refer to both parties to the divorce.)" p. 217.

of the last letter, a *mem* into a *nun*) and correct the text accordingly, or give to the masculine suffix the value of a feminine suffix.[42]

The interpreters who think that our text prohibits polygamy (to have simultaneously two wives), can claim a good reason to understand (or even to correct) the text as a statement prohibiting marrying two women when both are alive (בחייהן): namely that the biblical phrase on which the expression is based is the text of Leviticus 18:18,[43] and this text employs the feminine pronoun בחייה, "in her life". Besides, the third of the proof-texts adduced in our fragment, the text of Deut 17:17 ("He [the king] shall not multiply wives for himself") is also quoted in the *Temple Scroll* 56:18–19, and a little later in this text it is interpreted in the following way:

> He shall take for himself a wife from his father's house, from his father's family. He shall take no other wife apart from her, because she will be with him all the days of her life. If she dies, he shall take for himself another from his father's house (11Q19 57:15–19).[44]

Here there is no doubt that polygamy is involved; this is the main issue, and the King is required to be monogamous. Divorce also may be involved, although indirectly, in so far as it is said that the wife shall remain with him all her life.[45] Remarriage after the death of the first wife is also clearly allowed (no doubt to assure that there is always a Queen).

Even before the publication of the *Temple Scroll*, this text was brought into the discussion of the meaning the *Damascus Document*.[46] And because here polygamy and possible divorce are clearly pro-

---

[42] R.H. Charles, in his translation of 1913, after noting that the suffix is indeed masculine, justified this understanding with the observation that "But not infrequently in the O.T. the masc. suffix is used in reference to feminine nouns", R.H. Charles (ed.) *The Apocrypha and Pseudepigrapha of the Old Testament. Volume II: Pseudepigrapha* (Oxford 1913, reprint 1973) 810.

[43] Which prohibits incest, forbidding taking the sister of the wife while she is alive.

[44] Text in Qimron, *The Temple Scroll*, 82; translation in García Martínez, *The Dead Sea Scrolls Translated*, 174.

[45] Schiffman, *art. cit.* 217 concludes "More difficult is the question of whether divorce is also prohibited by this law in the *Temple Scroll*". T. Holmén, *art. cit.* 401–402, interprets the phrase in the light of Deut 17:19 which is also applied to "the royal guard" and to the "royal council" in the *Temple Scroll*. He consequently understands "she will be with him all the days of her life" not as referring to divorce but as a description of the ideal wife of Prov 31:12 who watches upon the King and keeps him from evil "all the days of her life".

[46] Y. Yadin, "L'attitude essénienne envers la polygamie et le divorce", *RB* 79 (1972) 88–89.

hibited to the King, most of the interpreters concluded that the *Damascus Document* prohibits the same thing for everybody.

But in my view this conclusion is far from proven[47] and forgets two basic methodological points:—the text of CD as it stands yields perfect sense (even if it seems strange to us and it was indeed strange in the Jewish context of its time) and without very serious reasons should not be modified;—every text should be interpreted on its own, before importing into it the opinions of other (even if closely related) documents.

The first point was sufficiently emphasized by Murphy-O'Connor. The second point is especially important here, because the recently published[48] new fragments of the *Damascus Document* from cave four show without doubt that divorce was not only allowed, but clearly regulated.

A fragment which apparently implies divorce is a fragment of 4Q270, one of the copies of the *Damascus Document* which contains a penal code not preserved in the copy of the Genizah.[49] Among the sins punished with expulsion from the community we find the following:

> And whoever approaches to have illegal sex with his wife, not in accordance with the regulation, shall leave and never return (4Q270 7 1 12–13).[50]

The type of sin involved does not concern us here.[51] What is interesting is that only the man is expelled from the community, and not

[47] P. Davis, "Marriage and the Essenes", 77–78 correctly underlines the differences between the King and the rest of the male species both in the *Temple Scroll* and in rabbinic literature.

[48] By J.M. Baumgarten, *Qumran Cave 4. XIII: The Damascus Document (4Q266–273)* (DJD XVIII; Oxford 1996).

[49] First edited by J.M. Baumgarten, "The Cave 4 Versions of the Qumran Penal Code", *JJS* 43 (1992) 268–276. See Ch. Hempel, "The Penal Code Reconsidered", in M. Bernstein *et al.* (eds.), *Legal Texts and Legal Issues* (STDJ 23; Leiden 1997) 337–348 and *Eadem, The Laws of the Damascus Document. Sources, Tradition and Redaction* (STDJ 29; Leiden 1998) 141–148.

[50] *DSSS*, 616–617.

[51] A number of suggestions have been made on the exact nature of this offence. Baumgarten, "The Cave 4 Versions of the Qumran Penal Code", *art. cit.* 270, hesitantly suggests "illicit marital relations during the menses"; M. Kister, "Notes on Some New Texts from Qumran", *JJS* 44 (1993) 281, proposes "sexual relations without intention of procreation"; S. Talmon, "The Community of the Renewed Covenant", in E. Ulrich and J. VanderKam (eds.), *The Community of the Renewed Covenant* (Christianity and Judaism in Antiquity Series 10; Notre Dame IN, 1994) 9, interprets the text as referring to any kind of marital relation during the member's

the wife. The text does not tell precisely what happens with her, but it is difficult to imagine that she would be condemned to remain a deserted wife all her life because of a transgression committed by her husband. This could imply that in this case divorce would be imposed upon the man in order to free the woman, who apparently remained a member of the community when the husband was expelled.

This text certainly does not prove that divorce was practiced in the community of the *Damascus Document*, but it suggests a circumstance when divorce could be applied within the community. The proof that divorce was indeed practiced by this community is provided by fragment 9 iii from 4Q266,[52] which contains part of the tasks of the Instructor and allows us to complete the fragmentary lines of CD 13:15–14:2. The composite text reads:

> And likewise with regard to anyone who takes a wife; it should be with consultation. And likewise he (the Inspector of the camps) shall pay attention to anyone who divorces; he shall instruct their children [. . .] and their small children with aspirit of modesty and with compassionate love.[53]

Although in the composite text there remains a small gap[54] and the two manuscripts present a somehow different text,[55] the new fragment makes it clear not only that marriage and divorce took place in the community of the *Damascus Document*, but that these matters were duly regulated and that the "Inspector of the camps" took an active role in counselling in these matter. The unavoidable conclusion is that the regulation of CD 4:20–21 cannot be taken as a ban on divorce, because the same document recognizes and legislates its practice within the community. Even if the *Temple Scroll* contained

---

permanence in the "commune" [the settlement at Qumran]; J. Maier, *Die Qumran-Essener: Die Texte vom Toten Meer.* Band II (UTB 1863; München 1995) 229, indicates "Abweichung von der festen Sitte (v.a. von 'the missionary position')."; A. Tosato, "Su di una norma matrimoniale 4QD", *Biblica* 74 (1993) 401–10, understands the text differently, as prohibiting sexual relations with an illegitimate wife, referring the אשר not to the offence but to the wife: "E Colui che si avvicina per 'prostituzione' a sua moglie, la quale non è secondo la normative giuridica, dovrà uscire (dalla communità) e non far(vi) più ritorno."

[52] DJD XVIII, 70–71.

[53] *DSSS*, 572–573 (CD 13:16–18; 594–595 (4Q266 9 iii).

[54] Baumgarten, in DJD XVIII, fills it with "[and their daughters]".

[55] There is a variant, not recorded as such in the *editio princeps* (the omission of the verb יבן in the text from the Genizah which reads simply וכן למגרש), and in the same manuscript is a sizeable lacuna at the beginning of line 17 which cannot be filled with the words preserved in 4Q266 and which requires some additional text.

a ban on divorce,[56] the introduction of this meaning into the *Damascus Document*, a text which has its own position on the matter, would be unwarranted.

Strange as it could appear, the literal interpretation of CD 4:20–21, which gives to the masculine suffix its normal value, is the one which is most coherent with the rest of the document. We can conclude that what this text forbids is not only having two wives simultaneously, but also that it forbids two marriages in a single lifetime, be it after the death of the spouse or after having divorced her.

The text of Gen 1:27 (as well as Gen 7:9 and Deut 17:17) is used in our fragment to ground and bolster a halakhic rule peculiar to the group. The conflict with their opponents was a conflict of interpretation of the law and the quotations are an essential part of the argument, intended to prove that the interpretation followed by the group of the *Damascus Document* and the consequent halakhic position was the only correct interpretation of the biblical text. In this perspective, the use of the Eden narrative we find in this text does not differ essentially from the use of the same narrative in the Gospel of Matthew. The only difference is in the halakhic position adopted. In Matthew the same text is used to ban divorce, while in CD it serves to ban not only polygamy but every second marriage.

3. *4Q265 7 ii 11–17*

The second halakhic text in which the Eden narrative is used was presented by Joseph Baumgarten for the first time during the Paris congress of the IOQS.[57] The text, which has not yet been published

---

[56] Which, as said, is possible but far from certain, and in any case it would be restricted to the King. In 66:11, in the law of the seduced or raped woman, we find the precision "she will be his wife, since he raped her, and he cannot dismiss her all her life", which certainly asserts that in this case divorce is not allowed, but implies that in other normal cases it is allowed. Also in 54:4–5 when dealing with the laws of vows, the author quotes Numeri 30:10 "But any vow of a widow or of a divorced woman, etc." without making any restriction at all on the divorcee.

[57] J.M. Baumgarten, "Purification after Childbirth and the Sacred Garden in 4Q265 and Jubilees", in G.J. Brooke with F. García Martínez (eds.), *New Qumran Texts and Studies* (STDJ 15; Leiden 1994) 3–10, plate 1. As far as I am aware, the text has only been dealt with briefly in a study by E. Eshel, "Hermeneutical Approaches to Genesis in the Dead Sea Scrolls", in J. Frishman and L. van Rompay (eds.), *The Book of Genesis in Jewish and Oriental Christian Interpretation, A Collection of Essays* (Traditio Exegetica Graeca 5; Peeters: Luven 1997) 1–12, on pp. 10–11.

in the official DJD edition, is part of a very interesting composition which is somehow a cross between the *Rule of the Community* and the *Damascus Document*.[58] It contains a penal code similar to the one in the *Serek* but also sabbath rules similar to the rules preserved in the CD.[59] The first ten lines of the second column of fragment 7 contain the end of sabbath rules, including the limit of two thousand cubits which a man can walk with animals on the sabbath, followed by a reference to the council of the community. And then, probably motivated by the desire to provide a rationale for the laws of purification after giving birth which the rest of the column addresses, the author introduces an elaboration on the Genesis narrative of the garden of Eden. On line 11, after a *blank*, starts the text which interests us here:

> [11] In the first week [. . . be-][12] fore he was brought into the garden of Eden. *Blank* And bone [from his bones . . .] was for her, before she was brought to his side [. . .] [13] [for] holy is the garden of Eden. And every shoot which is in its middle, is holy. Therefore (Lev 12:2–5) [a woman who conceives and bears a male child] [14] shall be impure for seven days; as in the days of her menstrual impurity, she shall be impure. And thir[ty-three days she shall remain in the blood of] [16] her purification. *Blank* But if she gives birth to a baby girl, [she shall be impure for two weeks, as in her menstruation, and sixty-six days] [17] [she shall re]main in the blood of her purification. No holy thing [shall she touch . . .] (4Q265 7 ii 11–17).[60]

Although the text is fragmentary and only can be reconstructed continuously from line 14 thanks to the quotation of Lev 12:2–5, the parallel offered by the book of *Jubilees* allows us to understand the general meaning of the first part in which the Eden narrative is thrust. *Jubilees* 3:8–13 reads:[61]

> [8] In the first week Adam was created and also the rib, his wife. And in the second week he showed her to him. And therefore the commandment was given to observe seven days for a male, but for a female twice seven days in their impurity.

[58] *DSSS*, 546–549.

[59] For the studies on the penal code see the references given in note 49; for a listing of the most important studies on the Sabbath law see L. Doering, "New Aspects of Qumran Sabbath Law from Cave 4 Fragments", in M. Bernstein *et al.* (ed.), *Legal Texts and Legal Issues* (STDJ 23; Leiden 1997) 251–274.

[60] *DSSS*, 548–549.

[61] In the translation of O.S. Wintermute, in J.H. Charlesworth (ed.), *The Old Testament Pseudepigrapha*. Volume 2 (Doubleday: Garden City NY, 1985) 59.

> [9] And after forty days were completed for Adam in the land where he was created, we brought him into the garden of Eden so that he might work it and guard it. And on the eightieth[62] day his wife was also brought in. And after this she entered the garden of Eden. [10] And therefore the command was written in the heavenly tablets for one who bears. "If she bears a male, she shall remain seven days in her impurity like the first seven days. And thirty-three days she shall remain in the blood of her purity. And she shall not touch anything holy. And she shall not enter the sanctuary until she has completed these days which are in accord with (the rule for) a male (child). [11] And that which is in accord with (the rule for) a female is two weeks—like the two first weeks—in her impurity. And sixty-six days she shall remain in the blood of her purity. And their total will be eighty days."
>
> [12] And when she finished those eighty days, we brought her into the garden of Eden because it is more holy than any land. And every tree which is planted in it is holy. [13] Therefore the ordinances of these days were ordained for anyone who bears a male or female that she might not touch anything holy and she might not enter the sanctuary until these days are completed for a male or female.

This parallel shows that the main points of our fragment are precisely the points which characterize the rewriting of the Eden narrative as it appears in *Jubilees*, some of which were until now only attested in this composition.[63] Which inevitably leads us to conclude that the author of 4Q265 is using the Eden story precisely in the rewritten form found in *Jubilees* as the source or inspiration of his narrative; in other words, our text appears to give us a summary of the story as retold in *Jubilees*. These main points are:

1) The creation of Adam and Eve outside the garden of Eden,
2) The garden as sanctuary,
3) The explanation of the period of purification after birth as a consequence of the time elapsed between the creation and the entrance into the Garden respectively of Adam and Eve.

Because all these points have been discussed in detail in the analysis of the narrative of *Jubilees* by J. van Ruiten, we only need to underline how these points appear in our text.

1) The creation of Adam and Eve outside the Garden.

Our text begins with something that happened "in the first week". The parallel with *Jubilees* and the remains of line 12 allow us to

[62] Wintermute mistakenly print "eighth".
[63] See the contribution of J. van Ruiten to this volume.

reconstruct in line 11, as does Baumgarten, the editor, "In the first week Adam was created" (as in the first sentence of *Jubilees* 3:8, which clearly specifies that Adam and Eve were created in the first week). This allows us to determine the subject of the verb on line 12, the person who is brought into the Garden. This line 12 states explicitly that whatever happened in line 11 happened before the entrance into the garden of Eden. We cannot know which event is referred to, but the negative construction used (עד אשר לא) before "he was brought" (הובא) suggests that the situation is seen in a negative way, contrasted with the new situation attained once the protagonist is introduced into the Garden. The same construction and the same verb are used on line 13 (this time in a feminine form) suggesting a similar negative situation of the second (feminine) protagonist.

After a *Blank* a new section starts in our text, of which only the word "bone" has been preserved. Again, in light of *Jubilees* 3:5 and 3:8 it is possible to complete this line, as does the editor, as referring to the creation of Eve from a bone of Adam. In our text, as in *Jubilees*, Adam and Eve are not granted immediate access to the Garden but need to wait for a certain time outside. The reason for this delay is specified in line 14 and is the same reason put forth by *Jubilees* 3:12: the Garden is holy and access to holiness requires purification.

2) The garden as sanctuary.

This holiness of the Garden leads the author of *Jubilees* to equate it with the Temple. *Jubilees* also presents Adam as priest.[64] Although *Jubilees* 3:27 ("And on that day when Adam went out from the garden of Eden, he offered a sweet-smelling sacrifice") explicitly locates the first sacrifice of Adam after his expulsion from Eden, there is no doubt the Garden is presented as a prototype of the temple. The interdiction to enter the temple that Leviticus 12:3–5 imposes upon the parturient is here transferred to Adam and Eve who are not allowed to enter the Garden before the period of purification has been completed. Besides, *Jubilees* not only affirms that the garden "is more holy than any land" (Jub 3:12), but it identifies explicitly the Garden with the Temple: "And he [Noah] knew that the garden of

[64] See J.R. Levison, *Portraits of Adam in Early Judaism. From Sirach to 2 Baruch* (JSPS 1; Sheffield 1988) 92–95. On the priesthood of Adam in *LAB* see C.T.R. Hayward, "The Figure of Adam in Pseudo-Philo's Biblical Antiquities", *JSJ* 23 (1992) 1–20.

Eden was the holy of holies and the dwelling of the Lord" (8:19).[65]

This idea was until now not found explicitly in the writings of Qumran. M. Wise[66] is the only one who has interpreted the disputed expression מקדש אדם of *4QFlorilegium* as meaning "Temple of Adam", although giving to it an eschatological meaning, based on the *Urzeit/Endzeit* typology and on the well-attested relationship of "Paradise" and Temple in Jewish tradition. But the new fragment of 4Q265 shows that the equation in *Jubilees* of Eden with the Temple was not only known, but was used for the same purpose as in *Jubilees.* 4Q265 7 ii 14 reads almost as a direct translation of the second part of Jub 3:12.

3) The explanation of the period of purification after birth.
In *Jubilees* 3:8–12 the idea of the Garden as Temple is used to explain the difference in length of the period of purification after childbirth in the case of a boy and of a girl required by the law of Lev 12:3–5. There it is established that a parturient should fulfil seven and thirty-three days of purification for a boy child before approaching the sanctuary in order to offer the prescribed sacrifices. During this time, the text specify that "she shall not touch anything sacred nor enter the sanctuary". For a baby girl, she should wait fourteen and sixty-six days.

This difference has always been difficult to explain, and *Jubilees* is the first known attempt to supply a rationale for it: that the origin of this difference is to be found in the different period of time that Adam and Eve expended before being allowed to enter the Garden, forty days for Adam and eighty for Eve. The underlying reason is that Adam and Eve need purification before being allowed to enter the Garden.[67]

Jubilees makes this etiological explanation of Leviticus explicitly, quoting the biblical text as if it was written in the "Heavenly Tablets,"[68]

---

[65] See D.W. Parry, "Garden of Eden: Prototype Sanctuary", in *Idem* (ed.), *Temples of the Ancient World* (Utah-Provo 1994) 126–151.

[66] M. Wise, "4QFlorilegium and the Temple of Adam", *RevQ* 15/57–58 (1991) 103–132.

[67] According to Jub 3:6 Adam has intercourse with Eve ("knew her") when she is presented to him the day of her creation, outside the Garden. On this see G. Anderson, "Celibacy or Consummation in the Garden? Reflections on Early Jewish and Christian Interpretations of the Garden of Eden", *HTR* 82 (1989) 121–148.

[68] See F. García Martínez, "The Heavenly Tables in the Book of Jubilees", in

although it is not completely clear how the author arrived at this etiology. In *Jubilees* the week and the two weeks (the seven and fourteen days) are related to the first week (in which Adam was created)[69] and to the second week (in which Eve was created and shown to Adam); and the forty and eighty days are related to the time of the respective entrances into the garden. The reason for observance of seven days for a male and "twice seven days" for a female is given (the difference in the time of the creation of Adam and Eve), but no reason is given for the difference of the additional 33 or 66 days for the male and the female other that the total of days that Adam was outside the Garden was 40, while 80 was the total of the days Eve needed to wait before being introduced into Eden. This would imply that the numbers in *Jubilees* are introduced expressly for the purpose of justifying the numbers given in the law of Leviticus.

If the way in which the author of *Jubilees* arrived at his conclusion is not completely clear, there is no doubt about his reason, the typological identification of the Garden with the Temple: "because it [the Garden of Eden] is more holy than any land, and every tree which is planted in it is holy." This is the same identification we find in 4Q265 which uses the same etiological explanation for the period of purification after childbirth. The only difference is that 4Q265 gives this reason as part of the narrative (lin. 14).[70]

4. *Summary*

The two halakhic texts we have examined show two different approaches to the biblical text, although in both the biblical narrative of the Garden of Eden is used in order to base a halakhic rule. Both approaches are grounded in the centrality of Scripture for the Community of Qumran.

In CD, the text of Gen 1:27 (as well as Gen 7:9 and Deut 17:17) is adduced to ground and bolster a halakhic rule peculiar to the group and to prove that the halakhah followed by the opponents of

M. Albani *et al.* (eds.), *Studies in the Book of Jubilees* (TSAJ 64; Mohr Siebeck: Tübingen 1997) 243–260.

[69] But also the rib, from which Eve will be formed, which the text defines as "his wife".

[70] Although כי is reconstructed, the available space in the lacuna makes the reconstruction unavoidable and almost certain.

the group is clearly wrong; the biblical narrative is used to justify a sectarian interpretation. 4Q256, on the contrary, uses a rewritten version of the Eden narrative (known to us only in the book of *Jubilees*) in order to justify a halakhic rule undisputed but unexplained in the biblical text.

PARADISE AS PARADIGM: GOOD AND EVIL IN RABBINICA AND KABBALAH

Wout Jac. van Bekkum

I

Jewish attitudes toward the Garden of Eden or Paradise reveal a richness of values and ideas which represent the plurality of Jewish life and thought. Paradise as a paradigm for good and evil in Rabbinics and Kabbalah will lead us to the dialectic between the recognition of Paradise as a place of beauty and perfection and the theological conception of Paradise as a place from which sin and death came forth. A tradition in the central work of Kabbalah, the Zohar, states that Adam, the First Man, appears before each dying man: כלהו בני עלמא חמאין ליה לאדם הראשון בשעתא דמסתלקי מן עלמא לאחזאה סהדותא דבנין חובוי דבר נש איהו אסתלק מעלמא ולא בגיניה דאדם כמה דתנינן אין מיתה בלא חטא—"When the dying person sees this vision, he cries out, It is because of you that I must die! The First Man answers this angry accusation by saying, It is true that I once sinned, a sin for which I was severely punished. But you, my son, how many sins have you committed?" A list of the dying man's misdeeds is revealed, certainly not making him happier in these circumstances, ending with the phrase, "There is no death without sin."[1]

Here one can already see the categories of sin and death expressed in specific rabbinic and mystical notions. Throughout the ages there has been considerable concern with these issues far beyond the Paradise story, as evidenced, for example, by the books of Ecclesiastes and Job. Although the term "sin" is used frequently in both biblical and rabbinic or kabbalistic sources, these texts deliberately contain little if any systematic reflection on the related questions of good and evil. The same is true for commandment and transgression, reward and punishment, life and death, body and soul, the Garden of Eden and Gehinnom, or Paradise and Hell, all of them dialectic conceptions placed within a dualistic ontological structure which time

[1] *Zohar* I, Genesis 57b; BT *Shab* 55a.

and again needed to be elaborated and refined in Jewish thought. Mainstream rabbinic teaching and central doctrine recognised the use of these antonymic categories as parts of an all embracing complex of ideas and values. Gan Eden, the Garden of Eden itself takes on ideas and meanings only as it interweaves with other ideas and intentions of the Paradise narrative which gradually became more explicit in Late Antiquity and during the Middle Ages; the narrative itself has never become a central issue. It is the purpose of this article to assemble some sources on this subject and to describe and explain them.

II

The Paradise story seems to revolve around two poles, good and evil, blessing and curse, reflected in the protagonists of the story, God and man, man and woman, God and serpent. Some essential aspects of the relationship between God and man or the divine and the human, and between Adam and Eve, male and female, are symbolized by one significant object: the tree of the knowledge of good and evil. In the eyes of some Sages this tree represents the existence of good and evil before man knew it. It is therefore said by Rabbi Pinhas ben Yair, עד שלא אכל ממנו אדם הראשון לא נקרא שמו אלא עץ בלבד כשאר כל העצים אבל משאכל ועבר על גזירתו של הקב״ה נקרא העץ עץ הדעת טוב ורע על שם סופו—"This tree, as long as the First Man did not eat from it, he only called עץ, tree, just like all other trees. After he had eaten and transgressed the decree of the Holy One, blessed be He, the tree was called the Tree of the knowledge of good and evil in accordance with its destination."[2] This tree is called after its function in the narrative, עץ הדעת טוב ורע, a name which fits the situation of the First Man after he had eaten of the tree of which God had commanded him "You shall not eat of it". The עץ הדעת טוב ורע appears in conjunction with the tree of life, first in a small summary in Gen 2:9, ועץ החיים בתוך הגן ועץ הדעת טוב ורע—"The tree of life in the midst of the garden, and the tree of knowledge of good and evil"; secondly in Gen 3:22 when God speaks or rather talks to Himself, הן האדם היה כאחד ממנו לדעת טוב ורע ועתה פן ישלח ידו ולקח גם מעץ החיים ואכל וחי לעלם—"The man

[2] *Ozar Midrashim* 474.

has become like one of us, knowing good and evil; and now, lest he put forth his hand and take also of the tree of life, and eat, and live for ever"; the conclusion continues in indirect speech, וישלחהו ה׳ אלהים מגן עדן—"Therefore the Lord God sent him forth from the Garden of Eden."

Midrashic expositions try to clarify which tree is the most essential. The prohibitive commandment firstly applies to the tree of knowledge of good and evil and not to the tree of life. This tree may retain its function as the guarantee of eternal life for Adam and Eve as long as good and evil are God's private knowledge. The reality of goodness is the core of the Creation account in which man can live in Paradise without knowing about evil or the origin of evil. Biblical and Rabbinic authors also describe God as good, and it is postulated in all the Jewish sources that God desires the good for His creatures and urges them to struggle against evil.

The abstract problem of why a benevolent God should have created evil and suffering in the first place is hardly touched upon until the Middle Ages. The question then is how it can be maintained at the same time that God is wholly good and almighty and that evil is a reality, not, as some Jewish thinkers have argued, an illusion or a negation of the good. The great thirteenth-century philosopher Maimonides refrains from ascribing goodness to God's essential nature and declares that, from the human angle at least, God is good and hates evil: שהשם יתעלה לא יאמר עליו סתם שהוא עושה רע בעצם כלל ר״ל שיכוין כונה ראשונה לעשות רע זה לא יתכן אבל פעולותיו כלם טוב נמור שהוא אינו עושה רק מציאות וכל מציאות טוב.[3] The way out of this severe problem for the majority of Jewish thinkers is the free-will defence. If God is to grant free will to His creatures, the world must be the arena in which free will can be exercised. This involves the creation of a world that provides for the conflict between good and evil and hence necessitates the existence of evil. The tree of knowledge of good and evil precedes the actual world where people have to find proper ways of choosing the good. Man's free will avoids the appearance that he is instrumental; his choice for מעשים טובים or good deeds is creative and fosters the realisation of goodness. In the words of Maimonides, God Himself is not evil, but He brought it into the world, as it is said in Is 45:7: יוצר אור ובורא חשך עשה שלום ובורא רע אני ה׳ עושה כל אלה—"I form light and create darkness, I

[3] *The Guide of the Perplexed* III,10.

make peace and create evil, I am the Lord, who does all these things." The medieval exegetes were in a great hurry to delimit the meaning of this dangerous verse and to apply it strictly to the context of chapter 45, which is addressed to Koresh or Cyrus: "I make peace for the sake of Persia, I create evil for Babylon."

III

It is clear from the above-mentioned observation that the First Man is not an instrument in the hands of God and possessed the power of knowledge and the ability of defining, as can be read in Gen 2:20, ויקרא האדם שמות לכל הבהמה ולעוף השמים ולכל חית השדה.. וכל אשר יקרא לו האדם נפש חיה הוא שמו—"The First Man gave names to all cattle, and to the birds of the air, and to every beast of the field"; v. 19: "Whatever the man called every living creature, that was its name." Various traditions cherish the concept of human wisdom to the disadvantage of angels who do not possess any knowledge. In *SOR* 21 the First Man is said to have prophetic qualities, but most sources allude to his wisdom by which he succeeded in naming the creatures and objects, as it is said, "The wisdom of Adam displayed itself to the greatest advantage when he gave names to the animals. Then it appeared that God, in combating the arguments of the angels who opposed the creation of man, had spoken well, when He insisted that the First Man would possess more wisdom than they themselves. When Adam was barely one hour old, God assembled the whole world of animals before him and the angels. The latter were called upon to name the different kinds, but they were not equal to the task. Adam, however, spoke without hesitation: O Lord of the world! The proper name for this animal is ox, for this one is horse, for this one lion, for this one camel! And so he called all in turn by name, suiting the name to the peculiarity of the animal. Then God asked him what his name was to be, and he said Adam, because he had been created out of *adamah*, dust of the earth. Then, God asked him His very own name, and he pronounced the Tetragrammaton, *YHWH Elohim*, because You are Lord over all creatures."[4] One version of this tradition in GenR 24:7 goes even

[4] Peter Schäfer, *Rivalität zwischen Engeln und Menschen, Untersuchungen zur rabbinischen Engelvorstellung*, Berlin and New York 1975.

further by bestowing on Adam additional talents, ר׳ תנחומא בשם ר׳ אלעזר ר׳ מנחמה בשם רב כל אומניות אדם הראשון לימדם מה טעם וחרשים המה מאדם מאדם הראשון—"Rabbi Tanhuma in Rabbi Eleazar's name and Rabbi Menahamah in Rab's name said, Adam taught mankind all forms of craftsmanship. What is the proof? It is to be found in Is 44:11: וחרשים המה מאדם—'And the craftsmen skilled above men', literally *me-Adam*, here interpreted to denote source or origin and to be translated as 'they are craftsmen from Adam', that is, taught by the First Man. Rab said, Adam also taught the art of writing and he invented all the seventy languages, as it is said, זה ספר תולדות אדם—'This is the book of the generations (plural: different generations) of Adam.'" (Gen 5:1).[5]

IV

However, it is to be noted that all these extraordinary qualities of the First Man seem not primarily to pertain to the very essence of his experience of good and evil. As such, the term that summons up this very essence is דעת. The verbal stem from which this infinitive has been derived is ידע, and when one considers how ידע is used within the biblical corpus itself, some patterns and distinctions do emerge. Two of the possible connotations are brought together in the commentary on Genesis by Nahmanides who combines the meaning "to discern", "to distinguish" with "to be lustful". Eating of the fruit from the tree of knowledge increased the wisdom of the First Man with the ability to distinguish between the sexes, involving both sexual desire and shame about nakedness; secondly, this דעת leads to the matter of choosing whether one's deed or action could be right or wrong. Choice means making distinctions and the First Man was not supposed to have the talent to decide for himself what is good and what is bad or what he liked or disliked about his own conduct and appearance. Nahmanides' view requires us to examine particularly the consequences of this דעת: האדם חטא בפרי עץ הדעת תחתון

[5] Peter Schäfer, "Adam in der jüdischen Überlieferung", in: W. Stolz, *Vom alten zum neuen Adam: Urzeitmythos und Heilsgeschichte*, Freiburg, Basel and Vienna: Herder 1986, pp. 69–93; Michael A. Stone offers a general overview in: *A History of the Literature of Adam and Eve*, Society of Biblical Literature, Early Judaism and Its Literature 3, Atlanta, Georgia: Scholars Press 1992, pp. 84–123: The Secondary Adam Literature.

ועליון במעשה ובמחשבה—"The man has committed a sin by means of eating fruit from the tree of knowledge below and above, in practice and in thinking." This exegetical-mystical reflection clarifies that sin is not to be treated as a separate, independent entity. Despite the existence of so many definitions of an endless variety of sin, and despite the stern reproof voiced by the Sages against sin and sinners, theological and even Kabbalistic concern with sin itself does not intend to formulate concepts in their own right. Adam's sin is a transgression of מצוה, a commandment, demonstrating in the first place that Paradise was not a pretext for a life without God's rule or religious practice. It is not an abstract value or dogma which is communicated to the First Man but a concrete and well-defined מצוה, one positive, "You shall freely eat of every tree of the Garden" (Gen 2:16), and one negative, "But of the tree of knowledge of good and evil you shall not eat" (2:17).[6]

It goes without saying that the Sages adduce many interpretations of Adam's disobedience, but none of these views corroborate the concept of original sin. This is to some extent surprising because of the general tendency to consider the conduct of the First Man as a paradigm for human conduct in general and to identify Adam as the father of humanity. MSanh 4:5 suggests a number of lessons to be drawn from the fact that the whole world is said to be descended from one man,

> לפיכך נברא אדם יחידי ללמדך שכל המאבד נפש אחת מישראל מעלה עליו הכתוב כאלו אבד עולם מלא וכל המקיים נפש אחת מישראל מעלה עליו הכתנב כאלו קיים עולם מלא ומפני שלום הבריות שלא יאמר אדם לחברו אבא גדול מאביך ושלא מינין אומרים הרבה רשויות בשמים ולהגיד גדולתו של הקדוש ברוך הוא שאדם טובע כמה מטבעות בחותם אחד וכולן דומין זה לזה ומלך מלכי המלכים הקדוש ברוך הוא טבע כל אדם בחותמו של אדם הראשון ואין אחד מהן דומה לחברו לפיכך כל אחד חייב לומר בשבילי נברא העולם.

> Therefore but a single man was created in the world, to teach that if anyone brings about the death of even one person Scripture considers it as if he had brought about the destruction of the whole world, and whoever saves the life of a single person Scripture considers it as if he had saved the whole world. Again for the sake of peace among human beings, that none should say to his fellow, My father was greater than your father; also that the heretics should not say, There are many

[6] Alexander Altmann, "The Gnostic Background of the Rabbinic Adam Legends", *Jewish Quarterly Review* N.S. 35, 1944–45, pp. 371–391.

> ruling powers in heaven. Again to proclaim the greatness of the Holy One, blessed be He, for man stamps many coins with the same seal, and they are all like one another; but the King of Kings, the Holy One, blessed be He, has stamped every man with the seal of the First Man, yet none of them is like another. Therefore every person must say, For my sake was the world created.

Whatever the exemplary value of the First Man may be, his acquaintance with good and evil is not equal to the דעת or knowledge his offspring have to acquire in order to differentiate between good and bad[7]. It is exactly the opposite: Adam's disobedience should not be copied, because his transgression against the prohibition of eating the fruit of the tree of the knowledge of good and evil established unequivocably the causal nexus between sin and punishment. The first sin brought into the world death, birth pangs, toil and fatigue. The story of Adam's sin does not purport in the Bible to explain men's sins and weaknesses. Furthermore, the entire episode is nowhere alluded to subsequently. A very explicit statement can be found in Ben Sira 25:24, "From a woman did sin originate, and because of her we all must die." However, these words occur in a chapter that discusses woman in general. Ben Sira states only that iniquity began on account of woman and because of her, death came into being, but there is no allusion to the concept of "original sin" and predestination whatsoever. On the contrary, he expressly states in 15:11–15: אל תאמר מאל פשעי כי את אשר שנא לא עשה—"Do not say, Because of God I left the right way; for you will not do what He hates"; פן תמאר הוא התקילני כי אין צורך באנשי חמס—"Do not say: It was He who led me astray; for He has no need of sinful men"; רעה ותועבה שנא ה׳ ולא יאננה ליראיו—"God hates all abominations, and they are not loved by those who fear him"; אלהים מבראשית ברא אדם וישתהו ביד חותפו ויתנהו ביד יצרו—"God created man from the beginning, and placed him in the hands of his enemy, in the hands of his own inclination, his "יצר"; אם תחפוץ תשמור מצוה ואמונה לעשות רצונו אם תאמין בו נם אתה תחיה—"If you will, you can keep the commandments, and it is His wish to act faithfully, if you will believe Him, then you will live . . ."; v. 17: לפני אדם חיים ומוות אשר יחפוץ יינתן לו—"Before each man are life and death, and whichever he chooses will be given to him . . ."; v. 21: לא צוה אנוש לחטוא ולא החלים אנשי כזב—"God has

[7] Ephraim E. Urbach, *The Sages, Their Concepts and Beliefs*, Jerusalem: The Magnes Press 1979.

not commanded anyone to sin, and He has not given anyone permission to do evil."

Ben Sira's words are consistent with the views of the Rabbis that the episode of Adam and Eve marks the moment when death came into being. Death came with Adam's fall, but not the necessity to sin. Natural death is imminent and inevitable but the orientation toward life and death also has a divinely conceived moral dimension, as it is written in Deut 30:15, ראה נתתי לפניך היום את החיים ואת הטוב ואת המות ואת הרע—"See, I have set before you this day life and good, death and evil", and 30:19, והמות נתתי לפניך הברכה והקללה ובחרת בחיים למען תחיה אתה וזרעך החיים—"I have set before you life and death, blessing and curse; therefore choose life, that you and your descendants may live."

The word יצר or inclination in Ben Sira was strongly stereotyped by the Sages in two phrases, יצר הטוב, the good inclination, and its antithesis יצר הרע, the evil inclination. Divergent approaches can be attributed to the concept of the evil inclination culminating in an explicit personification of יצר הרע as a corrupting agent in the world like the serpent in Paradise or Satan or the Angel of Death, however, mainstream teaching has it that the Torah is of great help in the struggle against the evil inclination. Whoever resists its power is called a righteous one, a צדיק.

Much more can be said about human righteousness and its redeeming power, but interesting for our discussion today is the reason why Gan Eden is not generally seen as a place where fruit has been stolen (מכל עץ הגן זה הגזל כמה דאת אמ׳ ומעץ הדעת טוב ורע לא תאכל ממנו) and a commandment has been ignored.[8] The Garden of Eden itself escapes a harsh judgment for a number of reasons. First, it is a place created by God in Eden (Gen 2:8). Second, God is present in Eden (3:8). He puts the man whom He had formed in the garden (2:8; GenR 16:5: ויניחהו as a Sabbath commandment connected with the noun מנוחה: God establishes that man rest and enjoy the Sabbath in Gan Eden). Lastly, He sends the man forth from the garden (3:22: וישלחהו). From then on the garden is a protected and well-guarded place (3:24). The word Eden bears connotations of fruitfulness and delight, and because of the topographical and geographical descriptions in relation to Gan Eden Martin Buber translates this expression

[8] *Pesikta de Rav Kahana*, ed. B. Mandelbaum, New York: Jewish Theological Seminary of America 1962, vol. I, *piska* 12, pp. 202–203.

with "Üppigland", which is quite nice.[9] The garden as a simile for a pleasant place within a futural context is found in Jer 31:12, ובאו ורננו במרום ציון ונהרו אל טוב ה׳.. והיתה נפשם כגן רוה—"They shall come and sing aloud on the height of Zion, and they shall be radiant over the goodness of the Lord . . . their life shall be like a watered garden", or in the context of threat as in Joel 2:3, כגן עדן הארץ לפניו ואחריו מדבר שממה—"The land is like the Garden of Eden before him (the enemy), but after him a desolate wilderness". The opposite is found in Ez 36:35 in the vision of the rebuilt land of Israel, ואמרו הארץ הלזו הנשמה היתה כגן עדן—"And they will say: this land that was desolate has become like the Garden of Eden." The same book, Ezekiel, contains in chapter 28 a lamentation over the king of Tyre who is said to have been in Eden, the garden of God where every precious stone was his covering and gold his settings and engravings and where he remained until iniquity was found in him, as it is said (28:16), ברוב רכולתך מלו תוכך חמס ותחטא ואחללך מהר אלהים ואבדך כרוב הסוכך מתוך אבני אש—"In the abundance of your trade you were filled with violence, and you sinned; so I cast you as a profane thing from the mountain of God, and the guardian cherub drove you out from the midst of the stones of fire." In these latter passages the Garden of Eden is a place of retribution in order to announce death to king Chiram of Tyre[10].

In Rabbinic Judaism Gan Eden and its opposite Gehinnom became names given to the places of reward and punishment of the soul after the death of the body. This is a major shift from Scriptural retribution which clearly belongs to the terrestrial world: if someone keeps the commandments of the Torah he will prosper in this world and be blessed here, but the Sages make people aware of heavenly retribution by which the righteous will live forever. In Hag 15a, Elisha ben Abuyah explains in the name of Rabbi Akiba that for everything God has created He also created its counterpart, ברא הרים ברא גבעות ברא ימים ברא נהרות. . . ברא צדיקים ברא רשעים ברא גן עדן ברא גיהנום. . . זכה צדיק נטל חלקו וחלק חברו בגן עדן נתחייב רשע נטל חלקו וחלק חברו בגיהנם—"He created mountains, and created

[9] Martin Buber und Franz Rosenzweig, *Die fünf Bücher der Weisung*, Heidelberg 1981, p. 13: "Er, Gott, pflanzte einen Garten in Eden, Üppigland, ostwärts, und legte darein den Menschen, den er gebildet hatte."

[10] As it is argued in GenR 9:5.

hills; He created seas, and created rivers . . . He created righteous, and created wicked; He created the Garden of Eden, and created Gehinnom . . . The righteous man, being meritorious, takes his portion and his fellow's portion in the Garden of Eden. The wicked man, being guilty, takes his portion and his fellow's portion in Gehinnom."

The Sages of the Talmud were aware of the problems that belief in divine reward and punishment raised. In various *derashot* there is considerable ambiguity on whether the souls of the righteous are in what later was called "the higher Gan Eden", meaning, in heaven, or in "the lower Gan Eden", on earth. An additional problem is whether the expression העולם הבא is to be identified with a kind of Hereafter or whether it is literally the World to Come as a reference to this world which will be renewed? In most teachings the otherworldliness of העולם הבא predominates as the saying of Rab in Ber 17a illustrates: לא כעולם הזה העולם הבא העולם הבא אין בו לא אכילה ולא שתייה ולא פרייה ורבייה ולא משא ומתן ולא קנאה ולא שנאה ולא תחרות אלא צדיקים יושבין ועטרותיהם בראשיהם ונהנים מזיו השכינה—"In the World to Come there is no eating nor drinking nor propagation nor business nor jealousy nor hatred nor competition, but the righteous sit with their crowns on their heads feasting the brightness of the Shekhinah." Very striking, however, is the saying in Ber 57b that three things afford a foretaste in miniature of the bliss of the World to Come: the Sabbath, a sunny day, and sex"—שלשה מעין העולם הבא אלו הן שבת שמש ותשמיש. The Gemara is doubtful whether sex should be included since it results in exhaustion of the body!

V

Paradise figures in one specific tradition in Hag 14b–15a as a פרדס, a garden as a figurative expression for heaven, according to the commentary of Rashi. The account of four men entering this *pardes* can also be found in *Heykhalot* literature in many different versions, as Peter Schäfer has shown in his famous *Synopse zur Hekhalot-Literatur*. "Simeon ben Azzai, Simeon ben Zoma, Acher and Rabbi Akiba entered the pardes. Rabbi Akiba said to them: When you arrive at the stones of pure marble (giving the illusion of water), do not say: 'water, water!' For it is said in Ps 101:7: 'No man who utters lies shall continue in My presence.' Ben Azzai cast a look and died instantly. Of him Scripture says in Ps 116:15: 'Precious in the sight of God is the death of his saints.' Ben Zoma looked and was stricken (became insane). Of him Scripture says in Prov 25:16: 'If you have found honey, eat only enough for you, lest you be sated with it and vomit it.' Acher (the so-called 'Other', the aforementioned Elisha ben Abuyah) severed the young shoots (usually explained as: he defected or apostatized). Only Rabbi Akiba returned unharmed."[11] Leaving all the interpretive difficulties aside, in modern research two tendencies can be discerned with regard to this famous *barayta*: one defends a pure Rabbinic stand taking the account as a purely intellectual exercise and defining it as a *mashal*, a parable; the second accepts this account as a mystical voyage to heaven which emerged from gnostic and mystical sources. The late tenth-century Babylonian Gaon Hay equated this *pardes* with Gan Eden as a hiding place for the righteous. The place is to be found in the seventh layer or the uppermost of the firmaments called ערבות where the souls of the righteous are brought together. One sage did not reach the ערבות alive; the other not in good mental health; the third did not accept the idea of the voyage; only the fourth ascended safely and descended safely. Both Hag 14b–15a and the mystical tractate *Merkabah Rabbah*, par. 671–672, read that when Acher or Elisha ירד למרכבה, descended to the chariot he saw the angel Metatron, who had been given permission to sit and write down the merits of Israel one hour a day. Elisha said: "The sages taught that above there is no standing and no sitting, no jealousy and no rivalry, and no support and no affliction" (another version of the words of Rab). He meditated: "Perhaps there are two powers in heaven?" Immediately God took Metatron outside of the celestial curtain (מפרגוד) and he (Metatron) was given sixty fiery blows, saying to him: "Why did you not rise before him when you saw him?" (that is to say, Metatron should have observed the rules of heaven). However, permission was given to Metatron to strike out the merits of Elisha. A heavenly voice went out and told him: "Return (repent) o faithless sons!" (Jer 3:14:22) except Acher (so that he was barred from *teshuvah* in the future and would die as a heretic).[12]

---

[11] Texte und Studien zum Antiken Judentum 2, Tübingen 1981; cf. also Yehudah Liebes, *The Sin of Elisha'*, Jerusalem: Akademon 1990.

[12] Annelies Kuyt, *The "Descent" to the Chariot*, Tübingen 1995, pp. 314–332.

Pardes in this early mystical and later Kabbalistic context is the heavenly Garden of Eden or Paradise, and the main writings of Kabbalah set both earthly and heavenly Gardens of Eden on high because in this גן עדן של מעלה the central object is the Tree of Life which is the Tree of the Sefirot, the ten revealed attributes or powers of Divinity. The problem of evil is central in the doctrine of the Sefirot, because it is Adam's sin which caused disharmony within the divine attributes eventually leading to an existence of a separate manifestation of evil outside the structure of the Sefirot. This *sitra achra*, the other side, is no longer an organic part of the world of the Sefirot, and although evil emerged from one of the attributes of God, it cannot be an essential part of Him. This view became dominant in mainstream Kabbalah through the treatises of the Zohar: a salvationary scheme has to be constituted in which Adam's soul, the soul of all souls so to speak, plays the main role. It is obvious that the fulfillment of a Torah commandment strengthens the side of holiness and brings harmony of the divine emanations nearer, but at first it is Adam as the *Adam Kadmon* or Primordial Man, who has to restore what he has broken. In later Lurianic Kabbalah, in the teachings of Rabbi Isaac Ashkenazi Luria (sixteenth century), Adam is held responsible for the fragmentation of souls. Each of his descendants has a mere ניצוץ or holy spark from Adam's great soul, and each has to help restore harmony in the Sefirotic realm by keeping the precepts of the Torah. Gan Eden in this context is the result of restoration and the reclamation of the holy, a symbol for cosmic redemption and the coming of the Messiah, and, above all, the reunion of Adam and *Shekhinah*, male and female, human and divine, both perfecting one another, filling one another, both returning after a long exile to the Garden of Eden. This is the Paradise of primal and future perfection which is hidden somewhere in the multistoried structure of Jewish thought, belief and hope.

A VISIT TO PARADISE: *APOCALYPSE OF PAUL* 45 AND ITS BACKGROUND

A. Hilhorst

In the apocryphal *Apocalypse of Paul*, chapter 45, the Apostle is treated to a guided tour of Paradise. The description runs as follows:

> And after that the angel said to me, "Have you seen all these things?" And I said, "Yes, sir." And he said to me, "Follow me, and I will lead you into Paradise, that the just who are there may see you, for lo, they hope to see you, and they are ready to come to meet you in joy and gladness!" And I followed the angel by the swiftness of the Holy Spirit, and he placed me in Paradise and said to me, "Do you see these things, this place? This is Paradise in which Adam and his wife erred." I entered Paradise and saw the beginning of waters, and the angel beckoned to me, and he said to me, "Observe the waters, for this is the river of Pison which surrounds all the land of Evila, and the second is Gion which surrounds all the land of Egypt and Ethiopia, and the third is Tigris which is over against the Assyrians, and another is Euphrates which waters the land of Mesopotamia." And when I had gone inside I saw a tree planted from whose roots water flowed out, and from this was the beginning of the four rivers. And the Spirit of God rested on that tree, and when the Spirit blew, the waters flowed forth, and I said, "My lord, is it this tree itself which makes the waters flow?" And he said to me, "From the beginning, before the heavens and earth were manifested, all things were invisible and the Spirit of God hovered upon the waters, but from the time when at the command of God the heaven and earth appeared, the Spirit has been resting upon this tree; wherefore, whenever the Spirit blows, the waters flow forth from the tree." And he held me by the hand and led me near the tree of knowledge of good and evil, and he said, "This is the tree by which death entered into the world, and Adam, receiving of it through his wife, ate, and death entered into the world." And he showed me another tree in the midst of Paradise and said to me, "This is the tree of life."[1]

[1] The translation is from J.K. Elliott, *The Apocryphal New Testament: A Collection of Apocryphal Christian Literature in an English Translation*, Oxford 1993, 639–640, with some retouches, mainly to adapt it to the text in T. Silverstein and A. Hilhorst, *Apocalypse of Paul: A New Critical Edition of Three Long Latin Versions* (Cahiers d'Orientalisme 21), Geneva 1997, 164.

The Apocalypse of Paul is a Christian apocryphon probably of the third century in which the visit is described which the Apostle Paul made to Paradise and to the place of the damned. It is inspired by the famous text in 2 Corinthians 12:2–4, in which Paul speaks in mysterious language about his being caught up into the third heaven: "I know a man in Christ who, fourteen years ago, was caught up—whether still in the body or out of the body, I do not know; God knows—right into the third heaven. I do know, however, that this same person—whether in the body or out of the body, I do not know; God knows—was caught up into paradise and heard things which must not and cannot be put into human language."[2] As Augustine suggested, it is paradoxical to write a whole book about things which must not and cannot be put into human language,[3] but this was no hindrance to the book's success in later times. The Apocalypse was even one of the sources of inspiration of Dante's *Divina Commedia.* Thus it had an important afterlife. On the other hand, the text itself was a depository of many earlier biblical, Jewish and Christian traditions. Chapter 45, just cited, is a case in point. Indeed it is possible to explain its background by sketching the development of the idea of Paradise in the literature of the Second Temple period and early Christianity; which is what I shall do in this paper.

This is not to say that the passage contains only well-known elements. First of all, while there are many earlier texts mentioning Paradise inhabited by the just, and at least several describing distinguished biblical characters visiting Paradise, I am unaware of any text before the *Apocalypse of Paul* stating that the just in Paradise are eager to meet the visitor. A second peculiar element is what we might call the water management of Paradise. The association of water with trees is nothing unusual; in Psalm 1, the happy man who finds his pleasure in the Law of the Lord is compared with "a tree that is planted by water streams", and the same image occurs in Jeremiah 17:8. More particularly, water welling up from the roots of a tree is paralleled in other apocryphal texts.[4] Again, the Spirit

---

[2] Scriptural quotations are drawn from The Jerusalem Bible.

[3] *In Ioh. tract.* 98.8 (PL 35,1885; CCSL 36,581).

[4] *Passion of Matthew* 9: *de ea uirga exierat harbor inmanis et desub harbore exiit fons; Gospel of Pseudo-Matthew* 20.2 (Jesus speaking to the palm:) *"Aperi autem ex radicibus tuis uenam quae absconsa est in terra, et fluant ex ea aquae ad satietatem nostram." Et statim erecta est palma, et coeperunt per radices eius egredi fontes aquarum limpidissimi et frigidi et dulcissimi nimis.* Cf. also A.M. Schwemer, *Studien zu den frühjüdischen Prophetenlegenden* Vitae

of God hovering upon the waters is familiar from the second verse of the Bible. On the other hand, to my knowledge there are no precedents of the Spirit resting on the tree from which the rivers spring "from the time when at the command of God the heaven and earth appeared". The most curious feature, however, is the way water is made to flow. This seems to be an intermittent process: "whenever the Spirit blows, the waters flow forth from the tree." Generally speaking, I know of no earlier mentions of the Spirit of Genesis 1:2 set to work in Paradise.

Thus, these seem to be exclusive features of the *Apocalypse of Paul.* My subject, however, is the Jewish and Christian traditions underlying that apocryphon; in other words, the history of the concept of Paradise in biblical and para-biblical texts roughly until the third century AD. Clearly it is impossible to give this a proper treatment within the compass of a short paper. All I can do is to trace some lines and to make some comments, hoping that the picture is not too much of a distortion. The difficulties are formidable. We have to consult many texts, many of which are in a bad state of transmission and hard to date exactly. Moreover, many passages contain only casual references to Paradise, so that we cannot know, for instance, whether Paradise is located on earth or in some extraterrestrial place, in heaven or somewhere else.

To get a grip on the elusive subject-matter, I shall distinguish three stages: Earthly Paradise as the abode of Adam and Eve, Earthly Paradise after the Fall, and Heavenly Paradise.

1. *Earthly Paradise as the abode of Adam and Eve*

The classical picture is, of course, Genesis 2 and 3. This account may be subdivided into the description of the Garden as a place of bliss and the story of the fall of the first couple.

Prophetarum, I (Texte und Studien zum Antiken Judentum 49), Tübingen 1995, 98, on the combination of tree, source and cave, and R. Bauerreiß, *Arbor vitae: Der "Lebensbaum" und seine Verwendung in Liturgie, Kunst und Brauchtum des Abendlandes* (Abhandlungen der Bayerischen Benediktiner-Akademie 3), Munich 1938, 28–31, for iconographical aspects.

a. *Earthly Paradise as a place of bliss*

The Old Testament has no depiction of the garden of Eden except the picture in Genesis 2; obviously this did not need to be repeated. But we do find Paradise as a proverbial concept of a delicious place: thus in Gen. 13:10, "Lot saw all the Jordan plain, irrigated everywhere . . . like the garden of Yahweh or the land of Egypt". Ezekiel uses the image to picture the prosperity of kings. In 28:13, the king of Tyre is addressed as follows: "You were in Eden, in the garden of God", and in 31, Pharaoh is compared to a cedar of Lebanon, cf. 31:8: "No cedar equalled it in the garden of God, no cypress had branches such as these; no plane tree could match its boughs, no tree in the garden of God could rival its beauty."[5] In Joel 2:3, the hostile army comes rushing along, eager to invade the country which is "like a garden of Eden ahead of them". The image is also used for consolation. In Isaiah 51:3, the prophet announces: "Yes, Yahweh has pity on Zion, has pity on all her ruins; turns her desolation into an Eden, her wasteland into the garden of Yahweh. Joy and gladness shall be found in her, thanksgiving and the sound of music." And Ezekiel has God speak as follows (36:35): "Everyone will say: This land, so recently a waste, is now like a garden of Eden." There are also references to the primeval Paradise in several parabiblical writings.[6]

In this connection a methodological remark may perhaps be made on the so-called paradise motifs, the features that are characteristic of Paradise. Joachim Jeremias, who contributed a rich article παράδεισος to the *Theological Dictionary of the New Testament*, mentions the following motifs:[7] great fertility, abundance of water, peace between peoples, peace between animals, peace between man and animal, advanced age, absence of illness and death, community with God. Each of these he illustrates using Old Testament passages. This demonstrates, he feels, the thesis "Endzeit ist gleich Urzeit". It should be observed, however, that none of the passages he mentions refers to the description of Paradise in Genesis. True, some of them may indeed be connected with it: fertility, abundance of water, possibly also advanced age, absence of illness and death, community with God. But others

[5] For a detailed discussion of Ezekiel 28 and 31, see the article by E. Noort in this volume.

[6] *Jub.* 2.7; *4 Esdr.* 6.2.

cannot be shown to be characteristic of Paradise: peace between peoples, peace between animals, peace between man and animal. On the other hand, some motifs left unmentioned by Jeremias do occur: sexual innocence (Gen 2:25; 3:7,21), absence of pain in childbearing (Gen 3:16), absence of toil (Gen 3:17–19). For the sake of precision, I would prefer to reserve the term "paradise motifs" for those features that do occur in Genesis 2 and 3.

b. *Fall of the first couple*

Here again, the account of Genesis was obviously sufficient, at least in the Old Testament. To my knowledge, there is only one allusion to it there, and it is oblique. It is the dirge in Ezekiel 28, in which the king of Tyre is portrayed as one who was once in Eden but was expelled from it because of his misbehaviour. In the para-biblical Jewish literature, however, the situation is different. Although most texts take the Genesis account for granted, here we come across the phenomenon of the rewritten Bible, whose aim is to give "a fuller, smoother and doctrinally more advanced form of the sacred narrative".[8]

There are at least four retellings of the fall in Paradise. The earliest of these is the version in the book of *Jubilees*, an originally Hebrew work from the second century BC. The story of the fall is told in 3.9–35.[9] The writer of *Jubilees* is anxious to root halakha in the events he narrates and indulges his interest in the number seven, so that, for instance, the fall takes place at the end of seven years in Paradise (3.17). To further illustrate the writer's use of expansions to the Genesis account I might mention the following three examples: first, that in Paradise all animals spoke with one another in one language (3.28), a detail also recorded by Josephus;[10] second, that Adam and his wife had the task of tilling the garden of Eden (3.15–16)—it was not a *dolce far niente* for them, as we might think;

[7] *Theologisches Wörterbuch zum Neuen Testament* V (1954), 764 n. 15. Add to the bibliography: J. Daniélou, "Terre et Paradis chez les Pères de l'Église", *Eranos-Jahrbuch* 22, 1953, 433–472; B. Otzen, "The Paradise Trees in Jewish Apocalyptic", in P. Bilde, H.K. Nielsen and J. Podemann Sørensen (eds.), *Apocryphon Severini presented to Søren Giversen*, Aarhus 1993, 140–154.

[8] E. Schürer, G. Vermes and F. Millar, *The History of the Jewish People in the Age of Jesus Christ (175 B.C.–A.D. 135)*, III.1, Edinburgh 1985, 308.

[9] For a detailed study of the passage, see the contribution of J.T.A.G.M. van Ruiten in this volume.

[10] *Ant.* 1.41, cf. L.H. Feldman, *Studies in Josephus' Rewritten Bible* (Supplements to the Journal for the Study of Judaism 58), Leiden-Boston-Köln 1998, 2–3.

and finally, that after their expulsion from Paradise, Adam and his wife "dwelt in the land of Elda, in the land of their creation" (3.32).[11]

Next comes the paraphrase in the *Life of Adam and Eve*, a Jewish or a Christian work possibly from the second century AD preserved in several languages including the probably original Greek.[12] In this work, the fall is narrated by Adam (7–8) and, in a much more detailed way, by Eve (15–30). There are many imaginative embellishments. Thus, before seducing Eve, the serpent itself has been persuaded by the devil to do so (16), and after Adam has eaten from the fruit, God comes to Paradise, seated on a chariot of cherubim (22.3).

Much closer to the literary habits of the Graeco-Roman world are the other two works to be mentioned here, first of all the *Jewish Antiquities* of Flavius Josephus, which in 1.35–51 has a description of the events of Eden. We must suppose Josephus meant to make the story palatable to Greek intellectuals but this did not stop him from telling such details as the formation of Eve from Adam's rib (35) or the order to abstain from the tree of life (37). A glance in Giancarlo Rinaldi's *Biblia Gentium* suffices to show that a more radical rewriting of the biblical account would have been necessary in order to prevent pagan readers from making fun of the narrative.[13] The other work is the poetic recasting in the *Sibylline Oracles*. This is a complex collection of hexameter poems from different times, partly written by Jews and partly by Christians. The suggestion is that a heathen prophetess, the Sibyl, formulates the biblical narrative in Homeric verses. The first two books consist of an original Jewish oracle and an extensive Christian redaction.[14] In the first book there are some 40 verses (1.22–64) devoted to the creation of Adam and Eve and to the fall. In these verses, there are no traces of Christian reworking;

[11] Quotations from Jewish apocrypha are taken from J. Charlesworth (ed.), *The Old Testament Pseudepigrapha*, 2 vols., New York 1983–1985.

[12] Specialists vary in their estimates about the work's original language, provenance and date. According to M. de Jonge and J. Tromp, *The Life of Adam and Eve and Related Literature* (Guides to Apocrypha and Pseudepigrapha 4), Sheffield 1997, the work was originally written in Greek (67), probably between AD 100 and 400 (77) and probably by Christians (74).

[13] G. Rinaldi, *Biblia Gentium: Primo contributo per un indice delle citazioni, dei riferimenti è delle allusioni alla Bibbia negli autori pagani, greci e latini, di età imperiale. A First Contribution towards an Index of Biblical Quotations, References and Allusions Made by Greek and Latin Heathen Writers of the Roman Imperial Times*, Rome 1989, 207–227. Origen was less naive than Josephus, cf. P.G.J.M. Raedts, "Het aards paradijs: De tuin als beeld van het geluk", in R.E.V. Stuip and C. Vellekoop (eds.), *Tuinen in de Middeleeuwen* (Utrechtse bijdragen tot de mediëvistiek 11), Hilversum 1992, 35–50, esp. 38.

[14] J.J. Collins in J. Charlesworth (n. 11), I, 1983, 330.

there are, for instance, no allusions to Christ as a second Adam or Mary as a better Eve. Touching details include the remark that Adam, while alone in Paradise, "desired conversation" (1.27), whereupon God created Eve, and the observation that Adam and Eve "conversed with wise words which flowed spontaneously, for God had taken care of everything" (1.33–34).

In addition, the Pseudepigrapha have a number of shorter references to the events in Paradise. Some of these use the same context as the passage in the *Apocalypse of Paul* we began with: Paradise is shown to a visionary. This is the case in *1 Enoch* 32.3,6, in a part of the work written before 170 BC. Here Enoch is granted a visit to Paradise, a Paradise clearly situated on earth. The same occurs to Moses in a much later Jewish work, Pseudo-Philo's *Biblical Antiquities*, which was probably written, according to its latest editor, in the first half of the second century AD.[15] Another context is the discussion a prophet has with the Almighty. This occurs in a Jewish work of the late first century AD, *4 Esdras* 3.4–7, cf. ib. 7.116–124, and in two much later Christian apocalypses, *Apocalypse of Esdras* 2.10–17 and *Apocalypse of Sedrach* 4.4–5.3.[16] Furthermore, the fall is alluded to in the Pauline corpus (Rom 5:12–14; 1 Cor 15:22; 1 Tim 2:13–14) and in the late second-century Christian *Tractate to Diognetus* 12.3–8. *Acts of Philip*, a Christian apocryphon of the fourth or fifth century, contains a confession by the serpent (11.3).

2. *Earthly Paradise after the Fall*

The belief in the existence of Paradise in some region of the earth never has died out. There are a number of ancient and medieval texts speaking about expeditions aimed at retrieving earthly Paradise.[17] Here, however, our concern is with the Bible and para-biblical literature, which do not record attempts of the kind. Three features

---

[15] 13.8–9. Cf. H. Jacobson, *A Commentary on Pseudo-Philo's* Liber Antiquitatum Biblicarum: *With Latin Text and English Translation* (Arbeiten zur Geschichte des Antiken Judentums und des Urchristentums 31), Leiden-New York-Köln 1996, 209–210. A passing reference to Adam in Paradise before the Fall may befound in 26.6.

[16] D. Ellul, in F. Bovon and P. Geoltrain (eds.), *Écrits apocryphes chrétiens I* (Bibliothèque de la Pléiade 442), [Paris] 1997, 550 and 576, dates them to the second half of the fourth century and "before 635" respectively.

[17] Cf. the contributions by C. Auffarth and S. Brouwer in this volume; furthermore G.J.M. Bartelink, "De terugkeer naar het paradijs: Paradijsverhalen uit de Oudheid", *Hermeneus* 62, 1990, 203–208, esp. 207–208.

draw our attention: the location, the just in Paradise, and Paradise as a dwelling of God.

Paradise, after having been left by Adam and Eve, continues to exist on earth. Earlier I quoted Genesis 13:10, "Looking round, Lot saw all the Jordan plain, irrigated everywhere—this was before the Lord destroyed Sodom and Gomorrah—like the garden of the Lord or the land of Egypt." The garden of the Lord and the land of Egypt are bracketed together in such a way that we can hardly suppose that the one (Paradise) is lost while the other (Egypt) exists. Later Jewish literature is more explicit. In the *Life of Adam and Eve*, Eve and Seth walk towards the regions of Paradise to fetch from there the oil of mercy, in order to anoint the sick Adam. *Jubilees* 8.16 (cf. also 8.21) states that the territory of Sem borders on the Garden of Eden, and *Jubilees* 4.24 declares that the deluge flooded the whole world except Eden. Pseudo-Philo, *Biblical Antiquities* 32.8, informs us that during the establishment of the Covenant on Mount Sinai, "Paradise, giving off the scent of its fruit, and the cedars of Lebanon were shaken from their roots".

The second feature is earthly Paradise being inhabited by the just, an idea we find in the *First Book of Enoch*, in the section chs. 37–71 known as the Similitudes and dating from the first half of the first century BC. Chapter 60.8 of that section speaks of a "desert whose name is Dundayin, east of the garden of Eden, wherein the elect and the righteous ones dwell". The fact that the context in question alludes to Enoch's voyage to the ends of the earth makes clear that terrestrial Paradise is meant here. Likewise, in the *Apocalypse of Abraham* 21.6, a Jewish work of the first or second century AD, but preserved only in an Old Slavonic translation, Abraham is shown "the garden of Eden and its fruits, and the source and the river flowing from it, and its trees and their flowering, making fruits, and I saw men doing justice in it, their food and their rest". Immediately before, he has seen the earth, the abyss, the sea and the rivers; so we may assume, I think, that Paradise is here on earth.

The third feature, the view that earthly Paradise is God's abode, is most clearly present in *Jubilees*. Thus *Jubilees* 8.19 states that Noah "knew that the garden of Eden was the holy of holies and the dwelling of the Lord".[18] Possibly this idea makes explicit what was

[18] For a more detailed discussion, cf. section 2.4, "Eden as a Temple", of the contribution by J.T.A.G.M. van Ruiten in this volume.

implied in Genesis 3:8, where God is walking in the garden, and in Genesis 13:10 and Ezekiel 28:13 and 31:8, which speak of Eden as "the garden of the Lord" or "the garden of God". On the other hand, in *Jubilees* 4.26 Paradise shares this privilege with three other places; the passage runs as follows: "For the Lord has four places upon the earth: the garden of Eden and the mountain of the East and this mountain which you are upon today, Mount Sinai, and Mount Zion." One cannot help thinking of the supreme god of the Greeks, Zeus, who dwells in ether (αἰθέρι ναίων Homer, *Iliad* 2.412), but also on Mount Olympus (ib. 1.494–495) and in Ethiopia (ib. 1.423–424).

The three features combine in a passage in *Jubilees* which mentions Enoch's transfer to the garden of Eden. Indeed, as 4.23 points out, because of his being there none of the water of the Flood came upon the land of Eden. This means that we have here earthly Paradise as a dwelling of God and at the same time as the abode of at least one just man. So, in principle, our sources know of a Paradise on earth which is the dwelling both of God and of the righteous.

In the long run, however, people might grow uneasy with the idea of Paradise on earth. Why, after all, if Euphrates and Tigris spring from it, can it not be found? And is it appropriate for the just, let alone for God, to dwell on earth? Therefore, it comes as no surprise that many texts situate Paradise in heaven.

3. *Paradise in heaven*

Again, we will have a look at three features: location, abode of the just, abode of God.

First of all, the location. In many texts the place of Paradise is not indicated. Thus, in Jesus' word to the good thief in Luke 23:43: "Today you will be with me in paradise", we cannot know for sure whether Jesus locates Paradise on earth or in heaven. Although I take for granted that Paradise is in heaven, the Gospel is silent about this question. The same applies for a passage like *2 Enoch* 71.1 (*2 Enoch* is a Jewish writing from the first or second century AD, preserved in an Old Slavonic translation): "The Lord said to Michael, 'Go down onto the earth to Nir the priest, and take my child Melkisedek, who is with him, and place him in the paradise of Edem for preservation.'"

Other texts, however, indicate that a heavenly place is meant. Thus, *4 Esdras* 4.7–8 (MS. L) states: "I never went down into the deep, nor as yet into hell, neither did I ever ascend into heaven nor did I enter into Paradise." We especially read about Paradise in the third heaven. As already discussed, the *Apocalypse of Paul* is entirely based on Paul's second letter to the Corinthians, ch. 12:2–4.[19] There are, however, many more echoes of it. A curious example may be found in a work falsely attributed to the pagan author Lucian, the so-called *Philopatris*, where in ch. 12 Paul is represented in a satirical way as a wizard "who had walked on air into the third heaven".[20] But the idea is not specifically Christian; it is also in *2 Enoch* 8–9, especially 8.1, where Enoch speaks as follows: "And the men took me from there. They brought me up to the third heaven. And they placed me in the midst of Paradise."

This Paradise in heaven is the abode of the just. Thus in the *Testament of Abraham* 20.14, a Jewish text probably from the second century AD, God orders: "Take, then, my friend Abraham into Paradise, where there are the tents of my righteous ones."

The third feature, heavenly Paradise as the abode of God, will hardly need demonstration. A classical witness is Rev 2:7: "Those who prove victorious I will feed from the tree of life set in God's paradise." The last nine words are a quotation of Gen 2:9, except precisely the word "God's". Even in many cases where Paradise is not explicitly mentioned, e.g. *1 Enoch* 70.1: "And it happened after this that his [Enoch's] living name was raised up before that Son of Man and to the Lord from among those who dwell upon the earth", we may be pretty sure that it is meant.[21]

Having come to the end of this brief outline, we may return to the *Apocalypse of Paul* and ask what light our findings shed on its chapter 45. In general, it has become clear, I trust, how much our text owes to the conceptual universe of early Judaism. There is, however, a question that is not so easy to answer, and that is whether

---

[19] Cf. *Apocalypse of Paul* 3, 19, 21.

[20] Cf. A. Hilhorst, "Paganism and Christianity in the *Philopatris*", in H. Hokwerda, E.R. Smits and M.M. Woesthuis (eds.), *Polyphonia Byzantina: Studies in Honour of Willem J. Aerts*, Groningen 1993, 39–43, esp. 41–42.

[21] In Ecclesiasticus 44:16, the Vulgate renders Ενωχ εὐηρέστησεν κυρίῳ καὶ μετετέθη by *Enoch placuit deo et translatus est in paradiso*. The addition *in paradiso* seems to make explicit what was implied in the Septuagint.

its Paradise should be situated on earth or in heaven. In the introductory part of this paper, we pointed out that the *Apocalypse of Paul* is an expansion of the passage in 2 Cor 12:2–4, where Paul speaks about his being caught up into the third heaven. So it seems clear that the Paradise in the *Apocalypse of Paul* is itself in heaven. Reality, however, is more complicated than that. First of all, the passage in 2 Corinthians mentions not only third heaven, but also Paradise; it is possible that different locations are meant, one in heaven and one on earth, or, at least, that the passage has been read like that.[22] Furthermore, Paul's other-worldly tour brings him to a bewildering variety of places: firmament (chs. 11–18), third heaven, and via second heaven back to firmament (chs. 19–21), land of promise and City of Christ in the extreme East, beyond the Ocean (chs. 21–30), place of punishment, at the opposite side of the inhabited world (chs. 31–44), Paradise (chs. 45–51). Finally, the witnesses to the text do not always agree; thus, unlike the other texts, the important Paris MS. calls the gate of third heaven "the gate of Paradise" (ch. 20); and many witnesses omit chs. 45–51 altogether. Chapter 45 offers no obvious clues to settle the question; we shall have to consider the text as a whole for a clarification.

Recently, two theories have been put forward. Claude Carozzi argued that Paradise in ch. 45 is earthly Paradise. To him, the chapter itself is eloquent in this respect: it is Paradise in which Adam and Eve erred and which is still provided with its trees and rivers. Moreover, chs. 45–51 are the seventh and last part of a sophisticated structure which begins with the element of Creation (chs. 3–6, which describe the appeal of Creation to God against sinful man); thus we have here a return *ad initium*.[23] Some years before, Jean-Marc Rosenstiehl had voiced a different view; unfortunately, Carozzi, who mentions this study in his bibliography, does not take it into consideration while developing his own opinion. Rosenstiehl, after analyzing the structure of the *Apocalypse*, concludes that an earlier

[22] Cf. J.-M. Rosenstiehl, "L'itinéraire de Paul dans l'Au-delà: Contribution à l'étude de l'Apocalypse apocryphe de Paul", in P. Nagel (ed.), *Carl-Schmidt-Kolloquium an der Martin-Luther-Universität Halle-Wittenberg 1988* (Kongress- und Tagungsberichte der Martin-Luther-Universität Halle-Wittenberg; Martin-Luther-Universität Halle-Wittenberg, Wissenschaftliche Beiträge 1990/23 (K 9)), Halle-Wittenberg 1990, 197–212, esp. 209 n. 84.

[23] C. Carozzi, *Eschatologie et Au-delà: Recherches sur* l'Apocalypse de Paul, Aix-en-Provence 1994, 33, 40–46, 130.

katabasis of Paul has been transformed into the present work by inserting chs. 19–21, which corresponds to 2 Cor 12:2 (third heaven), and 45–51, which corresponds to 2 Cor 12:4 (Paradise). According to him, third heaven and Paradise are different places, and since chs. 45–51 do not contain any topographical indications, we cannot know where to situate Paradise.[24]

Neither theory is entirely convincing. Carozzi's idea of a return to the origins is highly artificial; even if the first chapters deal with the elements of Creation, they have nothing to do with Paradise, and Paul is completely absent in them. As for the trees and the rivers, they are as imaginable in heavenly regions as is Jerusalem or its Temple. Rosenstiehl rightly denies the occurrence of topographical clues for Paradise in chs. 45–51, but he is on less sure ground affirming that Paradise is different from third heaven, either in 1 Cor 12:2–4[25] or in *Apocalypse of Paul* 19–21 and 45–51. In particular, he overlooks that at least one of the Old Testament righteous figures both in chs. 19–21 and 45–51, namely Elijah (chs. 20 and 51). Therefore, in the end there is still good reason to equate third heaven and Paradise, and good old Montague Rhodes James may have been criticised too hastily for labeling chs. 45–51 as "Second vision of Paradise".[26]

---

[24] Rosenstiehl (n. 22) 204–210.

[25] M.E. Thrall, "Paul's Journey to Paradise. Some Exegetical Issues in 2 Cor 12,2–4", in R. Bieringer (ed.), *The Corinthian Correspondence* (Bibliotheca Ephemeridum Theologicarum Lovaniensium 125), Leuven 1996, 347–363, comes to the following conclusion: "Since the arguments on either side are somewhat evenly balanced, it is difficult to make a decision. Nevertheless, there is some weight to the claim that there is little point in the mention of the third heaven (and no other) unless it is regarded as the location of Paradise. And if this is so, Paul would be describing a one-stage rapture. That Paradise, in Jewish thinking, could be so located is attested in the *Apocalypse of Moses* [37.5], where the archangel Michael is instructed to take Adam up 'into Paradise to the third heaven'. Similarly in *2 Enoch* [8.1] Enoch speaks of his being brought to the third heaven and placed in the midst of Paradise."

[26] M.R. James, *The Apocryphal New Testament, being the Apocryphal Gospels, Acts, Epistles, and Apocalypses with Other Narrations and Fragments Newly Translated*, Oxford 1924, 526. Cf. Rosenstiehl (n. 22) 198 and 206.

A RESISTANT INTERPRETATION OF THE PARADISE STORY IN THE GNOSTIC *TESTIMONY OF TRUTH* (NAG HAMM. COD. IX.3) 45–50

GERARD P. LUTTIKHUIZEN

In several narrations of the classic Gnostic myth of origins ample use is made of Genesis stories of the creation of man and the early history of humankind.[1] The biblical accounts, however, are reinterpreted in such a way that they fit into the Gnostic story line. It is a characteristic feature of this story line to present the primeval events as episodes in an ongoing combat between good and evil forces.[2] The creator of the material world, who is considered an inferior and ignorant demiurge (he has no knowledge of the fully transcendent supreme God), is the chief ruler of the evil forces. The biblical creator-God is identified with this demiurgical figure. Of course, this identification has far-reaching consequences for the Gnostic evaluation of biblical and post-biblical Jewish traditions.

In spite of his supposed ignorance, the demiurge seems to understand that *gnosis*, the insight of human beings into their inner relationship with the true God, makes them spiritually superior to himself.[3] Therefore his effort is to prevent the first humans and their spiritual offspring from becoming acquainted with the truth.

On the good side of the mythical combat we find the unknowable most high God and the light powers sent by Him into the world of the demiurge with a view to informing spiritual humanity of its true Godlike identity and, eventually, to bringing back to the divine world the Gnostics whom the demiurge detains in his dark cosmos. In their attempts to reach human beings, the powers from the world above use various tricks. In *The True Nature of the Archons* and *On the*

---

[1] Notably the versions of the myth in the second part of *The Secret Book (Apocryphon) of John*, in *The True Nature (Hypostasis) of the Archons* and in *The Revelation of Adam*.

[2] See further my article "Biblical Narrative in Gnostic Revision" in: *Interpretations of the Flood* (Themes in Biblical Narrative I), 109–23).

[3] Cf. the opening words of the Gnostic story of Noah and the Flood in *The Secret Book of John* (BG 71,14–72,2): "The Chief Archon realized that they (the first human beings) surpassed him in the height of their wisdom . . ."

Origin of the World, for instance, we are told how the female spirit (or: spiritual woman) who comes from the imperishable world to bring *gnosis* to Adam and Eve changes herself into a tree or enters into a tree (either the tree of knowledge or the tree of life).[4] Also the wise serpent of the Paradise story is depicted as a temporary dwelling of the female spirit.[5] As we shall see, the serpent in the rewritten Paradise story of *The Testimony of Truth* is interpreted typologically as a manifestation of Christ.[6]

There is another ingredient of the thought pattern underlying the Gnostic myth that calls for special attention in a study dealing with the interpretation of the biblical Paradise story in a Gnostic text. In Gnostic conviction, human beings are not at all responsible for the bad conditions of human existence. The Gnostic myth in *The Secret Book of John* explains how imperfection and evil originated from a series of tragic events in the supramundane and prehistoric world *before* it speaks about the creation of man and the history of spiritual humankind (the creative retelling of Genesis stories about Adam and Eve, Noah and the Flood, etc. occurs in the second part of the myth). Thus, the origin of evil and suffering is not related to misbehaviour of human beings. In fact, Adam and Eve are not viewed as causers of evil but rather as the very first victims of evil. When the creator of the physical world found out that Adam possessed a portion of divine light or *pneuma* he brought him down deep into the dark cosmos and he enclosed Adam's *pneuma* in a material and mortal body. There he was bound to live fully isolated from his divine origin. These basic Gnostic convictions will help us to understand the rewriting of the biblical Paradise story and the subsequent critical comments in *The Testimony of Truth.*

1. *The Testimony of Truth*

TestTr is the third and last writing of codex IX of Nag Hammadi. It is also the most extensive writing of this codex. It begins on

[4] *HA* 89,25; *OrW* 116,28–29: "She entered the tree of knowledge and remained there". Cf. I.S. Gilhus, *The Nature of the Archons*, Wiesbaden 1985, 69–72.

[5] *HA* 89,31–32: "The female spirit entered the serpent, the instructor".

[6] In *SecrBookJn*, the risen Christ reveals to John, the son of Zebedee, that it was not a serpent but he himself who induced Adam and Eve to eat from the tree of knowledge (BG 57,20–58,1).

p. 29 and originally must have covered some 48 to 50 pages of the Coptic manuscript. However, the last part of the manuscript survives in a very fragmentary condition. Some complete papyrus leaves are even lost. The damaged part of the manuscript begins on p. 49, at the end of the critical comments on the Paradise story. The few remains of this damaged second half of the text suggest that on these pages the author was engaged in a controversy with other Gnostic groups.[7] This is a very rare phenomenon in surviving Gnostic literature. It is regrettable that we do not possess this part of the text in a better state.

Indeed a characteristic feature of *TestTr* is the explicit and detailed polemics with Christian groups: with Gnostic Christian groups but also and primarily with ecclesiastical or catholic Christianity. We already find a sharp polemic against catholic Christianity in the better preserved first half of our writing. This controversy with emerging mainstream Christianity and with such Gnostic schools as the Valentinians is of some help in dating the original text of *TestTr*. In his introduction to the edition of the Coptic text, Birger Pearson suggests that the writing was composed at the end of the second or the beginning of the third century.[8] We shall see that polemics against ecclesiastical Christianity are also a prominent feature of the Paradise text in *TestTr*. For this reason I will pay some attention to the nature of this polemic.

In *TestTr* ecclesiastical Christians are blamed for their obedience to the Old Testament creator-God and his Law. It is highly significant that for the author of our text, the Old Testament Law is summed up in the commandment to the first humans to procreate. Obviously the purpose of the text is to contrast the strongly ascetic or rather encratite lifestyle of the author's Gnostic group (its encratism included the rejection of marriage) with the allegedly worldly, licentious ethics of mainstream Christianity. In the opinion of the author, the worldly ethics of catholic Christians springs from their belief in the Old Testament God and from their obedience to his Law. This contrast between the Gnostic and the ecclesiastical positions is displayed on the first pages of the text:

---

[7] The damaged pages still reveal the names of several Gnostic teachers and schools: Valentinus and his disciples (56,1f.5), [Basilid]es and his son Isidorus (57,6–8), the Simonians (58,2).

[8] S. Giversen and B. Pearson, *Nag Hammadi Codices IX and X*, Leiden 1981, 118.

> (**29**,22) No one who is under the Law will be able to look up to the truth, for they will not be able to serve two masters.[9] For the defilement of the Law is manifest, (**30**) while undefilement belongs to the light. The Law commands (one) to take a husband (or) a wife, and to beget, to multiply like the sand of the sea. But passion which is a delight to them constrains the souls of those who are begotten in this place (. . .) in order that the Law might be fulfilled through them. And they show that they are assisting the world and they turn away from the light.

A relatively long section on pp. 41 to 44 can be read as an encomium or eulogy of the true Gnostic, the person who renounces the world, who subdues desire everywhere in himself, and who is filled with wisdom. Apparently the first main part of the text aims at drawing a clear line between the ideology of the author's group and that of mainstream Christianity and at upgrading and lauding the author's system of values at the expense of those of others.[10] In this first part of the text, the author addresses fellow members of his own Gnostic group. It is plausible that this part is concluded with the following words on pp. 44–45:

> (**44**,30) This, therefore, is (**45**) the true testimony (*marturía*):[11] When man knows himself and God who is over the truth, he will be saved, and he will be crowned with the unfading crown.[12]

2. *The creator-God and the serpent*

The retelling of the events in Paradise begins on p. 45, line 23. It is preceded by a question:

> (**45**,19) Why, then, do you [err] and not seek after these mysteries which were prefigured for our sake?[13]

---

[9] Matt 6:24 par.

[10] For this type of rhetoric see D.L. Sullivan, "Establishing Orthodoxy: The Letters of Ignatius of Antioch as Epideictic Rhetoric", *The Journal of Communication and Religion* 15 (1992), 71–86.

[11] The statement, "This is the true testimony", has a Johannine ring, cf. esp. John 5:32. The present title of the document was assigned by modern editors on the basis of this passage. Due to the loss of the last papyrus sheet we do not know which title was given to our text in the Coptic manuscript. (In many writings of the Nag Hammadi collection, the title is added at the end of the text.)

[12] Cf. 1 Pet 5:4.

[13] The wording of this question is reminiscent of Paul's view of the Scriptures: according to Paul the Scriptures contain a cryptic message "for our sake", cf. esp. Rom 4:23–4 and 15:4.

I quote this introductory question because it shows that the present part of the text (which begins after the first lines of p. 45, cited above) is no longer addressed to Gnostic fellow-spirits but to others: to readers, that is, who do not seek seriously after the real meaning of the events mentioned in the Scriptures.[14]

We will see that *TestTr* does not reject the biblical Paradise story as all stuff and nonsense. In fact, the actual events are not doubted.[15] The controversy concerns the identity of the actors appearing in the story (the creator, the serpent and the first human beings) and the real meaning of what was said and what was done.[16]

> (**45**,23) As to this it is written in the Law—when God gave Adam the commandment—"*You may eat from every tree, but do not eat from the tree in the middle of Paradise. For on the day that you eat from it you will surely die.*" (Gen 2:16–17)

It may be noted that the preceding section of the Genesis story—the description of the garden of Eden—is omitted. Also the account of the creation of Eve, the subsequent episode in the Genesis text (Gen 2:18–24), is left out. The Gnostic rewriting continues with a paraphrase of Gen 3:1. The author seems to confine himself to those elements of the story that lend themselves to his critical comments.

> *Now the serpent was wiser* (**46**) *than all the* animals in Paradise. (Gen 3:1a)

Notice the words that are not italicized: the serpent is not called a θηρίον as in the LXX but a ζῷον which is a word with more favourable connotations (an animal instead of a beast). Moreover in this rewriting the serpent does not belong to the earth (LXX: ἐπὶ τῆς γῆς) but to Paradise. In a subtle way, in this Gnostic paraphrase the serpent is upgraded. In contrast, as we will see presently, the biblical God is slightly degraded mainly by means of a further emphasis on the anthropomorphic features attributed to him.

> (**46**,2) And he persuaded Eve, *saying, "On the day that you eat from the tree in the middle of Paradise, the eyes of your mind will be opened."* And Eve obeyed, and *reached out her hand and took* from the tree *and ate. And she*

[14] Pearson, *o.c.* (above, n. 8), 102.

[15] P. Nagel, "Die Auslegung der Paradieserzählung in der Gnosis", in: K.-W. Tröger, *Altes Testament—Frühjudentum—Gnosis*, Gütersloh 1980, 49–70 (50).

[16] By using italics I will indicate where, in the retelling of the Paradise story and in the ensuing commentary, we come upon more or less literal quotations of the Bible text or upon clear allusions to biblical texts.

> *gave to her husband who was with her. And* immediately *they realized that they were naked. They took fig leaves and put them on themselves as aprons. And in the* [*evening*] *God* came *walking through* the middle [*of*] *Paradise.* And when Adam saw him *he hid himself. And he said, "Adam, where are you?" And he answered and said,* "[I] have gone under the fig tree." And in that moment God knew that *he had eaten from the tree of which he had commanded him not to eat. And he said to him, "Who* (**47**) informed *you?" Adam answered, "The woman whom you gave me." And the woman said, "It was the serpent who* informed *me."* And he *cursed* the serpent and called him "devil". (Gen 3:4–14)

In small but significant details this retelling deviates from the LXX version of the Genesis story. Our text does not affirm that the serpent deluded or seduced Eve (in the LXX version Eve says: ὁ ὄφις ἠπάτησέν με, "the serpent seduced me"; cf. 1 Cor 11:3 and 1 Tim 2:14). He persuaded and informed her and he explained that her inner eyes would be opened.

On the other hand, the anthropomorphic features of the creator are emphasized. In this way the reader is being prepared for the negative comments that follow soon. The text continues:

> (**47**,7) *And he said, "Behold, Adam has become like one of us, knowing evil and good."* So he said, "Let us *throw him out of Paradise lest he take from the tree of life and eat and live forever.*" (Gen 3:22–23)

Whereas the biblical story merely reports that God threw man out of Paradise, the Gnostic retelling quotes a deliberate decision by God himself: "Let us throw him out of Paradise . . ."

We now turn to the Gnostic author's comments on this rewritten story of the events in the Paradise garden.

> (**47**,14) What sort of God is this? First [he] was envious of Adam that he should eat from the tree of knowledge. And secondly he said, "*Adam, where are you?*" So God did not have foreknowledge? That is, he did not know this from the beginning? And later on he said, "Let us *throw him out of this place lest he eat from the tree of life and live for ever*". Thus he has shown himself to be a malicious envier.
>
> (**48**) What sort of God is this? Indeed, great is the blindness of those who read (this) and have not recognized him![17]

[17] The Coptic text allows other translations. Giversen-Pearson, *o.c.* (above, n. 8), 165: "For great is the blindness of those who read. And they did not understand it". K. Koschorke, "Der gnostische Traktak 'Testimonium Veritatis'", *ZNW* 69 (1978) 91–117, 108: "Denn gross ist die Blindheit derer, die (zu ihm) rufen; nicht haben sie ihn erkannt (oder: die (dies) lesen und ihn doch nicht erkannt haben)."

This last sentence betrays that the polemic is actually directed to people, most likely Christians of the Church, who believe in the Old Testament creator-God.

> (**48**,4) And he said, "*I am a jealous God. I bring the sins of the parents upon the children for three, four generations*" (Ex 20:5). And he said, "*I will cause their heart to become hardened and I will cause* their mind *to be blind, so that they might not* understand or comprehend what is said" (cf. Isa 6:10). These are the things he said to those who believe in him and serve him!

The author has added two Old Testament passages (quotations of the biblical God) that are supposed to confirm the jealousy and the wickedness of the creator-God. The last sentence ("These are the things he said to those who believe in him and serve him") once again shows that the polemic is directed to believers in the Old Testament God.

The selection of Old Testament passages addressing the alleged jealousy and wickedness of the biblical God has a counterpart in a selection of Bible texts speaking about certain serpents. This final section is seriously damaged. I quote one lacunal passage:

> (**48**,23) "(. . . .) [*and the rod*] *which was in the hand of Moses became a serpent. It swallowed the serpents of the magicians*" (cf. Ex 7: 10–12). Again it is written, "*He made a serpent of bronze (and) hung it upon a pole*" (cf. Num 21:9) (49) [5 lines damaged] this bronze serpent [. . .] For this is Christ. [Those who] believed in him, have [. . .] Those who did not believe [. . .] What, then, is this [belief? They] do not serve [13 lines missing].

This passage underlines that the serpents of the relevant Moses stories possessed miraculous saving powers. Apparently the serpent of Num 21 is explained typologically as a manifestation of Christ. The serpent of the Paradise garden is associated with these estimable serpents. Whereas the creator-God is exposed as a malevolent being, the serpent definitively is on the side of the good forces.

3. *Historical context*

How are we to explain the selective and coloured rewriting of the Paradise story and the subsequent resistant comments in *TestTr*? As I indicated in the introduction to this article, it is my contention that Gnostic authors were able to thoroughly revise biblical traditions just by bringing these traditions into agreement with their own mythological convictions.[18] I should add, however, that this explanation is not undisputed in scholarly literature. Actually, one of the editors of the Coptic text, Birger Pearson, explains the rejection of the biblical God in this text in a completely different way. I will discuss his suggestion as well as one other remarkable explanation of the critical attitude towards the Jewish God and the Jewish Scriptures in Gnostic literature before I elaborate on the above solution.

At the conclusion of his essay "Jewish Haggadic Traditions in *The Testimony of Truth*",[19] Pearson states that our text may be very significant for what it can tell us about Gnostic origins. He observes that the factor of Judaism in the early development of Gnosticism is attracting more and more scholarly attention. In fact Pearson himself is an influential and authoritative representative of a scholarly tradition that looks for an inner-Jewish origin of ancient Gnostic mythology. With respect to the Genesis interpretation of *TestTr*, he argues: "One can hear in this text echoes of existential despair arising in circles of the people of the Covenant faced with a crisis of history, with the apparent failure of the God of history: 'What kind of a God is this?' (48,1); 'These things he has said (and done, failed to do) to those who believe in him and serve him!' (48,13ff)."

In Pearson's opinion, the words, "These things he has said to those who believe in him and serve him", are an exclamation by Jews who felt abandoned by their own God.[20] The resistant, negative comments on the biblical Paradise story in *TestTr* are explained as a reaction of disappointment by Jews. Pearson takes this very seriously as evidenced in his remark: "Such expressions of existential

---

[18] Cf. also my paper "The Thought Pattern of Gnostic Mythologizers and their Use of Biblical Traditions", in: J.D. Turner and A. McQuire, *The Nag Hammadi Library after Fifty Years*, Leiden 1997, 89–101.

[19] In: J. Bergman *et al.*, *Ex Orbe Religionum* I, Leiden: Brill 1972, 457–70, repr. in B.A. Pearson, *Gnosticism, Judaism, and Egyptian Christianity*, Minneapolis 1990, 39–51.

[20] Pearson can maintain this because he assumes that the paraphrase of the Paradise story and the subsequent comments (in his view, a "Gnostic midrash", see below) were borrowed by the Christian Gnostic composer of *TestTr* from an earlier Jewish source. It is not my intention to go into this source-critical question. I just wish to state that the negative and polemical comments in our section of the text are in perfect agreement with the rejection of the Old Testament God and his Law and with the controversy with catholic Christians in other parts of *TestTr*. J.-D. Kaestli, "Une relecture polémique de Genèse 3 dans le gnosticisme chrétien: le Témoignage de Verité", *Foi et Vie* 1976, 48–62, 52: "Loin d'être un corps étranger, le développement sur le Dieu de la Genèse et sur le serpent est rattaché au reste du *TemVer* par des liens évidents."

anguish are not without parallels in our own time 'after Auschwitz'." Indeed before and after Pearson there have been various attempts to find a period in the history of Second Temple Judaism where such a revolt could have occurred.[21] Pearson himself surmises that the alleged inner-Jewish rebellion originated in the first century BCE or in the first century CE.[22]

In his essay Pearson points to another explanation of the critical attitude towards the Jewish Bible and the rejection of the biblical creator-God in Gnostic literature. This alternative explanation is connected with the name of Hans Jonas. What Jonas' views have in common with those of Pearson and others is the stress he lays on the element of revolt in Gnosticism. But whereas Pearson, as we have seen, thinks of an inner-Jewish revolt—a protest, that is, of Jews against their own God and against their own Scriptures—Jonas sees in Gnosticism a pagan revolt against Judaism: "Gnosticism originated in *close vicinity* and in partial reaction to Judaism."[23] Jonas insists that the critical use of Jewish traditions by Gnostic mythologizers was motivated by an anti-Jewish attitude: "The nature of the relation of Gnosticism to Judaism—in itself an undeniable fact—is defined by the anti-Jewish animus with which it is saturated."[24] Jonas even uses the expression "metaphysical anti-Semitism" to characterize the supposed hostility of Gnostics towards Judaism.[25]

In spite of this fundamental difference, both Pearson and Jonas understand the critical use of biblical traditions in Gnostic literature as a kind of "protest exegesis", a deliberate negation, that is, of the traditional interpretation. But exactly this idea—the idea that the critical interpretation of biblical texts was prompted by a mood of

---

[21] Cf. the survey of social crises related to Gnostic origins in M.A. Williams, "The demonizing of the demiurge: The innovation of Gnostic myth", in: M.A. Williams *et al.* (eds.), *Innovations in Religious Tradition*, Berlin-New York 1992, 73–107, 84. In my article "The Thought Pattern" (above, n. 18) I refer to a proposal made by D. Parrott in an unpublished paper, "The reign of John Hyrcanus as the Seedbed for Sethian Gnosticism" (short summary in the *SBL Abstracts* of 1994).

[22] *Art. cit.*, 51.

[23] "Delimitation of the gnostic phenomenon—typological and historical", in: U. Bianchi, *The Origins of Gnosticism*, Leiden 1967, 90–104, 102. Jonas surmises that "the this-worldly spirit of the Hebrew religion made it the natural target of gnostic dislike". He explains the anti-Judaism as "one form of expression of the anti-cosmic spirit as such, *i.e.*, of the gnostic revolt against the world and its gods."

[24] "Response to G. Quispel's 'Gnosticism and the New Testament'", in: J.Ph. Hyatt (ed.), *The Bible in Modern Scholarship*, Nashville 1965, 279–93, 288.

[25] *Ibid.*

rebellion against the biblical God, either among Jews or among anti-Jewish pagans—is questionable.

It may be recalled, to begin with, that Gnostics were not the only ones or the first ones to have great problems with some biblical texts, notably with texts that assign anthropomorphic qualities and actions to God. The Genesis account of the events in Paradise is such a text. Generations of Jewish and Christian commentators and theologians have been puzzled about the way God makes his appearance in this story and about the emotions and actions attributed to him. They have tried to explain away the problematic elements of this and other stories either by means of allegorical interpretation (*e.g.* Philo of Alexandria and the Christian theologians of Alexandria), by rewriting and emending the biblical text (*e.g.* in such translations as the Septuagint and the Targums and in such books as *Jubilees* and *Genesis Apocryphon*), or by declaring the texts in question to be later corruptions (notably in Pseudo-Clementine literature).[26]

It should further be noted that pagan polemicists made clever use of such notoriously difficult passages to demonstrate the inferiority of the Jewish and Christian God. The second-century Platonist philosopher Celsus, for instance, more than once ridicules the attempts made by Jews and Christians to allegorize the anthropomorphic features of the biblical God.[27] Another and more striking instance can be found in a surviving fragment of the treatise *Against the Galileans* (75A–94A), written by the fourth-century Roman emperor Julian, surnamed "the Apostate" because he broke with his Christian upbringing and, after his ascent to the throne, strove for a revival of pagan religion in the empire. In a similar fashion to the author of *TestTr*, he recapitulates the biblical Paradise story, interlarding his selective summary with some quotations, and he concludes that this story discloses the ignorance, the jealousy and the wickedness of the God in whom Christians believe.[28] Incidentally, Julian argues that the ignorance of the creator-God appears above all in the fact that precisely the one whom he meant to be a helper to Adam turned out to be the cause of Adam's fall.

26 M.A. Williams, *Rethinking "Gnosticism". An Argument for Dismantling a Dubious Category*, Princeton 1996, 64–7.

27 Origenes, *Contra Celsum* IV 3,48–51.89. Williams, 67.

28 K. Koschorke, *Die Polemik der Gnostiker gegen das kirchliche Christentum*, Leiden 1978, 150f.

Pagan philosophers as well as early Jewish and early Christian exegetes took offence at the anthropomorphisms and the moral inequalities of the biblical God. I surmise that this observation gives us a clue to understanding the negative comments on the biblical Paradise story in *TestTr.* Here I come back to the explanation proposed before. I do not see special grounds for relating the resistant interpretation of the Genesis story in our text to feelings of disappointment and despair on the part of Jews or to explain this interpretation from a supposed hostile attitude towards Jews and their God on the part of pagan outsiders. The resistant interpretation of the Paradise story just demonstrates that in the conviction of the Gnostic author, the God who figures in the biblical Paradise story cannot possibly be equated with the fully transcendent and perfectly good God in whom Gnostics believed. In the God of this story Gnostics could but recognize the features of the ignorant demiurge, the creator of the dark world who tries to prevent spiritual humanity from returning to its origin in the world above.

Supposing that this explanation is basically correct, we are facing a further question: if it is true that Gnostics could not recognize in the biblical creator-God their own supreme Godhead and if for that reason they rejected the Old Testament revelation, why, then, were they interested at all in the Old Testament? Why did they make such frequent and extensive use of biblical traditions? I propose that also in this case a key to the answer is given in *TestTr.*

Pace Pearson, I take it for granted that the critical comments added to the rewritten Paradise story are an organic, integrated part of the polemic with other Christians—in particular catholic Christians—that permeates through the whole of the surviving text.[29] The words at the beginning of p. 48, "What sort of God is this? Indeed, great is the blindness of those who read (this) and have not recognized him!" and, a few lines further on, "These are the things he said to those who believe in him and serve him!", were worded by Christian Gnostics who blamed Christians of the Church for their belief in the Old Testament creator-God and his commandments. We are dealing with a difference of opinion, in fact a sharp and bitter discussion, between Gnostics and other Christians about the revelatory value of the Old Testament. Whereas mainstream Christians believed

[29] Cf. above, n. 20.

in the identity of the God revealed by Jesus Christ as the creator of heaven and earth,[30] Gnostic Christians considered the creator a demonic figure and, accordingly, rejected the creator-God of the Old Testament and all texts testifying to his greatness and holiness. In their conviction, the truth about the creator of the material universe, about the history of spiritual humanity and, above all, about their supreme Godhead and his world of light, could not be found in the Jewish Scriptures.[31]

4. *A Gnostic midrash?*

Since Pearson's article, it is usual to refer to the Paradise text of *TestTr* as a "Gnostic midrash".[32] Apparently, this designation is based on the literary form of our text segment: a quotation of Scripture followed by a pronouncement upon this quotation.[33] But the question is whether in defining midrash we should pay attention exclusively to formal characteristics. The term should be reserved for those instances of the above literary form that give expression to the typically Rabbinic approach to Scripture.[34] The designation "Gnostic midrash" is a *contradictio in terminis* if we apply this additional criterium.[35]

---

[30] The unity of the two Testaments and the identity of the God of Jesus Christ with the Old Testament God are underlined *e.g.* in Irenaeus' *Adv. Haer.*, book III *passim.*

[31] Cf. the recurrent statement in *The Secret Book of John*, "It is not as Moses said but" . . . (then the allegedly correct account of what happened follows).

[32] Pearson was probably the first to call the text a Gnostic Midrash. His designation was adopted by others, cf. the studies by M.A. Williams and J.-D. Kaestli mentioned in notes 19, 20, 25.

[33] For the literary form of the midrash see esp. A. Goldberg, "Form-Analysis of Midrashic Literature as a Method of Description", *JJS* 36 (1985), 159–74.

[34] Ph. Alexander, "Midrash and the Gospels", in: C.M. Tuckett (ed.), *Synoptic Studies* (Journal for the Study of the New Testament, Suppl. Series 7), Sheffield 1984, 1–18. Cf. L. Teugels, "Midrasj in, en op de bijbel? Kritische kanttekeningen bij het onkritische gebruik van een term", *Nederlands Theologisch Tijdschrift* 49 (1995), 273–90.

[35] Cf. Pearson's statement: ". . . it is axiomatic that once Gnosticism is present Judaism has been abandoned", *art. cit.* (above, n. 18), 51. It is necessary to make a clear distinction between the usual Gnostic attitude towards the Jewish writings and midrashic, *i.e.* early Rabbinic, methods of exegesis. After all, in Midrashic literature the Rabbis interpreted their own Scripture. For the rest, they were not less critical and negative about Gnostic schools and ideas than Gnostics were about biblical and post-biblical Jewish traditions. Cf. A.F. Segal, *Two Powers in Heaven: Early Rabbinic Reports about Christianity and Gnosticism*, Leiden 1977.

I surmise, by the way, that this literary form, (biblical) quotation + commentary, also occurs outside (and independent from) Rabbinic traditions. An interesting example is the quotation of an early Christian christological creed emphasizing the suffering of Jesus in *The Letter of Peter to Philip* which is followed by the comments: "My brothers, Jesus is a stranger to this suffering. But we are the ones who have suffered through the transgression of the Mother (*i.e.* Sophia, the mother of the demiurge)", etc.[36] Just as in the Paradise text of *TestTr*, the quotation and the commentary are clearly separated, and the commentary corrects the information in the quoted text.

The Letter of Peter to Philip also bears witness to a controversy between Gnostics and (other) Christians, in all probability Christians of the Church. While in this writing the discussion is focused on the true meaning of the suffering of Jesus Christ (in relation to the suffering of the Gnostics), the polemic of *TestTr* is directed in particular, as we have seen, against the worship of the Jewish creator-God by ecclesiastical and other Christians and against their compliance with the order given by this God to Adam and Eve to multiply. The Paradise text served to underscore the Gnostic position in this controversy by exposing the inferior qualities, motives and actions of the biblical creator-God.

[36] Nag Hammadi cod. VIII,2,139,11–30. For a discussion of this section of *Ep.Pet.Phil.* in connection with Gnostic interpretations of early Christian traditions see my article mentioned in n. 18.

PARADISIACAL LIFE: THE STORY OF PARADISE IN THE EARLY CHURCH

H.S. Benjamins

The biblical story of paradise frequently appears in the writings of the Early Church Fathers.[1] The term "paradise" is used in a wide variety of meanings. "Paradise" refers, of course, to the Garden of Eden, but may also point to the Kingdom of God, Heaven, or the place where the blessed souls await their entrance into a higher heaven of supreme glory.[2] Some exegetes of the Early Church interpret the biblical narrative of Genesis 2–3 in a purely spiritual way, others suppose that the narrated events actually occurred, others again interpret the biblical story both literally and spiritually.[3] This obviously produces a manifold and sometimes contradictory account of the biblical story of paradise in the early Christian tradition. There is unanimity, however, in one respect. Paradise, having been lost when Adam was driven out of Eden, has now been regained by the work of Christ, the new Adam (cf. Rom 5:14–16; 1 Cor 15:45–48). Jesus told the crucified criminal that "today you will be with me in paradise" (Luke 23:43) and Paul knew a man who was caught up in paradise (2 Cor 12:2). Consequently, the Christian Church generally proclaimed that paradise had once more become accessible.[4]

This astonishing claim can be found in the works of Irenaeus, Tertullian, Methodius and others. Irenaeus says that ". . . men, if they do truly progress by faith towards better things, and receive the

---

[1] See the article "Paradise" by G. Filoramo in the *Encyclopedia of the Early Church*, produced by the Institutum Patristicum Augustinianum and edited by Angelo di Berardino, translated by Adrian Walford, Vol. II, Cambridge, 1992, 649–650; also the article "Paradis" by H. Leclercq in the *Dictionnaire d'archéologie chrétienne et de liturgie*, Paris, 1938, vol. 13–2, 1578ff.; also J. Daniélou, *Sacramentum Futuri, Études sur les origines de la typologie biblique*, Paris, 1950, 3–52: "Adam et le paradis".

[2] See G. Filoramo, *Encyclopedia* . . . and H. Leclercq, *Dictionn.* . . ., 1579–1583.

[3] See Augustine in *De Genesi ad Litteram* 8.1.1. Augustine rejects an exclusively spiritual interpretation, probably disassociating himself from the interpretation of Philo and Origen, see P. Agaësse and A. Solignac's note in *La Genèse au sens littéral*, Bibliothèque Augustinienne 49, p. 13, also the additional note on pp. 497–499.

[4] See J. Daniélou, *Sacramentum Futuri*, p. 15: "Or l'affirmation chrétienne, c'est le *Hodie* du Paradis. Dans le Christ, ce Paradis est désormais présent".

Spirit of God, and bring forth the fruit thereof, shall be spiritual, as being planted in the paradise of God".[5] According to Tertullian, man was "transferred into paradise, out of the world into the Church".[6] Methodius says that ". . . the tree of life which paradise once bore, the Church has now again produced for all . . .".[7]

Christians believed that paradise was regained and could be entered by entering into the Church. Christians live the life that Adam lived before the Fall. We can find the most vivid expressions of this bold belief in writings that concern Christian life more than Christian doctrine. Hence, it will be useful to consider the way in which paradise was understood in early Christian life and belief, prior to focusing on a scholarly interpretation of the biblical story, since that belief affected the learned interpretation as a matter of course.

In writings concerning the Christian faith, paradise is frequently associated with baptism, which is the entry into the Christian life, or with martyrdom, virginity and monasticism, which are its most distinguished expressions.

In the *Catechetical Lectures*, Cyril of Jerusalem gives instructions in the Christian religion to the catechumens, who will be baptized in due time. In an enthusiastic speech, Cyril introduces them to the forthcoming lectures and to baptism: "Then may the gate of paradise be opened to every man and every woman among you. Then may you enjoy the Christ-bearing waters in their fragrance. Then may you receive the name of Christ, and the power of things divine (. . .) Great is the baptism that lies before you: a ransom to captives; a remission of offenses; a death of sin; a new-birth of the soul; a garment of light; a holy indissoluble seal; a chariot to heaven; the delight of paradise; a welcome into the Kingdom; the gift of adoption!".[8] In the so-called *Lectures on the Mysteries*, Cyril continues his instructions, addressing himself to the newly baptized Christians in a lecture which was probably delivered on the Monday after Easter, the day baptism was administered. "I have long been wishing, O true-born and dearly beloved children of the Church, to discourse to you concerning these spiritual and heavenly mysteries; but since

[5] *Adversus Haereses*, V.10.1.
[6] *Adversus Marcionem*, II.IV.
[7] *Symposium*, IX.3.
[8] *Procatechesis* 15.16.

I well knew that seeing is far more persuasive than hearing, I waited for the present season; that finding you more open to the influence of my words from your present experience, I might lead you by the hand into the brighter and more fragrant meadow of the paradise before us; especially as you have been made fit to receive the more sacred mysteries after having been found worthy of divine and life-giving baptism".[9] Cyril explains what happens when the catechumens received baptism: "When therefore thou renouncest satan, utterly breaking all thy covenant with him, that ancient league with hell, there is opened to thee the paradise of God, which He planted towards the east, whence for his transgression our first father was banished . . .".[10]

Baptism is our entry into the "meadow of paradise", which is now open and accessible to us.[11] The same imagery is used by Methodius of Olympus in the *Symposium*. In this work, a failure in literary respect, Gregorion informs Euboulios about the orations of ten virgins, who were praising virginity and Christian spirituality by turns. Their banquet was held in a garden "with an eastern aspect", where "the air was diffused in soft and regular currents, mingled with pure beams of light, and a stream flowing as gently as oil through the very middle of the garden threw up a most delicious drink; and the water flowing from it, transparent and pure, formed itself into fountains, and these, overflowing like rivers, watered all the garden with their abundant streams; and there were different kinds of trees there, full of fresh fruits . . .".[12] Just in case somebody missed the abundantly plain suggestion, Methodius is willing to explain the meaning of this scene: "EUBOULIOS: You seem to me, my good friend, to be making a revelation of a second paradise. GREGORION: You speak truly and wisely".[13] The implication is obvious: The Christian virgins live the paradisiacal life.

---

[9] *Catechesis* XIX.1.

[10] *Catechesis* XIX.9.

[11] See also, for example, the *Discourse on the holy Theophany* 8, perhaps incorrectly ascribed to Hippolytus, in: Hippolytus Werke, erster Band, herausgegeben von G. Nath. Bonwetsch und Hans Achelis, GCS, Leipzig, 1897, and Gregory of Nyssa, *De Baptismo*, PG XLVI 420C and *In Baptismo Christi*, PG XLVI, 599ff., mentioned by J. Daniélou, *Sacramentum Futuri*, 17–18, who is summoning other places as well in his chapter "baptême et paradis", 13–20.

[12] *Symposium*, introduction.

[13] *Symposium*, introduction.

Virginity and paradise are also coupled together in the work of Gregory of Nyssa *On Virginity*. "We, then, who in our first ancestors were thus ejected, are allowed to return to our earliest state of blessedness by the very same stages by which we lost paradise". The last steps on the road leaving paradise should be the first steps returning to it. "Marriage, then, is the last stage of our separation from the life that was led in paradise; marriage therefore, as our discourse is suggesting, is the first thing to be left". Next we must retire from vain labour[14] and wisdom of the flesh, stand in the sight of our Creator and feel ceaselessly and continually the delight of it. "One might even be bold enough to say that this might be regarded as the way by which a man could again be caught up into paradise, out of this world which lieth in the evil, into that paradise where Paul was when he saw the unspeakable sights which it is not appropriate for a man to talk of".[15]

Paradise and paradisiacal life are not only closely connected with baptism and virginity but also with martyrdom and the monastic life. Cyprian of Carthage wrote an exhortation to martyrdom, *Ad Fortunatum*. In this treatise, he describes the glory of martyrs. "If to soldiers of this world it is glorious to return in triumph to their country when the foe is vanquished, how much more excellent and greater is the glory, when the devil is overcome, to return in triumph to paradise, and to bring back victorious trophies to that place whence Adam was ejected as a sinner, after casting down him who formerly had cast him down".[16] In the acts of the Christian martyrs, their death is usually depicted as a victory and a completion of the faith, and sometimes it is also told that they enter Heaven or paradise. Bishop Fructuosus did not want, according to *The Martyrdom of Bishop Fructuosus and his Deacons, Augurius and Eulogius*, to break his fast before martyrdom. "And so on Friday, he was hastening joyfully and confidently to break his fast with the martyrs and prophets in paradise, which the Lord has prepared for those who love Him" (1 Cor 2:9).[17]

---

[14] See note 4, p. 423 in *Grégoire de Nysse, Traité de la virginité*, intr., texte, trad., comm., et index par Michel Aubineau, Sources Chrétiennes 119, Paris, 1966.

[15] *De Virginitate*, XIII.1. Cf. Sources Chrétiennes 119, note 5, p. 425: "GNys. fait très souvent allusion à ce paradis, à ce troisième ciel où Paul fut ravi . . .". Jerome, like Gregory of Nyssa, also couples virginity with paradise in his letter *Ad Eustochium* (letter 22.18–19).

[16] *Ad Fortunatum* 13.

[17] See H. Musurillo, *The Acts of the Christian Martyrs*, Oxford 1972, 180.

In the *Passion of Perpetua and Felicitas* Saturus has a vision of paradise after martyrdom: "We had died, he said, and had put off the flesh, and we began to be carried towards the east by four angels who did not touch us with their hands. But we moved along, not with our backs facing upwards but as though we were climbing up a gentle hill. And when we were free of the world, we first saw an intense light. And I said to Perpetua (for she was at my side): 'This is what the Lord promised us. We have received his promise'".[18]

Since monks live the celibate life and are usually taken to be the successors to martyrs, it seems almost logical that their way of life would also be seen as a restoration of the life Adam lived in paradise.[19] In a homily on the Gospel of Matthew, John Chrysostom speaks in praise of the monks: "And their work is what Adam's also was at the beginning and before his sin, when he was clothed with the glory, and conversed freely with God, and dwelt in that place that was full of great blessedness. For in what respect are they in a worse state than he, when before his diobedience he was set to till the garden? Had he no worldly care? But neither have these. Did he talk to God with a pure conscience? This also do these; or rather, they have a greater confidence than he, inasmuch as they enjoy even greater grace by the supply of the Spirit".[20]

The quotations mentioned above, witnessing the claim that Christians live the paradisiacal life that Adam lost, may have been lengthy, broad and various, but they had to be expressed in order to prove the vigorous belief of the Early Church that paradise had been regained. This believe formed the context of a learned tradition of early Christian exegesis of the biblical story of paradise, and it moulded that tradition quite naturally. We can become acquainted with this learned tradition by studying *De Paradiso*, written by Ambrose of Milan.[21]

[18] *Passio Perpetuae et Felicitatis*, IV.1, in: H. Musurillo, *The Acts* . . ., 118–120.

[19] The Hymns of Ephraem the Syrian *De Paradiso* sometimes deal with this subject, e.g. hymn 6.3: "Gepriesen sei das Paradies das in sich sammelt die Versammlung der Wachenden und Fastenden". Edition and translation by E. Beck, CSCO, vols. 174–175, Louvain, 1957.

[20] *Homily on the Gospel of Matthew* 68.3, PG 58, 643ff. See also G.J.M. Bartelink, *De bloeiende woestijn, de wereld van het vroege monachisme*, Baarn, 1993, 89–92, "Het monnikenleven als herstel van de paradijselijke toestand voor de zondeval—De terugkeer naar het paradijs".

[21] Sant' Ambrogio, *Opere esegetiche II/I*, Il Paradiso Terrestre, Caino e Abele, introduzione, traduzione, note e indici di Paolo Siniscalco, Milano, Roma, Bibliotheca

De Paradiso is probably the first of a series of relatively short exegetical treatises which Ambrose, a former civil servant, wrote at the beginning of his career as a bishop in Milan. The question whether these treatises, *De Paradiso, De Cain, De Noe, De Abraham II* and *De Fuga,* are elaborated sermons or were originally written for a reading public cannot be resolved.[22] It is abundantly clear, however, that *De Paradiso* is the work of a beginner.[23] Ambrose himself admits that he wrote this work when he was not yet a "veteranus sacerdos",[24] at a time when he had to teach before he could learn.[25] Ambrose's inexperience may well explain the unbalanced composition of *De Paradiso,* which was written around 377 AD, only about three years after the beginning of his ecclesiastical career.

De Paradiso consists of two different parts. An allegorical interpretation of the story of paradise is interrupted by a dialectical section in which the objections raised by Apelles to the biblical story are refuted. The unity of the treatise is seriously damaged by the diversity of these constituent parts, but the incoherence of this work is also very illuminating, since it clarifies the difficulties Ambrose had to face as he interpreted the biblical story.[26] The imbalance of *De Paradiso* explains Ambrose's own development as an exegete, as H. Savon demonstrated,[27] and it can also reveal two different ways of dealing with the biblical story in the early Christian tradition. For this latter reason, an examination of *De Paradiso* will be presented in this context.

Ambrose's allegorical interpretation of paradise is largely dependent on the interpretation of Philo in the *Legum Allegoriae* and the *Questiones in Genesin.*[28] E. Lucchesi suggested that Ambrose depended on intermediary sources, namely Origen and Hippolytus, for his knowledge of Philo's allegorical interpretation.[29] But although there

Ambrosiana 1984. English translation by John J. Savage in: Saint Ambrose, *Hexameron, Paradise, and Cain and Abel,* "The Fathers of the Church, a new translation", Washington, D.C. 1961. Quotations of *De Paradiso* in this article are from Savage's translation.

[22] See Hervé Savon, *Saint Ambroise devant l'exégèse de Philon le juif,* Paris, 1977, Tome I (Texte), 15–16.

[23] Cf. Hervé Savon, *op. cit.,* 37: ". . . le *De Paradiso* est le travail, sans doute hâtif, d'un débutant".

[24] *Epistula* 45.

[25] *De Officiis Ministrorum* I.1.4.

[26] See H. Savon, *op. cit.,* 25–54.

[27] H. Savon, *op. cit.,* 25–54.

[28] References to Philo in *Opere esegetiche II/I* by P. Siniscalco.

[29] Enzo Lucchesi, *L'Usage de Philon dans l'oeuvre exégétique de saint Ambroise,* Leiden, 1977.

was a broad reception of Philo's allegory in the Early Church and although Ambrose may have been influenced by some Christian author passing on the Philonic allegory,[30] it still seems most likely that Ambrose was directly dependent on Philo, whose interpretation is followed at large, although not slavishly.[31]

Harnack tried to show that the dialectical part of *De Paradiso* was dependent on Origen's lost *Commentary on Genesis*.[32] Harnack's opinion is hard to prove, but easy to believe, and has, to the best of my knowledge, not been refuted by any serious scholar. In the dialectical part of *De Paradiso*, Ambrose tries to argue that the narrated events of the biblical story make sense and do not conflict with a sound doctrine of God and His commandment. About one-and-a-half centuries earlier, Apelles, a pupil of Marcion, tried to ridicule the biblical story of paradise, showing it was full of absurdities. Origen refuted Apelles and Ambrose incorporated both Apelles' objections and Origen's refutation in his own treatise on paradise, once again probably following his source at large, although not dogmatically.[33]

Apelles may not have been an important figure in the days of Ambrose, but his objections were probably re-echoed by non-Christians and heretics, perhaps Manicheans, who also took the biblical story as an irrationality. Ambrose probably had to deal with their rationalist criticism which was very similar to the polemics of Apelles.[34] H. Savon argued that we can grasp the unity of Ambrose's treatise

[30] Wolfgang Karl Bietz, *Paradiesvorstellungen bei Ambrosius und seinen Vorgängern*, Diss. Gießen, 1973, gives a systematic account of the concept of paradise in the works of Philo, Clement, Origen, Gregory of Nyssa, Tertullian and Ambrose. Bietz concludes: "Insgesamt erwies sich die Übernahme philonischen Gutes durch Ambrosius als grundlegend wichtig, eine Übernahme allerdings, die Zwischenglieder in der Traditionskette ebensowenig ausschließt wie ambrosianische Modifikationen an der Vorlage im Sinne der christlichen Anschauungen. Wiederholt konnten auch Traditionslinien von einzelnen Kirchenvätern zu Ambrosius hin verfolgt werden, für die philonisches Ursprungsgut nicht aufzudecken war", p. 125.

[31] Ambrose refers to Philo by name in *De Par.* 4.25 and also hints at Philo in *De Par.* 2.11 with the phrase "quidam ante nos", cf. H. Savon, *op. cit.*, 23ff. Savon rejects the suggestion of Lucchesi in *op. cit.* tome II (notes), 15–16, n. 44.

[32] A. v. Harnack, *Sieben Bruchstücke der Syllogismen des Apelles*, TU 6.3, Leipzig, 1890, 109–120. See also A. v. Harnack, *Marcion, Das Evangelium vom fremden Gott*, TU 45, Leipzig, 1921 (Berlin, 1960) 177–196, Beilage VIII, 404ff.

[33] See H. Savon, *op. cit.*, 51: "Il est vraisemblable qu'Ambroise pratique déjà ici ce qui sera sa méthode ordinaire: ne jamais pousser l'imitation jusqu'à la reproduction servile. Si Origène est bien à la base de cette section du *De Paradiso*, l'évêque de Milan le réinterprète et l'adapte comme il fait ailleurs pour Philon".

[34] H. Savon, *op. cit.*, 45–48.

once we see him dealing with this rationalist criticism. Ambrose tries to refute its objections on a literal level of comprehension, but then shifts the method of interpretation to an allegorical way of understanding, thereby evading the difficulties on the literal level.[35]

If we now ignore any further philological questions, we may get the following, slightly simplified[36] picture. Ambrose's interpretation of the story of paradise consists of two main parts. There is a dialectic part, probably dependent on Origen, arguing on a literal level of understanding, and an allegorical part, probably dependent on Philo, arguing on a spiritual level.[37] These parts are meant to refute rational criticism and to evade that criticism while searching for a hidden meaning. Both parts will be presented below.

In *De Paradiso* 5.28 Ambrose refers to Apelles' criticism of the biblical story of paradise.[38] Up until now, Ambrose has explained the text of Gen 2:8–15, but now he has to face some serious problems concerning the tree of knowledge in Gen 2:16–17. Apelles asks the following questions:

1) If eating from the tree of knowledge implies death, how can it be that the tree of life has more power for giving life than the breath of God?
2) If man is supposed to acquire virtue for himself, does he not seem to gain more than God had bestowed on him?
3) If man has not yet known death, how can he fear the punishment of death that God inflicts?[39]

These questions clearly show Apelles' intention: he wants to ridicule the biblical story and to show that it holds impossible ideas about

[35] H. Savon, *op. cit.*, 25–54, especially pp. 50ff.

[36] In *De Paradiso*, Ambrose follows the text of Genesis 2:8–3,19, and this text is commented upon by superficially using the method of the *questiones et solutiones*, cf. H. Savon, *op. cit.*, Tome I, pp. 27–29. Within this structure, however, a dialectical and an allegorical part can be distinguished as the main parts.

[37] It is an intriguing question, of course, why Ambrose probably follows Philo's allegorical interpretation even though he might have followed the exegesis of Origen which he must have known if the refutation of Apelles is dependent on him. It may be impossible to answer these questions since 1) Ambrose followed Greek examples never quoted literally in his own Latin writings, 2) Ambrose's sources e.g. Origen's *Commentary on Genesis* are partly lost and 3) Ambrose's reception of the tradition is creative. On Ambrose and Origen, see the contribution of Christoph Markschies, *Ambrosius und Origenes* to the Colloquium Origenianum Septimum, to be published in the Acts of the Conference, *Origeniana Septima*.

[38] Strictly speaking, Ambrose refers to "Plerique . . . quorum auctor Apelles . . .".

[39] *De Paradiso* 5.28.

God and his commandment. Apelles probably inherited Marcion's exegetical acumen and a gnostic dislike of a limited and narrow-minded Creator.[40] Hence, Apelles thinks it was not wrong to disobey the commandment of such a God and, on the other hand, it was also narrowness or deceit on His behalf to give such a stupid order. The fourth point shows this clearly. Apelles says that it is good not to obey a wicked order. The order to prevent man's knowledge of good and evil was wicked, because God had that knowledge too, and what God has is good.[41]

It seems, Apelles next anticipated the apology that God dealt with man in his childhood and that the command was appropriate for that reason. The command was not appropriate, Apelles maintains, for

5) a man who does not know the difference between good and evil is like a child, not guilty of crime and
6) a person without knowledge of good and evil does not know that disobedience is an evil, and deserves to be excused.[42]

These objections claim that even if God dealt with man in his childhood, the punishment of a childlike man was unjust.

Four more questions are raised concerning the biblical story:

7) Did Adam's death come from the tree or from God?[43]
8) Did God have prior knowledge of whether or not Adam was going to violate the commandment?[44]
9) Suppose God established in the mind of man an implanted notion of good and evil, was He then maleficent since he knew man would fall into sin, or was He not prescient?[45]

These questions try to prove that the benevolence and foreknowledge or omnipotence of God are incompatible. The last objection to the story may not be derived from Apelles.[46]

---

[40] See A. v. Harnack, *Marcion* . . ., pp. 194–5: "Die Lehre des Apelles . . . ist eine interessante Verbindung des Marcionitismus mit dem Gnostizismus auf Kosten des ersteren (. . .) Sie ist Korrektur des Marcionitismus durch eine mit der valentinianischen verwandte Spekulation.

[41] *De Paradiso* 6.30.

[42] *De Paradiso* 6.31–32.

[43] *De Paradiso* 7.35. If from the tree, then its power is superior to the power of the breath of God. If from God, then God is either devoid of beneficence, if he has the power to pardon but does not wish to, or he lacks the power to pardon.

[44] *De Paradiso* 8.38. If God did not have this prior knowledge, he was limited. If God did have it, his providence gave an unnecessary order since Adam was going to violate it anyway.

[45] *De Paradiso* 8.40.

[46] See P. Siniscalco, *Sant' Ambrogio, Opere esegetiche II/I*, p. 103, note 1.

10) It was unworthy of God to prohibit the consumption of a certain food, unless you take this food "in a prophetic sense".[47]

This objection was probably not raised by Apelles, who took the story literally and ridiculed it in that way, but rather by an opponent trying to show that the story should be taken allegorically. This objection served Ambrose quite well, since it gave him a reason to continue his treatise in an allegorical way, taking the story in a prophetic sense, and indeed leaving Apelles' questions behind.

Ambrose, of course, tries to refute Apelles' objections.[48]

1) There is no distinction between the breath of God and the fruit of the tree of knowledge;
2) no man gets more than was granted to him by God and
3) man feared death even when he was not mortal, for there is an innate fear of death in every creature.
4) Ambrose denies that it was good to acquire knowledge of good and evil by disobedience, because "man ought to obey the command. A failure to obey is a violation of duty".[49]
5,6) Even if Adam was childlike, nevertheless, "since the creator of such mighty things had declared that one should not eat of the tree of good and evil, loyal adherence should be given to Him who gave the command".[50]
7) Man knew it was wrong to disobey, since the woman answered the serpent that she was not allowed to eat from the tree of knowledge. Man himself was the agent of his death by his own disobedience, not the tree nor God.
8) Of course God knew what was going to happen, but his command was not superfluous, even if he knew it would not be observed. God did not want Adam to sin, nor caused him to sin, even though he knew that Adam would sin.
9) God permitted man to die, but he is benevolent and gave men the means to be saved.

Ambrose did not leave Apelles unanswered, but his reply lacks systematic unity and force. There is no account of a universal history of salvation in which Adam's sin was a first misdirected step, nor a systematic exposition of the unity of God and the compati-

[47] *De Paradiso* 9.42.
[48] Cf. H. Savon, *op. cit.*, Tome I, 35–42.
[49] *De Paradiso* 6.30, *Opere esegetiche II/I*, 82.
[50] *De Paradiso* 6.32, *Opere esegetiche II/I*, 86.

bility of his benevolence, foreknowledge and omnipotence, even though the Greek Christian theology might have provided Ambrose with these concepts, as in the works of Irenaeus and Origen, for example. Ambrose's dialectical arguments are only developed as occasion arises and he is clearly more at ease with the allegorical explanation of the biblical story.

An allegorical interpretation of the story of paradise is developed from the second chapter of Ambrose's treatise. According to Gen 2:8–9, a garden was planted in a place called delight, where man was placed. In this spot, the devil, the snake, also exists. In order to make sense of this evil creature in the garden of Eden, Ambrose gives an allegorical explanation. "We maintain that the figure of the serpent stands for enjoyment and the figure of the woman for the emotions of the mind and the heart. The latter is called by the Greeks *aisthesis*. According to this theory, when the senses are deceived, the mind, which the Greeks call *nous*, falls into error. Hence, not without reason the author to whom I refer[51] accepts the Greek word *nous* as a figure of man and *aisthesis* as that of a woman".[52] This introduction of Philo and his allegorical exegesis opens the way to understanding paradise planted with trees as a description of the soul adorned with virtues: "Paradise is, therefore, a land of fertility—that is to say, a soul which is fertile—planted in Eden, that is, in a certain delightful or well-tilled land in which the soul finds pleasure. Adam existed there as *nous* and Eve as sense".[53] In this paradise of the soul, the mind became deceived by the senses seeking pleasure.

The fount, which Gen 2:10 says irrigated the land of paradise, is interpreted in the same way. "Is not this stream our Lord Jesus Christ, the fount as well as the father of eternal life?" This fount "irrigates paradise, that is to say, the soul's virtues that blossom because of their eminent merits".[54]

The river is separated into four branches (Gen 2:10–14). These four rivers symbolise the four principal virtues: prudence, temperance, fortitude and justice.[55] The river Phison, the Ganges, encircles

[51] Ambrose refers to Philo, see K. Schenkl, *CSEL*, 32, 1, xxi.
[52] De Paradiso 2.11, *Opere esegetiche II/I*, 50–52.
[53] *De Paradiso* 3.12, *Opere esegetiche II/I*, 52.
[54] *De Paradiso* 3.13, *Opere esegetiche II/I*, 52–54.
[55] Cf. Hervé Savon, *op. cit.*, pp. 215–241: "Les quatre fleuves du paradis", comparing Ambrose's interpretation with Philo's allegory in *Legum Allegoriae* and *Questiones in Genesin*.

all the land of Hevila, where there is gold. This river stands for prudence and wisdom, hence it has pure gold, for we often refer to wise discoveries as gold.[56] The river Gihon, the Nile, refers to the place where the law was given. The name of the river signifies an opening of the earth. An opening of the earth absorbs the earth and the defilements in it, just as the law absorbs carnal sin and chastity consumes the passion of the body. Gihon is a figure of chastity.[57] The third river, Tigris, is the swiftest of all rivers. "Hence, those who by their fortitude hold in check the guileful vices of the body and direct themselves to higher things are thought to have something in common with this river".[58] The Euphrates, the fourth river, means in Latin "fecundity and abundance of fruits". It represents justice, the nourishment of every soul. Scripture does not report the regions through which the Euphrates flows; which means that it is not known in part, since justice, representing the unity of all virtues, is not divisible into parts. Justice is, "as it were, the mother of all virtues".[59]

Ambrose also connects the virtues, represented by the four rivers, with different ages.[60] The first age, from the beginnings of the world up to the time of the flood, is the age of wisdom.[61] The second age is the age of Abraham, Isaac, Jacob and the other patriarchs, a period of pure and temperate religion.[62] The third age is the time of Moses and the other prophets who stand as types of fortitude.[63] The fourth age is the time of salvation, the time of the coming of Christ who said: "Permit us to fulfill all justice" (Matt 3:15).[64]

The biblical story next mentions that God put man in the garden of Eden and forbade him to eat of the tree of the knowledge of good and evil (Gen 2:15–17). This gives Ambrose an opportunity to refute Apelles' objections against the biblical story in the dialectic part of the treatise which was dealt with above. The story of Genesis then deals with the creation of the beasts of the field and the birds

---

[56] *De Paradiso* 3.15.
[57] *De Paradiso* 3.16.
[58] *De Paradiso* 3.17, *Opere esegetiche II/I*, 60.
[59] *De Paradiso* 13.18, *Opere esegetiche II/I*, 62.
[60] Cf. Viktor Hahn, *Das wahre Gesetz, eine Untersuchung der Auffassung des Ambrosius von Mailand vom Verhältnis der beiden Testamente*, Münster, 1969, 231–235.
[61] *De Paradiso* 3.19.
[62] *De Paradiso* 3.20.
[63] *De Paradiso* 3.21.
[64] *De Paradiso* 3.22.

of the air, to whom man gives names (Gen 2:18–20). Ambrose, however, first treats the creation of Eve from the rib of Adam.[65] The creation of Eve is not interpreted allegorically and this is surprising, since there was a Latin tradition that saw the creation of Eve out of Adam's rib as a typological reference to the birth of the Church out of the pierced side of the crucified Christ.[66] Ambrose only explains that Eve was made out of Adam, because God wanted human nature to be a unity, derived from one identical physical nature.[67]

The allegorical interpretation is again picked up when Ambrose treats the beasts and birds which are brought to Adam to be given names (Gen 2:19). The beasts and the birds refer to the passions of the body and the vanity of thoughts. Ambrose says: "The beasts of the field and the birds of the air which were brought to Adam are our irrational senses, because beasts and animals represent the diverse emotions of the body, whether of the more violent kind or even of the more temperate. What else are we to consider the birds of the air if not as representations of our idle thoughts which, like winged creatures, flit around our souls and frequently lead us by their varied motions now in one direction, now in another?"[68]

Ambrose's treatise illustrates how the biblical story of paradise allegorically refers to the soul of man. The soul consists of sense and mind, depends on Christ to be virtuous, and should be fighting and resisting pleasure, emotions of the body and idle thoughts.[69] This learned interpretation, then, is clearly connected to the Christian belief that paradise is accessible once more. Christians, purified from sin by baptism, live the virtuous life of the paradisiacal soul, a life

[65] *De Paradiso* 10.

[66] Cf. J. Daniélou, *op. cit.* 37–44, chapter IV: "Le sommeil d'Adam et la naissance de l'église".

[67] In *De Paradiso* 14.72, however, Ambrose connects the story of Adam and Eve with the mystery of Christ, with reference to Gen 3:16 which concerns the rebuke of Eve: "and he (Adam) shall rule over you". Ambrose explains: "I see clearly here the mystery of Christ and his Church. The Church's turning toward Christ in times to come and a religious servitude submissive to the word of God—these are conditions far better than the liberty of this world", *Opere Esegetiche II/I*, 156.

[68] *De Paradiso* 11.51, *Opere Esegetiche II/I*, 118, 120.

[69] Jean Daniélou, *op. cit.*, is very critical of this allegorical interpretation: ". . . ce qui importe pour nous, c'est de reconnaître qu'il s'agit d'une interprétation étrangère à la tradition commune de L'Église, qui se rattache à l'enseignement des didascales et qui doit donc être absolument distinguée de l'exégèse typologique" (p. 52). In my opinion it is not as easy to distinguish typological from allegorical exegesis as Daniélou suggests. The proposition that an allegorical interpretation is "étrangère à la tradition commune de l'Église", is an evaluation and certainly not a description.

which is exemplified by virgins, martyrs, and monks. To put it briefly: on the one hand, paradise refers to the pure and virtuous soul, on the other hand, the purified and virtuous Christian soul lives a paradisiacal life.[70]

There remain, I think, some concluding remarks concerning the very obvious question as to how paradise, which in the Early Church had again become accessible for a while, once more got lost. This question can only be answered by glancing through some of the fundamental and most influential notions of Augustine's theology.[71]

In the course of his life, Augustine came to realize that, even after baptism, he did not possess a free, pure and virtuous state of soul. Looking back at the turmoil of his own inner life, he became aware that he had been led to the point where he was now in the grip of some other force driving him in that direction. In the process of introspection, he came to regard his own human nature, and from there that of humanity as a whole, as something miserable, lost and in conflict, incapable of salvation by its own force of will.[72]

Translating this experience into theological terms, Augustine formulated his concept of an original sin. Adam once lived a life without sin, but had been seduced into acting on the basis of his own disobedient free will and got trapped in a life of conflict and tension. Augustine illustrates this conflict at the foundation of human life with his favourite example of the body's movement of sexual desire and arousal. Our own rebellion against God is mirrored in the rebellion of our flesh and sexual desire, arising independently and involuntarily against our will.[73] It is exactly this conflict that keeps us out of paradise and the paradisiacal life.

We cannot overcome this conflict was the view Augustine ardently defended against the Pelagians in his later years. He even turned

---

[70] Cf. Claudio Morino, *Il Ritorno al Paradiso di Adamo in S. Ambrogio*, Rome, 1952, describing the journey of the soul towards paradise: "Perciò il ritorno si deve verificare nella sostanza stessa dell'anima (ritorno ontologico), nella pratica delle virtù corrispondenti (ritorno ascetico) e nella congrua esperienza di questa partecipazione e perfezione (ritorno mistico)", p. xv.

[71] See for an elaborated treatise on this theme E. Pagels, "The Politics of Paradise: Augustine's Exegesis of Genesis 1–3 versus That of John Chrysostom", in: *Harvard Theological Review* 78, 1985, 67–100.

[72] See especially Augustine's *Confessiones*. Cf. P. Brown, *Augustine of Hippo, a Biography*, Berkeley, 1967.

[73] See especially *De Civitate Dei* XIV.

baptism, which was formerly seen as a purification and an entry into paradise, into a proof of his own ideas. Augustine argued that the ecclesiastical habit of infant baptism could only point to his own concept of an original sin, for which other sin could be cleansed in the baptism of infants? Augustine claimed that baptism, even though it remits all sins, leaves concupiscence, which is not a sin itself, but worse, a source of sin, conflict and tension.[74]

Baptism, therefore, is not an entry into paradise and neither do the saints live a paradisiacal life. "On what ground is 'the possession of paradise' restored to us?", Augustine asks in the dialogue with the Pelagians (and, in fact, with the Early Church as a whole). "How are we restored to paradise if we have never been there? Or how have we been there, apart from being there in Adam?".[75] Only "in Adam" did we live in paradise, but "in Adam" we were driven out as well.[76] Augustine's theology thereby turned the story of paradise into the story of the Fall. This reinterpretation of the biblical story may have been very realistic and necessary for a growing Church that could not live up to its own standards of virtue and holiness. The present paradisiacal life, however, that the Early Church proclaimed, got lost when the story of paradise became the story of the Fall.

---

[74] See especially *De peccatorum meritis et remissione et de baptismo parvulorum* and *Contra duas epistulas Pelagianorum* I.26–28.

[75] *Contra duas epistulas Pelagianorum* IV.24.

[76] Cf. John M. Rist, *Augustine, Ancient thought baptized*, Cambridge, 1994, 121ff. "Our life in Adam, a restored dimension".

PARADISE NOW—BUT FOR THE WALL BETWEEN SOME REMARKS ON PARADISE IN THE MIDDLE AGES*

CHRISTOPH AUFFARTH

1. *Paradise as an "otherworld"*

Paradise provided the people of the Middle Ages with a place into which they could project their wishes and plans for utopia. These individuals were not frozen in a holy order, unable to transcend their boundaries. This assumption is, as it turns out, a prejudice held by those who used the "otherness" of the "time before" to construct anti-modernity. According to them, modernity begins with the Utopia of Thomas More. But long before him, people of the Middle Ages constructed utopias using traditional imagery and metaphors; among them, paradise was prominent.[1]

"Paradise" does not refer only to the "historical" paradise which marks the beginning of human history. One could also call it "mythical", but in Holy History every event is an anti-type to *historia profana* and thus gains a quality of being "outside of time" and "outside of the world". It is part of an "otherworld" (*Gegenwelt*) which is neither part of reality nor a reconstructed time in the past when the most perfect order of things was still intact. This would be the function of charter myths. The paradise myth is of another type.[2] No one dreams of returning to a primordial paradise in the sense of a place without culture, but rather, to a place where justice and equality reign. The best model in biblical imagination is the utopia of Ezekiel, envisioned during the Babylonian exile: Jerusalem had been destroyed, but not by its enemies. They had only acted as God's instrument executing His inevitable judgement. God's people themselves destroyed

---

* Dedicated to Günter Kehrer, *collegae sexagenario*, inhabitant of paradise in its untamed form.

[1] Otto Gerhard Oexle: "Wunschräume und Wunschzeiten. Entstehung und Funktionen des utopischen Denkens in Mittelalter, Früher Neuzeit und Moderne." In: Jörg Calließ (Hrsg.): *Die Wahrheit des Nirgendwo. Zu Geschichte und Zukunft des utopischen Denkens*. (Loccumer Protokolle 93/12). Loccum 1994, 33–83.

[2] Fritz Stolz: "Paradiese und Gegenwelten". *Zeitschrift für Religionswissenschaft* 1 (1993), 5–24. Turner's term "antistructure" also comes to mind.

Jerusalem by oppressing the poor and profaning God's temple. As a result, God's people were cast out into the desert of Babylon. Conversion was the precondition for their return, but then it would be to a new Jerusalem with a new name and a new people living on equally divided plots of land. Along with the people, nature would be transformed as well: the bitter waters of the Dead Sea would be changed into fresh water and the wildnerness around it into a paradise garden nourished by a river springing from the temple. God would have to create the temple a second time. The world as it was could not be made better; an other, "new" world had to be created.[3]

Ezekiel's New Jerusalem is the plan for a new social order in a new, paradisiacal world. In the biblical book that transports this model into European religion, the Apocalypse of John, however, both human planning and the imagery of paradise are of minor importance.

In addition to primordial paradise on the one hand and eschatological paradise on the other, there is yet another paradise type in the Middle Ages, one which is neither closed off, nor in a distant future of uncertain reality.[4] There are only very few instances in the Bible that refer to a paradise existing in the present time, immediately accessible. Enoch and Elijah, the bosom of Abraham for poor Lazarus, and Jesus's words of consolation for the thief hanging on the cross beside him, "Today you will be with me in Paradise", are not representative of biblical theology, but are cited often by medieval theologians. The idea of paradise as real in the present time allowed it to be imagined as in the here and now (but at a far distance) or in the here and now, but with a wall dividing this world from the "otherworld".

---

[3] Ezek 40–48. Jürgen H. Ebach: *Kritik und Utopie. Untersuchungen zum Verhältnis von Volk und Herrscher im Verfassungsentwurf des Ezekiel, Kapitel 40–48.* Diss. Hamburg 1972. Christoph Auffarth: *Der drohende Untergang. "Schöpfung" in Mythos und Ritual im Alten Orient und in Griechenland am Beispiel der Odyssee und des Ezechielbuches.* RGVV 39. Berlin; New York 1991, 78–118.

[4] For a full bibliography of iconographical representations and of theological treatises, see: Hans Martin von Erffa: *Ikonologie der Genesis. Die christlichen Bildthemen aus dem Alten Testament und ihre Quellen.* 2 Vols. München 1989–1995. Reinhold R. Grimm: *Paradisus coelestis, paradisus terrestris. Zur Auslegungsgeschichte des Paradieses im Abendland bis um 1200.* (Medium Aevum 33) München 1977. P. Raedts: "Het aards paradijs. De tuin als beeld van het geluk". In: R.E.V. Stuip; C. Vellekoop (ed.): *Tuinen in de Middeleeuwen.* Hilversum 1992, 35–50.

2. *The historical paradise*

The historical paradise transported a negative message. The division between men and women of the Church on the one hand and the laity on the other hand began in paradise. Monks still lived an *angelikos bios*, in accordance with the life of the angels in the primordial garden, whereas the life of "normal" married people was considered bad, reiterating the fall of the first couple by sexual intercourse. Whereas Jews entered into matrimony preferably on the third day of the week, citing another verse of the creation story in which God says it is *tov tov* (very good), for Christians marriage was a necessity, but not the principal order. The most holy order was represented by the *continentes* and the *virgines*. In this case, the paradise myth functioned as a charter myth for the Christian dichotomy between unmarried clergy and married laity.[5]

But the case was not as easy and clearcut as it seemed to be. The virginity of Adam and Eve before the Fall was Jerome's justification for renouncing marriage and family. Augustine, however, who had lived for many years with a woman and fathered a child, could not accept this interpretation. He claimed that there was love and marriage in paradise, albeit "innocent" marriage, i.e. sex without lust.[6]

A later conflict provides another illustration of the salience of paradise imagery. The Cistercians regarded themselves as an army of God and preached the Crusade against the enemies outside of as well as within Christianity. A member of this order, Everwin of Steinfeld, watched a group of non-conformists in Cologne be put to death by local authorities and decided to ask the leader of his new order for advice. He wrote a letter describing what he had heard

---

[5] Innocent III changed the elements of the Church from two to three, including the married laymen and laywomen as members of the Church: Council of Lateran IV 1215, c. 1 (Denzinger, Enchiridion symbolorum, [37]1991, 802) at a cost: the loss of the laity's own way to salvation (see below 3.3): *Una est fidelium universalis ecclesia, extra quam nullus omnino salvatur.*

[6] Augustinus, *confessiones* 6. 15; *De civitate Dei* 14, 10; 14, 21. *Nupt.concup.* 1.1,1; 1.8,9.; *gen.litt.* 9,3. Gerhard Delling: "Geschlechtsverkehr." *RAC* 10 (1978), 812–829, 826f. Michael Müller: *Die Lehre des heiligen Augustinus von der Paradiesehe und ihre Auswirkungen in der Sozialethik des 12. und 13. Jahrhunderts bei Thomas von Aquin.* Münster 1954, 19–35. Reinhold Grimm: "Die Paradiesehe, eine erotische Utopie des Mittelalters". in: Franz Hundsnurscher; Ulrich Müller (Hrsg.): *"Getemperet und gemischet". Festschrift Wolfgang Mohr.* (GAG 65) Göppingen 1972, 1–25. Manfred Gerwing: "Paradiesehe". *Lexikon des Mittelalters.* 6 (1993), 1699–1700.

about the heretics to Bernard of Clairvaux. One of their ideas was that marriage should not be sanctified by Christian rite, arguing in full accordance with Jerome that God had created man and woman as virgins. In renouncing marriage and not consuming meat, these Cathars, as they were called, lived like monks. Everwin was full of admiration for their steadfastness.

Bernard replied in one of his sermons on the Song of Solomon warning against the "little foxes" referred to in the biblical text (Cant 2:15) and distributed it to all the monasteries of the new order. The Cathars were not monks by profession, they reversed the essential dichotomy: laymen and -women must work and procreate; only a minority must produce the "surplus" of salvation. They may not condemn a second union sanctified by the Christian rite of marriage. The Cathar argument based on the paradise narrative was outweighed by Pauline pronouncements and by textual exegesis: in the Bible it is not written that God created "virgins" but man and woman.[7]

Once the possibility of love in paradise is permitted, and moreover, an extraordinary love without the pains of childbirth, a "sexual revolution" was possible, if only in the imagination. Paradise images mingled with the *hortus conclusus* of the Song of Songs 4:12, the place where the loving couple comes together in a secure and secret place behind a wall.[8]

In medieval images of the world (*imagines mundi*) paradise is placed, unlike heaven and hell, within the world. There are a few instances of paradise located in the far west, as in the ancient tradition of the Garden of Hesperides or the Isle of the Blessed. Normally, however, it is located in the far east, following the text of Genesis: "God planted a garden in the east".[9] Since medieval maps were orientated, paradise was situated at the top. In the Ebstorf map, where the world is represented as the body of Christ, it is found near the head

[7] Everwin *MPL* 182, 676–680. Bernard of Clairvaux answers in *Sermo super canticum canticorum* 65 and 66; the relevant passage about virginity in paradise is 66,4 (*SBerO* 2, 180–181).

[8] Jean Leclercq: *Monks and Love in Twelfth-Century France. Psycho-Historical Essays.* Oxford 1979.

[9] Herma Kliege: *Weltbild und Darstellungspraxis hochmittelalterlicher Weltkarten.* Münster: Nodus 1991, 118–120. Jörg-Geerd Arentzen: *Imago mundi cartographica. Studien zur Bildlichkeit mittelalterlicher Welt- und Ökumenekarten unter besonderer Berücksichtigung des Zusammenwirkens von Text und Bild.* (MMS 53) München 1984, 206–214.

of Christ as the rising sun.[10] On other maps the *locus amoenus*[11] is separated from the Oikumene by the sea (as an island), by deserts, or by a wall of fire. Sometimes not (only) Adam and Eve are depicted as inhabitants of paradise, but Enoch and Elijah (as well). They do not,[12] however, act as eschatological figures, but are evidence that paradise is real in the present, for they are the two men who were taken into the place of the blessed without having to experience death.

The location of earthly paradise was so distant that very few people could ever entertain thoughts of going there. Even so, clues that would guide one to God's garden were deliberately confusing: Following the rivers of paradise back to their origin would lead one there. But the Tigris and Euphrates (named expressly in the Bible), as well as the Phison and Gehon (today called the Ganges and the Nile), flow for long distances underground, so that they could not aid in finding the earthly location of paradise. Nevertheless, there were sailors and travellers who felt they had found it. Christopher Columbus, for example, seeing himself as an actor in the eschatological drama, first discovered the island of Saint Brendan, which the saint had seen as a model of paradise, but which no one had ever found again since. And on his third voyage, as he sailed along the coast of South America and came to the mouth of the Orinoco, Columbus was sure that this must be the river of sweet water and the garden full of fruit (among them the *musa paradisiaca*, also known as bananas). The people there were naked without shame, innocent inhabitants of paradise.

3. *"Today you will be with me in Paradise"*

In one famous biblical quotation, the eschatological prospect of reward is reversed. To the criminal crucified at his side Christ says: "Today you will be with me in Paradise" (Luke 23:43). The problem of the temporal gap between an individual's death and the universal judgement of all humanity after the end of the world was in Christian

[10] Christoph Auffarth: "Finis terrae, finis mundi". In: Dieter Zeller (Hrsg.): *Weltbilder im Wandel der Kosmologien.* (Religionswissenschaft) Frankfurt [u.a.] 1998 (in print).

[11] Isidor *etymologiae* 14. 3,2.

[12] Contra Arentzen 1984, 213 *f* und Danielle Lecoq: "La mappemonde du liber floridus ou la Vision du Monde de Lambert de Saint-Omer". In: *Imago mundi* 39 (1987), 9–49; 41.

tradition normally solved in favour of the Last Judgement. But for performing rituals, preaching asceticism, or motivating others to special tasks, such a distant goal could not be as effective over a longer period of time as smaller and increasing demands and rewards could.[13] Christ's promise, "*Today* you will be with me in Paradise", could be cited as an immediate reward for those with special callings, such as nuns and monks, donators, penitents, or crusaders.

Unlike the Muslim paradise, the Christian paradise was not open to all; as a place of final rest it was restricted to but a few holy men and women. In a polemic against Muslims in 1241 Peter the Venerable reproaches Muhammed's coarse imagination of paradise for every man, for its bodily pleasures in the form of wine and women.[14] In Muslim tradition the future condition of an individual was decided in the grave, immediately after death; a simple affirmative answer to the name of God and the duties of a Muslim would open the door to paradise.[15] The Last Judgement would only confirm this decision. For Christians, as Peter maintains, the entrance was very narrow; following an ascetic life, one would enjoy spiritual rewards in paradise, not bodily pleasures.

But in the course of the eleventh century there was a change: the laity demanded its own path to salvation. The quarrel over lay investiture disturbed the Church's freedom in matters of religious life. The pope involved in this conflict, however, Gregory VII, was the very one who provided laymen an opportunity to achieve salvation through crusading. In 1096, his successor, Urban II, instigated the First Crusade. In later years, the promise of full remission of sins was restricted to secular punishments. In the first summoning, however, the pope promised both earthly and heavenly rewards. One historian of the

[13] From the angle of cultural anthropology (or more precisely: *Kulturwissenschaft*), I use the principle of "operationalizing" distant spiritual goals through signs in earthly experience in Christoph Auffarth: *Mittelalterliche Eschatologie. Religionswissenschaftliche Studien*. Diss. theol. Groningen 1996. [Published in extended form (including a chapter about paradise) under the title: *Geradewegs in den Himmel? Religionswissenschaftliche Studien zur mittelalterlichen Eschatologie*. (VMPIG 144) Göttingen 1999].

[14] Petrus Venerabilis: *Summa totius haeresis Saracenorum* 9; *Contra sectam Saracenorum* 2. 129 (Petrus Venerabilis: *Schriften zum Islam*. Ediert, ins Deutsche übersetzt und kommentiert von Reinhold Glei. (Corpus Islamo-Christianum SL 1) Altenberge: CIS-Verlag 1985).

[15] Abd ar-Rahim ibn Ahmad al-Qadi: *Das Totenbuch des Islam. Die Lehren des Propheten Mohammed über das Leben nach dem Tod*. [*Islamic Book of the Dead*. 1977; dt.] Freiburg 1993, 79f.

First Crusade, Albert of Aachen, says that Christ himself appeared in a vision to a noble pilgrim in the Church of the Holy Sepulchre, sending him to bring the pope a letter demanding an armed pilgrimage to Jerusalem. "Because after having passed dangers and temptations, the doors of paradise will be opened now for those who are called and chosen."[16] The pope called and thousands came.

Like the other historians of the First Crusade, Albert of Aachen wrote after Jerusalem had been taken and the crusaders had returned. In the meantime, during the expedition something back at home had happened that changed the path to salvation. The idea of finding the heavenly Jerusalem in the historical city on earth or of waiting for the Last Judgement at the location Jesus was said to come again had lost importance. During the siege of Antioch the hope faded that the crusaders would achieve the goal of their armed pilgrimage at all. One soldier after the other died, not at the hands of their enemies but from hunger and disease,[17] a meaningless, unnoticed death, far from home and family. And it got worse: the day after the city was conquered, a Turkish army arrived, encircling and besieging the crusaders. Caught in the trap of either waiting for death from hunger or being slaughtered by a merciless enemy, they created a new ideal for themselves: the Saints of Antioch. The Maccabees were extraordinary because they fought for God as laymen and as knights. The seven brothers died in the end as martyrs, the first and most influential model for ancient Christian and Jewish martyrdom.[18] God rewarded them by taking them immediately into the place of reward. Though the feast of the seven brothers has a long history in the Western Church, it was chosen in particular as a model for the laymen's own way to heaven because of two relevant points: 1) the extreme situation of Antioch and 2) because the crusaders had seen Jews in the pogroms at the beginning of the expedition who refused to be baptised, preferring to take their own lives while "sanctifying

[16] Albert of Aachen 1,4.

[17] Christoph Auffarth: "Die Makkabäer als Modell für die Kreuzfahrer. Usurpationen und Brüche in der Tradition eines jüdischen Heiligenideals. Ein religionswissenschaftlicher Versuch zur Kreuzzugseschatologie". In: Christoph Elsas [et alii] (Hrsg.): *Tradition und Translation. Zum Problem der interkulturellen Übersetzbarkeit religiöser Phänomene. Festschrift für Carsten Colpe zum 65. Geburtstag.* Berlin; New York 1994, 362–390. Auffarth, *Eschatologie* 1996, 67–89.

[18] Jan Willem van Henten: *The Maccabean Martyrs as Saviours of the Jewish People.* (JSJ-Suppl 57) Leiden [e.a.] 1997.

the name of God, *kiddush ha-shem*". They told one another the story of the Maccabees, how God saves those who choose tribulation and death instead of the good life.[19]

There was yet another way to bypass death and enter immediately into paradise, alive on a rapturous journey. With recourse to the words of St. Paul, mystics could declare their ecstatic and abnormal behaviour to be a journey into paradise. Paul is asked by his chaotic community at Corinth for his opinion on ecstatic speech (*glossolalia*). Paul does not forbid it and furthermore explains to the sceptics that these people are torn away into paradise.[20] Every mystic takes these words as authorisation for religious behaviour which would otherwise be forbidden. The biblical canon is complete and sealed; it does not allow for further revelation or further direct contact with God and heaven. God's word is written down and can be explained by professionals who have undergone exegetical instruction. With their visions, however, mystics reopen a direct connection to heaven and paradise and escape the institutions of scripture and censorship. They hear and repeat the tongues of angels, which are different from human language. The mystics of the High and Late Middle Ages used the sanctioned space of the *hortus conclusus* to utter bold images in outrageous words. But before those visions passed the exit of the *hortus conclusus* in the form of a written book, the father confessor checked it in order to avoid inquisition. The content of the vision was Love, nearly exclusively the images from the Song of Songs. The canonical interpretation of this biblical book as an allegory of the love between Christ and the Church was replaced during the twelfth century by a new mystic understanding of the individual soul longing for loving union with the bridegroom Christ.[21] The *hortus conclusus* is the place for lovemaking; a ladder is used to

---

[19] For further evidence see Auffarth: *Eschatologie* 1996, 85–87.

[20] 2 Cor 12:4.

[21] Friedrich Ohly: *Hohelied-Studien. Grundzüge einer Geschichte der Hoheliedauslegung des Abendlandes bis um 1200*. (Schriften der Wissenschaftlichen Gesellschaft an der Johann Wolfgang Goethe-Universität Frankfurt am Main, Geisteswissenschaftliche Reihe Nr. 1) Wiesbaden 1958, 121ff. See further his extensive commentary on: *Das St. Trudberter Hohelied*, Hrsg. von Friedrich Ohly unter Mitarbeit von Nicola Kleine. (Bibliothek des Mittelalters) Frankfurt a.M. 1997. Friedrich Wilhelm Wodtke: "Die Allegorie des 'Inneren Paradieses' bei Bernhard von Clairvaux, Honorius Augustodunensis, Gottfried von Straßburg und in der deutschen Mystik" in: Hugo Moser; Rudolf Schützeichel; Karl Strackmann (Hrsg.): *Festschrift Josef Quint, anläßlich seines 65. Geburtstages überreicht*. Bonn: Semmel 1964, 277–290.

get inside, the first rung of which is the fear of God and the last, the erotic union with Christ in the *unio mystica.* The garden surrounded by a protective wall was easily equated with the cloister.

4. *The cloister as paradise*

The mysticism of the twelfth century is deeply influenced by, or even originated with, Bernard of Clairvaux, the head of the reform group of monastics known as the Cistercians. They left their wealthy order in Cluny and symbolically changed their style of dress: instead of black cloaks they wore coarse garments of undyed, greyish, scratchy cloth. In the dispute between the old and the new order the Cistercians reproached the Benedictines for their luxurious lifestyle.[22] They in turn responded by accusing the Cistercians of wearing white clothes as a sign of superiority to human beings, of considering themselves to be angels. And indeed, in Bernard's works there are references to Clairvaux using the imagery of paradise: as a place of heavenly reward in the present day, securely protected by a wall.

In his "Life of Malachias" Bernard says that he founded his monastery "as if he were about to plant paradise anew".[23] The imagery of paradise is an often used image for monastic life. Living like angels, the *bios angelikos,* is also a traditional image. The "conventional" monasticism of the Middle Ages, an alternative form of life for members of the nobility, could be compared to a comfortable existence in a well-kept garden of pleasure. Cistercians, on the other hand, stressed the new community of men and angels, in which men (later: women as well) should live in perfect, angelic asceticism.

The traditional designation of a part of churches and monastaries as "paradise" has its origins in Late Antiquity. But there is also a connection between the paradise garden of the rulers of Islamic Spain and the cloisters (in the proper sense) of the Benedictine monasteries of Carolingian times. The garden with lines crossing in the middle, shadowy colonnades, and fountain was evidently of Mediterranean origin. It symbolised paradise as God's creation with all its wonders:

---

[22] Bernard of Clairvaux, *epistola* 1. See Adriaan Bredero: *Cluny et Citeaux au douzième siècle. L'histoire d'une controverse monastique.* Amsterdam; Maarssen; Lille 1985.

[23] Bernard of Clairvaux, *Vita Sancti Malachiae episcopi* 13 (SBerO 3. 322, 15). *Veluti quemdam replantaturus paradisum.*

plants from all over the world with fine-tasting fruits and herbs of wonderful effect demonstrated the greatness of God the creator.[24]

One of the gifts from God is offered to Muslims nowhere else but in paradise, namely wine. What is taboo for a Muslim on earth he can drink in great quantities in paradise, where it does not cause drunkenness, otherwise it would not be there. The biblical narrative puts the invention of wine outside of paradise, because of its dangerous effects if imbibed without precaution. The story of Noah is revealing in this regard. The myth of origins (*Urgeschichte*) thus connects the invention of wine with the beginning of culture. People without cultural knowledge are poisoned by it. But both Muslims and Christians found a way to prevent wine from being harmful. In the Muslim paradise, wine does not intoxicate.[25] For the Christians there are two religious restrictions. Wine is sacred as part of the Lord's supper and one is required not to drink too much of it: *Dignum et justum est.* But there is wine in the paradise of Bernard of Clairvaux, who quotes the bridegroom of the Song of Songs (5:1): "Eat, O friends, and drink: drink deeply, O lovers!" And he comments: "In the end, after the resurrection of our bodies, in the life of immortality, we will be inebriated and overflow in wonderful abundance. And the bridegroom intoxicates his friends. Hence results the inebriate sobriety, which is inebriated by truth, not by wine; which is soaked not in wine, but burns with God in eternity."[26] The famous oxymoron "inebriate sobriety" is used to describe the ecstasy of the mystical experience.[27]

Bernard approved of the Crusades as a form of *militia Christi*, which was formerly restricted to the "spiritual warfare" of monks. He recruited members of the nobility to join the army entering the Holy Land. Killing an enemy of Christ was, according to him, an act of salvation. God had made a special offer to win salvation through

---

[24] Christoph Auffarth: "Langeweile im Himmel? Das Paradies als Wunschraum und seine Engelsbewohner" in: *Symbolon, Neue Folge* 13. 1997, 125–146.

[25] Qoran, sure 52, 23.

[26] Bernard of Clairvaux, *De diligendo Deo* 11. 33 (*SBerO* 3. 147, 6). *Post mortem vero in vita spirituali iam bibimus suavissima quadam facilitate quod percipitur colantes; tandem redivivis corporibus in vita immortali inebriamur, mira plenitudine exuberantes. Haec pro eo quod sponsus in Canticis dicit: Comedite, amici, et bibite et inebriamini post ressurrectionem. Merito iam carissimi, qui caritate inebriantur; merito inebriati, qui ad nuptias Agni introduci merentur; edentes et bibentes super mensam illius in regno suo.* Cp. *Sermo super canticum* 30, 12: *modico.*

[27] Albert Henrichs: "The Sobriety of Oedipus: Sophocles *OC* 100 Misunderstood". *HSCP* 87 (1983), 87–100.

killing.[28] Bernard himself never joined a Crusade. His way of life was the better one.

He once defended a friend against the charges of a bishop as follows: A monk had placed himself under the obligation to join a Crusade. He joined an army starting from England, but at Clairvaux he decided to become a member of Bernard's community. The English bishop wrote the monk a letter to remind him of his vow. Bernard, however, who was always preaching that the crusaders should not remain in Europe and fight the enemies of God in their own countries, in this case defended the monk against the charges. He was not obliged to continue on his road to the earthly Jerusalem, Bernard argued, "because his feet are already standing in the heavenly Jerusalem. And in case you do not know what I mean: Clairvaux *is* Jerusalem."[29]

5. *Conclusion*

In this paper I stress those features which demonstrate the "translation" of biblical imagery into the medieval world, where paradise was to be seen, smelled, touched, and walked in.

I have differentiated four types of paradise in the present day:

1) the primordial paradise, which is used as a charter myth for the Christian dichotomy between the celibacy of monastics and priests and the married life of the laity on the one hand, but which is also a geographic location in the present, one that Christopher Columbus had in mind on his voyages;
2) the eschatological place of reward after the future end of the universe, represented in the present day in the architecture of cloisters as the garden of God's wondrous creation;
3) the bold and self-confident characterization by the Cistercians of their way of life, according to which monastic life is not ascetic "penitent" preparation to win future reward (as in the luxurious life of a Benedictine monk)—in their view, Cistercians were already among the angels in paradise.

---

[28] Bernard of Clairvaux, *epistola* 363,5 (*SBerO* 8, 315). M. Greeves (ed.): *The Second Crusade and the Cistercians*. New York 1992.

[29] Bernard of Clairvaux, *epistola* 64 (*SBerO* 7. 157, 11; 158, 2).

4) an unexpected form of "paradise now" in the Christian tradition: that of laymen and, moreover, soldiers being rewarded by God's taking them immediately after a death by disease or hunger into paradise—a new lay image which originated during the siege of Antioch.

The Church's response to the need among the laity expressed by these images was the invention of Purgatory to fill the void between the individual's demise and the universal end of time. Now a part of hell and a part of paradise were under the control of the Church, extending her realm into the afterlife. The doors of paradise were locked once again, and the key held in the hands of St. Peter's successors.*

* Many thanks to Monique Scheer for correcting my English.

RUSSIAN MEDIEVAL CONCEPTS OF PARADISE

Sander Brouwer

The Common Slavic word for paradise is "ray" (рай). This is a loanword from Old Iranian, Avestan rāy, "wealth, happiness", cf. Old Indian rāy, rās, "fortune, treasure, wealth". As a matter of fact, it is one of the two dozen or so words in Common Slavic that have been influenced by Iranian, in the period roughly between 500 BC and 200–300 AD; all these words belong to the sphere of mythology and religion. Other examples include the words for "repent", "heaven", "word", "bad" and even the word for God: bog (бог), that is etymologically connected with Avestan baγa: "Lord, god" and Old Indian bhαgas: "giver, lord".

From the times SS Cyril and Methodius began to translate parts of the Bible, in the second half of the ninth century, the Slavic word "ray" serves as a translation of the Greek παράδεισος, "enclosed park, garden",[1] but it carries connotations quite different from it: it points to a conception of paradise as a special state of earthly reality,[2] and misses the connotation of "seclusion" that is so prominent in the Greek. By the ninth century, the origin of the word was certainly forgotten, but still, the different semantic background helps to explain the fact that in the medieval Russian tradition, the notion of paradise as an enclosed garden was very weakly developed.[3] In the

[1] Apart from Gen 2 and 3, cf., for instance, Gen 13:10: "the region of the Jordan (. . .) was (. . .) like God's 'ray'"; Ezek 28:13 "You were in the sweetness of God's 'ray'", etc. According to his *Vita*, Methodius translated the whole Bible, but that text is not extant. Only those parts of the Bible were translated that were needed for liturgical use: those included in the Euchologion and the Lectionaries, and in Commentaries ("Tolkovye"). The first complete Russian Bible is the (printed) Gennadi Bible of 1499.

[2] Interestingly, the Common Slavic word for "wealthy", "bogat", is also connected with "bog", "god". A.P. Vlasto explains that this group of words contain "not so much loan-words as native words which acquired new senses in C[ommon] Sl[avic] through (. . .) cultural contact" (*A Linguistic History of Russia to the end of the Eighteenth Century*. (Oxford 1988) 253).

[3] According to D.S. Likhachev, the image was known in hymnography (as well as the image of the Virgin Mary as "hortus conclusus"), but he gives no examples (Д.С. Лихачев, *Поэзия садов.* К семантике садово-парковых стилей. Сад как текст. Изд. 2-ое, испр. и доп. (Санкт Петербург. 1991) 48–49).

Slavic Bible, the word that denotes an enclosed garden ("вертоград" or "вертоград заключен") was used only when a non-paradisical garden was meant (as in Esther 7:7, or S of S 4:12).

D.S. Likhachev has suggested that the tradition to regard monastery gardens as symbols of paradise, well known in Western Europe, can be traced in medieval Russia, as well.[4] This he indirectly reconstructs from icons, on which such gardens are adorned with the same stylized trees that we see in depictions of paradise. But there is a strange contradiction in Likhachev's arguments: on the one hand, he writes that monasteries were not depicted on icons before the fifteenth century;[5] but on the other, he mentions the fact that after that period, monastery gardens were no longer regarded as symbols of paradise.[6] To my view, in his otherwise brilliant book, Likhachev fails to show convincingly the existence of a tradition to regard monastery gardens as symbols of paradise before the seventeenth century, that is, before the influence of latinized culture. But that does not necessarily mean that his thesis is wrong. If it is true, however, there was a significant difference with Western cloisters: the enclosure of Russian monastery gardens was formed by the monastery walls themselves, and the gardens were not *adjacent* to the monastery: thus, the monastery *as a whole* was taken as a symbol of paradise, not the garden as such.[7] As places of religious worship and sanctity they thus show the same symbolism as churches and cathedrals, around which we often

[4] Likhachev 48–61.

[5] Likhachev 52–53.

[6] Likhachev 49. In the XIV and XV centuries, they were no longer constructed. Instead, under the influence of hesychasm monasteries began to be built predominantly in wild, deserted places, and much attention was paid to where, in what natural environment, the monastery itself was to be situated. In this period, paradise is conceived of as "the whole natural environment, that is not modified by sinful man. The saint and the righteous man should live amidst nature, that in itself is righteous" (ibidem).

[7] Likhachev 50. These monastery gardens have probably developed from the "holy woods" of heathen times, that were "christianized" by enclosure in a monastery (Likhachev 52). Furthermore, we know that sometimes Russian princes called their country courts "ray" (Likhachev 51). It is, however, difficult to say why this was: because the estates contained gardens, or for some other reason. In the case of prince Andrey Bogolyubski, B.A. Uspenski suggests that it may have been because the court was situated "over the water"; the name thus stresses that paradise is separated from the world by a stream (Б.А. Успенский, *Филологические разыскания в области славянских древностей* Реликты язычества в восточнославянском культе Николая Мирликийского. (Москва. 1982) 56). We may note that Daniil Galitski's and Vladimir Vasilkovich Volynski's town Ray was also situated on the shore of a lake.

find paradise trees depicted on Russian icons.[8] This can be connected with the circumstance, that the Eastern church elaborated the general Christian symbolism of the church as a "provisional paradise" into a symbolism of the church and its rituals as heaven on earth, as earthly paradise.[9]

S.L. Baehr has argued that this depiction of the church as earthly paradise "reflected a characteristic of Byzantine theological thought that John Meyendorff has called 'realized eschatology'—the assumption that the transfiguration and deification of man are accessible now, not just in the future."[10] Indeed, here we may see the background to what I would select as the typologically most characteristic feature of Russian conceptualizations of paradise: that it is spoken of in terms of presence, of familiar space, and may be located within the boundary of known geographical space, within the oecumene (this tendency can be noted in the Western tradition, as well, but there the case is somewhat different. We will return to that presently).

For an example of this last tendency, let us turn to the epistle of 1347 by Vasili Kalika, who was archbishop of Novgorod from 1330–1352, to Fyodor Dobry, bishop of Tver from 1342–1360 (a full translation of this text is given in the appendix).[11] What exactly provoked the epistle is not clear, but from some expressions in it we gather that it was written in reaction to a polemics in Tver on the status of paradise: "[We] learnt that a dispute over venerable paradise has risen in Tver." Further on in the epistle it becomes clear that Fyodor had maintained that paradise is to be understood only in a spiritual way: "I have heard, brother, that you say: 'Paradise, in which Adam lived, has perished'"; "And now, brother, you think that paradise is only spiritual." Vasili then proceeds to defend the

---

[8] Likhachev lists a number of them (Likhachev 53–54).

[9] *The Paradise Myth in Eighteenth-Century Russia.* Utopian Patterns in Early Secular Russian Literature and Culture (Stanford, Ca. Stanford University Press. 1991) 14–16; cf. literature in the notes to these pages. As representatives of this tradition, Baehr mentions St. Irenaeus († 202), Origen († 253–54), St. Ephraim Syrus († 373), St. Eusebius of Samosata († 378), St. Germanus (patriarch of Constantinople until 729); and a passage from a Christmas vesper hymn.

[10] Baehr 16.

[11] For a discussion of the place of this document in Russian medieval conceptualizations of earthly paradise see Б.А. Успенский, "Дуалистический характер русской средневековой культуры (на материале 'Хожения за три моря' Афанасия Никитина)," idem, *Избранные труды в 3–х томах* (2–ое изд., испр. и перераб. Москва. 1996) Т.I: 381–382, 403–406).

existence up to the present day of concrete, geographically located paradise, which "God planted in the East, in Eden". Although he does not deny the existence of that spiritual paradise, he holds that earthly, "planted" paradise exists as well:

> And if you say, brother, that "paradise is spiritual", let it be so, brother, the spiritual paradise exists, and will exist. But the paradise that has been planted has not perished either; it exists today. There is a light in it that shines of itself, but its grounds are inaccessible, one can only reach [the foot of] the mountains of paradise. But spiritual paradise, brother, will be when all earth is renewed by fire, as the apostle says: "We await a new heaven and a new earth, when the true light—Christ—will descend upon earth."

As a proof of this assertion, Vasili relates how some spiritual children of his have actually found the entrance to hell, and others the place where paradise is located:

> The location of holy paradise was found by Moislav from Novgorod and his son Iakov; they were all sailing in three boats, and one of them perished after it had lost its way and drifted about a long time, and the other two were carried criss-cross over the sea by the wind for a long time thereafter, until they were brought to high mountains. And they saw that on these mountains the Deisus[12] was painted with marvellous azure and lavishly adorned, as if created not by human hands but by God's blessing. And there was a light in that place that shone of its own accord, so that it is impossible to describe in human words.
>
> And they stayed long in this place, and they did not see the sun, but there was a light of manifold splendour, and it shone brighter than the sun. And from the mountains they heard triumphal singing, filled with joy. And they had one of their company climb up the mountain with a climbing-pole, in order to see where that light and those triumphal voices came from; and it so happened, that when he reached the top of the mountain, he immediately started to clap his hands and laugh, and he ran away from his friends, to where the voices came from. They were completely amazed by this and they sent up another man, giving him strict instructions to return and tell them about what was on the mountain. But he acted likewise; not only did he fail to return but he ran away from them with great joy. They became filled with fear, and started to ponder on the matter, saying to themselves: "Even if death should ensue, we would still like to know more about the shining light in this place". And they sent up a third man, having tied a rope to his foot. And this man wanted to act likewise: he

[12] An icon composition of Christ with the Virgin Mary and John the Baptist.

> cheerfully clapped his hands and started to run, but in his joy forgot about the rope on his foot. They pulled him down with the rope, but found that he had died. Then they hurried away from there: it was not given to them to behold that place any further, neither that inexpressible luminescence, nor to hear the joy and the triumph there. And to the present day, brother, the children and grandchildren of these seafarers are alive and well.[13]

This legend must have been quite persistent: still in the nineteenth century, the expression existed: "He has found the Novgorod paradise", meaning "he is telling tall stories".

It would be wrong to think that archbishop Vasili here expresses the official view of the Russian orthodox church on the status of paradise. In fact, it may be argued that his position is heretic; one investigator finds it close to the conception of paradise of the Nestorians and the Jacobites.[14] On the other hand, his views reflect notions that are well known from Russian medieval texts, in which men visit paradise and return from it. Vasili himself mentions a few of them, from the Russian *Prologue*:

– that on Enoch the Righteous;[15]

– the 12th–13th century *Journey of our father Agapi to paradise*, in which Agapi visits Elijah in paradise and receives a piece of bread from him, which he takes back;

– the *Tale of Macarius of Rome*, that was first translated from Greek into Russian in the 14th century, and in which three monks visit saint Macarius, who lives close to the entrance into paradise

– the *Tale of St. Yefrosin*, who took three apples back from paradise, that had healing power.

---

[13] A.N. Veselovski has pointed to a passage from Heinrich von der Neuenstadt's (von Neustadt) *Apollonius von Tyrus* (end of the thirteenth century), in which Apollonius and his men in almost exactly the same manner (mastpole, three attempts, joy and clapping of hands, third man with rope on foot is pulled down dead, hurried retreat) try to look over a high wall, behind which "dâ mac wol sîn ein paradîs." Later legends also contain the episode. (А.Н. Веселовский, "Эпизоды о рае и аде в послании новгородского архиепископа Василия. (Разыскания в области русского духовного стиха XIX)," *Сборник Отделения русского языка и Словесности имп. Академии Наук* Т. LIII, 1891, № 6, 93–97).

[14] А.М. Панченко, "Василий Калика", *Словарь книжников и книжности Древней Руси: XI—первая половина XIV в.* (Отв. редактор Д.С. Лихачев. Ленинград. 1987) 95.

[15] Parts of the Slavic version of the book of Enoch (it was probably translated in the 11th–12th cent.) were included in the Great Reading Menaion in the sixteenth centrury. Only later it became regarded as apocryphal (*Мифы народов мира.* Энциклопедия в 2-х томах. (Гл. ред. С.А. Токарев. Москва. 1987–1988) II, 436).

Furthermore, Vasili mentions the land of the "rakhmans" (a corruption of "brahman"), who live on inaccessible mountains that reach to the sky, and are located at the source of the Nile. This shows that he was familiar with the Slavic version of the romance of Alexander or with tales that were inspired by it, and that were very popular in medieval Russia: the Russian translation of the Prester John epistle,[16] and the *Journey of Zosima to the Rakhmans*, that was translated from the Greek already in the 10th century. Of course, many elements of Vasili's depiction are familiar from other written sources: the mountain, the ladder,[17] the halo of light (St. Ephraim Syrus); in another place Vasili mentions the well-known four rivers, etc.

Some of these works, especially the romance of Alexander, were very popular in Western Europe, as well. As I have said, in medieval Western Europe, the notion that paradise was an actual terrestrian location did exist. There, it can be traced back to St. Augustine, but in general it was of Eastern origin.[18] Until the fourteenth century, however, although authors maintained that paradise had actual existed and even persisted to the present (it may be located somewhere in the East, and descriptions may be given, though these remain fairly constant and clearly are of literary origin), they agreed that it was unreachable.

> No orthodox Christian in the Middle Ages—writes G. Kimble—doubted the existence of this original home of mankind as a fact of contemporary history. Many writers devote long chapters to the description of its delights, though none from first-hand enjoyment of them! Even Mandeville, the most romantic geographer of the age, confesses that he had not visited it on account of his unworthiness, but that he had derived his information about it from trustworthy men.[19]

---

[16] In Russia it was known as the *Tale of the Indian Empire* (Сказание о Индийском царстве); it was translated in the 13th or 14th century.

[17] See Patch, index ("ladder").

[18] Cf. H.S. Benjamins' contribution to the present collection. Of the Eastern authors, J. Delumeau mentions St. Theophilus of Antioch († 181), St. Irenaeus of Lyon († 202) and St. Hippolytus of Rome († 235), who both were of Eastern descent; Epiphanius of Constantia († 403), Theodorus of Mopsueste († 428), St. John of Damascus († 749), Moses Bar Cephas of Bethraman (ca. 900), Philostorgius of Cappadocia († 425), and Cosmas Indicopleustes (sixth cent.), who lived in Alexandria. Of the Western authors, apart from St. Augustine, he mentions Isidorus of Sevilla († 633/636), Beda Venerabilis († 735), Petrus Lombardus († 1160) (*Une histoire du paradis*. T.I: *Le jardin des délices*. [Paris: Fayard. 1992]; T.II: *Mille ans de bonheur* [Paris: Fayard. 1995] I: 28–30 and 60ff.).

[19] G.H.T. Kimble, *Geography in the Middle Ages* (London: Methuen. 1938) 184. Cf. 24–25, 31, 130, 184–185.

Departing from the twelfth century, tales appear of Alexander the Great's journey to paradise (*Iter ad paradisum*), but these are still accounts of a legendary past. In the thirteenth century, authors, like St. Bonaventura, Vincent of Beauvais and Joinville, and even an authority like Thomas of Aquino, begin to locate paradise somewhere very far away, e.g. below the equator, but not wholly unreachable in principle;[20] still, there are little traces that anyone has really ventured to actually reach the place.[21] Only from the end of the fourteenth century do authors report to have been close to paradise, or to know others who have. Authors like Kimble, Patch and Delumeau mention Johannes de Hese's *Itinerarium* (c. 1389), Giovanni Marignolli's *Cronica* (c. 1355), of course Mandeville, the *Polychronicon* of Ranulf Hygden († 1364), translated into English in 1385, Pierre d'Ailly's *Imago mundi* (1483), and Chistopher Columbus' firm belief that paradise can be found somewhere on earth.[22] But the sixteenth and seventeenth centuries "abandonnèrent progressivement la croyance en l'existence continueé du paradis terrestre".[23] The culmination of the belief that a real contact can be established between known geographical space and terrestrial paradise thus falls in the late fourteenth to sixteenth centuries. It is my conviction that although the active search for earthly paradise (however far away) presupposes the belief that paradise had or has a real earthly shape, these are actually quite distinct moods, just as the belief that at some unpredictable moment the world will cease to exist, all men will be judged and the New Jerusalem will come is distinct from the expectation that that moment is at hand. In the investigations that I have consulted this distinction is hardly made. To my mind, the sense of paradise being located somewhere within actual human reach is a form of the urge to realize the transcendental; in Western Europe, it should and can therefore be seen in the historical context of the widespread

---

[20] Delumeau I, 70–73.

[21] An exception is formed by the legendary voyages of Bran, son of Febal and of St. Brendan; the account of the British monks in the *Pantheon* of Gotofredo of Viterbo (XII century) may have been influenced by it (cf. H.R. Patch, *The Other World According to Descriptions in Medieval Literature.* (Cambridge, Mass.: Harvard University Press. 1950. Reprinted New York: Octagon Books. 1970) 159–160. For close parallels betwen passages of the St. Brendan voyage and Vasili Kalika's epistle see Veselovski 97–104.

[22] Delumeau I, 74–81. Cf. also Patch 165–174 for further examples.

[23] Delumeau I, 153.

eschatological mood of the fourteenth and fifteenth centuries, described by Norman Cohn.[24] Such moods are not documented in Russia until the end of the fifteenth century, and even then only for a relatively short time,[25] and the belief in the attainability of paradise cannot be explained by it. How then *can* it be explained?

Once again, I would argue that Orthodox theology creates a favourable atmosphere for such ideas. B.A. Uspenski stresses the importance of the Orthodox theology of the icon for an understanding of Vasili's position of merging the spiritual, the sacral, with the concrete and earthly: as far as dogma is concerned, the reverence of icons, that is, the idea that the image perceived by the senses is a direct reflection of the sacred person depicted, is the element that pre-eminently distinguishes the Orthodox from other Christian churches.[26] But the popularity of the works mentioned, and of Vasili's epistle as well, should also be explained by the fact that they reflected folk notions about the "other world", that is accessible for men. As N.I. Tolstoy writes: "Among all Slavs, first among them those of the South and the East, notions about the underworld from written (church) sources blend with folk notions."[27]

This can be demonstrated, first of all, by the fact that within both written and folk tradition, the idea of purgatory is absent.[28] In folk tradition, even hell and paradise are not always clearly distinguished. In fairy tales of the "wonder-tale" type, the "other world", which as a rule is visited by the main hero, is a general "reversed land", far

---

[24] *The Pursuit of the Millennium: Revolutionary Millenarians and Mystical Anarchists of the Middle Ages.* (Rev. and expanded ed. London: Temple Smiths. 1970); cf. Я.С. Лурье, Средневековый роман об Александре Македонском в русской литературе XV в., *Александрия. Роман об Александре Македонском по русской рукописи XV века.* (Изд. подг. М.Н. Ботвинник, Я.С. Лурье и О.В. Творогов. Москва-Ленинград. 1965) 155–157.

[25] It was connected with expectations of the end of the world in 1492, when the seventh era of thousand years would come to a close: according to medieval Russian chronography, the world was created in 5508 BC.

[26] "Древнерусское богословие: проблема чувственного и духовного опыта (представления о рае в середине XIV в.)," *Русистика. Славистика. Индоевропеистика: Сборник к 60—летию А.А.Зализняка* (Ред. коллегия А.А. Гиппиус, Т.М. Николаева (отв. ред.), В.Н. Топоров. Москва. 1996) 105–151.

[27] "Ад," *Славянская мифология* (Ред. В.Я. Петрухин и др. Москва 1995) 28. For the influence of Russian popular legends on Vasili Kalika's epistle, see A.D. Sedel'nikov, "Vasilij Kalika: L'histoire et la légende," *Revue des Etudes Slaves* VII, 1927, fasc. 3–4: 224–240.

[28] The importance of this point of difference from the (Catholic) West was already stressed by the nineteenth-century Slavophile Aleksey Khomyakov.

away, but accessible in principle.[29] In Russian spiritual verses, apocryphal tales and folk legends this land (ecqually accessible) acquires the traits of the land of the ancestors in general. In this "other world", hell and heaven, a region of punishment and a region of bliss and reward are often not clearly distinguished, a trait that clearly survived from pre-Christian times.[30] In fact, this may be regarded as one of the arguments in favour of the thesis that one of the typologically distinguishing traits of Russian folk culture—christianized in principle—was that it retained strong pagan elements (the phenomenon of "dvoeverie").[31]

Departing from the fifteenth century, the tendency to conceive of paradise as a region located somewhere on the earth may have influenced the notion that Muscovite Russia was the realization of the sacred "third Rome". This was the result of a complicated historical process, in which the fact that in 1453 Constantinople fell to the Turks and Russia remained as the only effective Orthodox empire played a major role, along with the beginning counteroffensive against the Islamic Tatars in the sixteenth century.[32] Here also, folk imagery, the notion of Russia as a sacred, "white" kingdom, blended with the "official" Byzantine heritage, "the doctrine that the ideal state is a theocracy, an empire guided by God."[33] In the seventeenth century, as a result of the renewed orientation of Muscovite culture toward Greek examples, to this process was added a strong tendency to

[29] See Е.Н. Елеонская, "Представление 'того света' в сказочной традиции," idem: *Сказка, заговор и колдовство в России. Сборник трудов* (Сост. и вступ. статья Л.Н. Виноградовой. Москва. 1994) 42–50 (first published in 1913);.

[30] See А.Н. Соболев, *Загробный мир по древнерусским представлениям* (Сергиев Посад. 1913); Успенский, *Разыскания* 144–149. Cf. this last publications for the notions of the "iriy/vyriy" (ирий/вырий), the land where birds as well as snakes were supposed to hybernate, and that consequently was located in the heavens and under the ground simultaneously.

[31] We may note that in Russian Church Slavonic texts, the words "poroda" (порода), litt. "race, sort, clan" and "rod" (род), "ancestors, clan" may denote resp. "paradise" and "underworld". The first word may be explained as a distorted loanword from Greek "παράδεισος", based on phonetic coincidence. The second is generally treated as a mistranslation from Greek γέεννα, "hell", that was mixed up with γέννα, γενεά, γέννησις, "birth", but Uspenski sees reasons to connect it to the identification in folk culture of the other world as a whole with the world of the ancestors (Успенский, *Разыскания* 147).

[32] For an introduction see A.V. Soloviev, *Holy Russia. The History of a Religious-Social Idea.* ('s-Gravenhage: Mouton. 1959. Musagetes 12).

[33] Baehr 16.

sacralize the tsar, a tendency that continued into the eighteenth century, and that helped contribute to the shaping of the Russian empire as the earthly paradise in this period (see Baehr, *passim*).[34]

On the other hand, there were those who did not want to accept the conformation to Greek examples and the massive correction of liturgical texts and details of ceremony that resulted from it. For these Old Believers, who in the nineteenth century numbered perhaps even up to 30% of the total Christian population in the Russian empire, Russia had betrayed its holy mission and had therefore turned into the empire of the Antichrist. It should be stressed that their fierce reaction to the reforms of the seventeenth century can only be explained if we take into account their conviction that the Russian empire was the realization of the eschatological Last empire.[35] Just because he was unworthy of his holy function, the tsar for them had become the Antichrist himself. As a consequence, during the seventeenth to nineteenth century, there appeared of veritable flood of self-proclaimed real sacred emperors and eschatological saviour-kings.[36] In the same period, the belief that somewhere on earth a traditional, pre-reform bishop was still living, in an edemic land where the true believer could safely wait for Judgment Day, acquired epidemic proportions. Great masses of Old Believers and others fled to the periphery of the empire and over its borders in search for this land. Legends of blessed regions abound in this period.[37] Even towards the very end of the nineteenth century, a group of Ural Old Believers set out to search this land, a journey that led them via Constantinople, India, Vietnam and Japan to the Bering Street.

[34] See B.A. Uspenskij, V.M. Živov, "Zar und Gott. Semiotische Aspekte der Sakralisierung des Monarchen in Russland," B.A. Uspenskij, *Semiotik der Geschichte*. (Wien: Verlag der Österreichischen Akademie der Wissenschaften. Philosophisch-Historische Klasse, Sitzungsberichte 579) 131–266.

[35] "the Schism itself had its roots in the widespread fear that [patriarch—SB] Nikon's reforms would somehow damage the purity of Orthodoxy, and thus render Russia unworthy of her Messianic task" (T. Szamuely, *The Russian Tradition*. (Ed. and with an Introduction by Robert Conquest. London: Secker and Warburg. 1974) 68–69).

[36] К.В. Чистов, *Русские народные социально-утопические легенды XVII–XIX вв.* (Москва. 1967) 24–236.

[37] E.g., those on Dauriya, the Silver Mountain, the Land of the Beard People, the River Darya, the Samara government, the town of Anapa, the "New Islands", the Nut-land etc. Most famous was the legendary land of Belovodye. See Чистов 237–326.

Thus we see that in some form or another, the belief in earthly paradise remained a factor of importance in Russian culture even in late stages of its development.[38]

Appendix

Archbishop Vasili of Novgorod's epistle to bishop Fyodor of Tver[39]

Vasili, by the grace of God archbishop of Novgorod, to the holy bishop Fyodor of Tver, his brother in the Lord: may the mercy and peace of God our Father Almighty be with your holiness, and with all the holy council, the abbots and the priests, and with your [spiritual] children.

Since our humble self and the holy council, the abbots and the priests, learnt that a dispute over venerable paradise has risen in Tver among you, the people of God, through the instigation and the counsel of the devil and of slick people—for that is what we heard—I have spent many days trying to penetrate the truth of God's laws. That which I have found I now write to you, because, brother, according to God's command we should write epistles to each other on the truth that we have gathered from the divine writings of the holy apostles and the great church teachers, just as the holy apostles themselves incessantly wrote epistles to each other; and this is appropriate for us as well for we have been appointed in their place. He who is called to a thing, let him abide by it.

I have heard, brother, that you say: "Paradise, in which Adam lived, has perished."[40]

---

[38] Of course, there have been speculations on the possible influence of this notion on Russian communism. Berdyayev held the opinion, that the eschatological urge to step out of secular history had spread from the Old Believers to the late nineteenth-century intelligentsia. For a detailed discussion of this problem see E. Sarkisyanz, *Rußland und der Messianismus des Orients*. Sendungsbewusstsein und politischer Chiliasmus des Ostens. (Tübingen 1955) 72–95.

[39] "Послание архиепископа новгородского Василия к владыке тверскому Феодору о рае," *Памятники литературы Древней Руси. XIV—середина XV века.* (Сост. и одщая ред. Д.А. Дмитриева, Д.С. Лихачева. Москва. 1984) 42–49. Translated by Sander Brouwer (with special thanks to Christine Crouwel).

[40] We do not know what exactly bishop Fyodor's position was; it may only be reconstructed from archbishop Vasili's letter. A.D. Sedel'nikov has suggested that the discussion may have been influenced by the contemporary palamite-barlaamite

But we, brother, have not heard of such a loss, nor did we find anything on it in those places of the Scripture that speak of that sacred paradise, but we all know from the Holy Scripture that God planted paradise in the East, in Eden, and He has led man into it, and commanded him, saying: "If you obey my word, you will live, but if you break it, you will pass away into death and enter into the ground from which you were taken." And he broke God's command, and was driven out of paradise, and he wept bitterly, exclaiming: "O sacred paradise, you that have been planted for my sake and locked because of Eve! Beseech your maker and my creator that I may one day enjoy the delight of your flowering again!" And therefore the Saviour said to him: "I do not want to do away with my creation, but I want to save it and lead it into true knowledge", and He promised him that he would once more enter into paradise.

And in the "Paremii"[41] four rivers are mentioned that flow from paradise: the Tigris, the Nile, the Thison and the Euphrates; the Nile is located in the region of Egypt, aloe trees are found floating in it,[42] and it springs from high mountains that reach from the earth into the sky, and that place is inaccessible to men, and on its top live the rakhmans.[43]

And you see, brother, that in the *Prologue* it is witnessed to all in the miracles of the holy archangel Michael, that he took Enoch the Righteous and brought him to venerable paradise.[44] And see, saint

controversy over hesychasm: whereas bishop Fyodor's position represents a simplified palamite view on "spritual paradise", archbishop Vasili's reflects Gregorius Sinaites' earlier insistence that paradise is "real" (perceptible to the senses), as well (А.Д. Седельников, "Мотив о рае в русском средневековом прении," *Byzantinoslavica* VII, 1937–1938, 164–173).

[41] That is, in the *Paremejnik*, a collection of readings from the OT, arranged according to their use in the Liturgy. Approximately one third of it consisted of passages from the Book of Proverbs, whence its name (from Greek "paroimia").

[42] The aloe trees from paradise floating in the Nile are mentioned by Joinville in his *History of Saint Louis* (Patch 161).

[43] For the location of earthly paradise on the top of high mountains in Western medieval literature cf. Patch *index*. The combination of the Ptolemaic Mountains of the Moon as the source of the Nile with the location of terrestrial paradise was made at approximately the same time (c. 1350) by an anonymous Spanish Franciscan in his *Libro del conoscimento de todos los regnos y tierras* (cf. Kimble 109–110). For the rakhmans see above (article) and cf. В.К. Шохин, "Страна рахманов: миф и реальность," idem, *Древняя Индия в культуре Руси* XI—середина XV в. (Москва. 1988) 225–253.

[44] The *Prologue* is a collection of short saints' lives and other works, arranged according to the calendar. The story of archangel Michael and Enoch the Wise is found under November 8.

Elijah lives in paradise, too; he was found there by saint Agapi, who received a morsel of bread from him. And saint Macarius lived twenty day's journey from holy paradise. And saint Yefrosim visited paradise, and he took back three apples from there, which he gave to his abbot Vasili, and many people were cured by them.[45]

And now, brother, you think that paradise is only spiritual, and everything spiritual is manifested only as a vision. But what Christ says on the second coming in the Gospel, do you hold that for only spiritual, as well? To those who stand to his right, He will say: "Come, you who are blessed by my Father, and inherit the kingdom that has been prepared for you before the earth was made." And to those who stand to his left, He will say: "Depart from me, you cursed ones, into the eternal fire that has been prepared for the devil and his servants." "It is not for you, He said, that I have prepared these torments, but for the devil and his servants."

Concerning these two places, John Chrysostom wrote: "God has planted paradise in the East, but in the West He has prepared the torments, just as inside the emperor's palace there is rejoicing and mirth, and outside it is the dungeon."

And this is what saint Patricius the martyr says: "God has prepared two places: the one is filled with things salutary, the other with darkness and fire."[46]

Furthermore, brother, God has not given to men to behold holy paradise, but [the place of] torments is to this day located in the West. Many of my spiritual children from Novgorod have seen it on the Blowing Sea (the White Sea and the Arctic Ocean—SB): an ever-watchful serpent, and gnashing of teeth, and a seething river called Morg, and the waters enter the underworld there and return from it three times a day.[47] And if these places of suffering have not

---

[45] The works in which these episodes are described are mentioned above (article).

[46] Probably Patricius, bishop of Prussa (Bithynia), martyred about the year 100. It is not likely that this is a reference to St. Patrick of Ireland, and that archbishop Vasili thus might have heard of "Patrick's Purgatory"; this saint became known in Russia only later, and I have not been able to find words that resemble the quotation in his writings.

[47] All these elements—the serpent, the seething river, waters entering the underground—are also familiar from western texts: cf. Patch *index*. In other manuscripts instead of a "seething" (молненая) river we find a "fiery" (смоляная, огненная) river. The presumption of the commentators of Vasili's letter (in the edition mentioned in note 39) that the motif of a warm river in the sea might somehow reflect a medieval explanation of the Gulfstream I find absurd.

perished, how then can that sacred place have perished, pray tell me, brother, in which the most pure Mother of God resides, and a multitude of saints, who after the resurrection of the Lord appeared to many in Jerusalem and re-entered paradise? And indeed they were told: "The fiery sword does no longer guard the gates of Eden;" for when my Saviour came, he exclaimed to the faithful: "Come and re-enter paradise."

And this, brother, is what it says in the Beatitudes:[48] "Through the tree's fruit the enemy led Adam out of paradise, but Christ led the robber into it through the cross."

And when the passing away of our Lady the Mother of God was drawing nigh, an angel brought some flowering branches of the date tree from paradise, thus indicating where she was to go. But if paradise is spiritual, then why did the angel bring this visible, not spiritual, branch? The apostles saw it, and a multitude of non-believing Jews saw this branch.

Not one single work of God is transitory, but all God's works are everlasting, I am witness to that, brother. When Christ was on his way to the suffering that He took upon himself voluntarily, He closed the town gates with his own hands—and to this day they stand closed. And when Christ fasted by the river Jordan—I saw his hermitage with my own eyes—He planted a hundred date trees; they are intact to the present: they did not perish, nor rot.[49]

Or do you perchance think like this, brother: if God planted paradise in the East, then why was Adam's body found in Jerusalem?[50] But surely you know, brother, the service of angels, how fast they carry things out; they serve God without words being spoken, in the twinkling of an eye they speed across the earth and scour the skies. Indeed, God is able with a single word to move Adam's body from paradise to Jerusalem; and He ordered the cherub to guard the gates of Eden, and after He had risen He ordered Adam to enter paradise,

---

[48] Archbishop Vasili here probably refers to the text of a troparion sung after the Beatitudes in the liturgy of Good Friday.

[49] Vasili had himself been in Jerusalem on a pilgrimage (therefore he can say that "he is witness"), most likely before he became an archbishop. His love of legends is testimonied by the "places of interest" that he mentions there: the town gates, forever closed by Christ on his way to Calvary hill, the date trees that He planted, and (presumably) a place where He fasted.

[50] According to legend, Adam's skull was buried in Golgotha.

and a multitude of saints with him. His word becomes deed in a moment.

And the location of holy paradise was found by Moislav from Novgorod and his son Iakov; they were all sailing in three boats, and one of them perished after it had lost its way and drifted about a long time, and the other two were carried criss-cross over the sea by the wind for a long time thereafter, until they were brought to high mountains.[51] And they saw that on these mountains the Deisus[52] was painted with marvellous azure and lavishly adorned, as if created not by human hands but by God's blessing. And there was a light in that place that shone of its own accord, so that it is impossible to describe in human words.

And they stayed long in this place, and they did not see the sun, but there was a light of manifold splendour, and it shone brighter than the sun. And from the mountains they heard triumphal singing, filled with joy. And they had one of their company climb up the mountain with a climbing-pole, in order to see where that light and those triumphal voices came from; and it so happened, that when he reached the top of the mountain, he immediately started to clap his hands and laugh, and he ran away from his friends, to where the voices came from. They were completely amazed by this and they sent up another man, giving him strict instructions to return and tell them about what was on the mountain. But he acted likewise; not only did he fail to return but he ran away from them with great joy. They became filled with fear, and started to ponder on the matter, saying to themselves: "Even if death should ensue, we would still like to know more about the shining light in this place." And they sent up a third man, having tied a rope to his foot. And this man wanted to act likewise: he cheerfully clapped his hands and started to run, but in his joy forgot about the rope on his foot. They pulled him down with the rope, but found that he had died. Then they hurried away from there: it was not given to them to behold that place any further, neither that inexpressible luminescence, nor to hear the joy and the triumph there. And to the present day,

[51] Herberstein in his memoir of the voyage to Muscovy (XVI century) mentions that in medieval Norway, the entrance to purgatory was located on the Shemekhan mountains in Lapland.

[52] An icon composition of Christ with the Virgin Mary and John the Baptist.

brother, the children and grandchildren of these seafarers are alive and well.

And if you say, brother, that "paradise is spiritual", let it be so, brother, the spiritual paradise exists, and will exist. But the paradise that has been planted has not perished either; it exists today. There is a light in it that shines of itself, but its grounds are inaccessible, one can only reach [the foot of] the mountains of paradise.

But spiritual paradise, brother, will be when all earth is renewed by fire, as the apostle says: "We await a new heaven and a new earth, when the true light—Christ—will descend upon earth."

Just think, brother, how bright in the book of Genesis the light is described that is enclosed by the mainland, but still more miraculous and bright is the true light of Christ, and with Him the nine bright orders that serve Him: the first order—the angels, the second—the archangels, the third—the origins, the fourth—the powers, the fifth—the forces, the sixth—the thrones, the seventh—the reigns, the eighth—the many-eyed cherubim, the ninth—the six-winged seraphim.[53] When our Lord appears on earth in the shining of His Godhead and the heavenly powers advance, the angels will cease their work and reveal their radiance, which is created by God; that then, brother, will be the spiritual heaven, when the whole earth is enlightened by the unspeakable light, and is filled with joy and pleasure, as the apostle Paul says, when he was exalted to the third heaven: "The eye has not seen, and the ear has not heard, and hearts of men have not experienced what God has prepared for those who love Him."

Of this spiritual paradise Christ said: "There are some among those who stand here, who will not know death before they have seen the kingdom of God which has come in all its might." And they who have seen the kingdom of God, brother, are these: Moses and Elijah, Peter, Jacob and John on Mount Tabor;[54] and when his disciples saw it, they prostrated themselves, for they could not behold the brightness of his Godhead.

---

[53] These are the nine heavenly spheres that are discerned by Pseudo-Dionysius in his work "On the heavenly Hierarchy". The works of Pseudo-Dionysius were well-known in medieval Russia. Cf. Г.М. Прохоров, *Памятники переводной и русской литературы XIV–XV веков* (Ленинград. 1987) 5–59.

[54] Archbishop Vasili's mentioning of the Tabor light is a strong argument in favour of Sedel'nikov's thesis about the influence of the hesychast controversy on his letter (cf. note 40).

Even to saints, brother, it is impossible to see spiritual paradise when they are in the flesh, and therefore, when these saints saw it, they were no longer able to stand and prostrated themselves.

And you too, brother Fyodor, do not doubt these words: the paradise in the East which was created for Adam has not perished. Do believe in these words, brother, and teach the whole holy council thus, and strengthen it with these wise considerations, as I pointed out to you from divine Scripture in this epistle.

Peace and love be with you in the name of God Almighty, our Lord Jesus Christ, praise be to Him for all ages. Amen.

MILTON AND GENESIS: INTERPRETATION AS PERSUASION

Helen Wilcox

Paradise is all around us. This is not so much a theological statement as an observation on a contemporary preoccupation of literature in English. Toni Morrison's most recent novel is simply entitled *Paradise*, and in Ted Hughes's newly published sequence of poems, *Birthday Letters* (written to his late wife, Sylvia Plath), we find the poignant comment, "You were never/More than a step from Paradise".[1] That one step, however, is enormously difficult to take, as the Groningen poet Maria van Daalen points out in her "Serpent Sonnet": "the entrance to Paradise and truth/is lost in winding lines".[2] My concern in this essay is to consider some of the "winding lines" through which the seventeenth-century English poet John Milton tried to rediscover that "entrance to Paradise and truth". The search for truth is in some sense always a quest for paradise, that stable reference-point of meaning and understanding. As the critic Northrop Frye mused in his study of Milton, "every act of the free intelligence, including the poetic intelligence, is an attempt to return to Eden, a world in the human form of a garden, where we may wander as we please but cannot lose our way".[3] The very act of interpretation, then, with which this volume is concerned, might be seen as a paradise-wish in itself.

This essay takes as its focus the reinterpretation of the Genesis account of Eden in Book IV of Milton's epic poem *Paradise Lost* (1667). The text in question thus differs in two crucial respects from most of the others considered in the preceding chapters: it is written in epic verse form—and is therefore a product of the literary imagination as well as reason and devotion—and it dates from after the Reformation. As a learned humanist, Milton knew the Bible in the original languages and was fully aware of the commentaries and

---

[1] Ted Hughes, "Child's Park", *Birthday Letters*, London 1998, 69.

[2] Maria van Daalen, sonnet 9, "The Serpent Sonnet", from *Thirteen Sonnets for a Lost Lover* AGNI (Boston Univ.) 48 (1998), 42, by kind permission of the author.

[3] Northrop Frye, *The Return of Eden: Five Essays on Milton's Epics*, Toronto 1965, 31.

debates around Genesis, but as a radical protestant he was also profoundly influenced by the range of recent English biblical translations, including the Authorised Version (1611).[4] The choice of his title, however, represented an act of interpretation in itself, for the word "paradise" only occurs three times in the Authorised Version, all of which are in the New Testament; his sense of Eden was, it is evident, strongly influenced by the promise of redemption. The second term in the title also alerts us to the context of Milton's interpretation; he was writing after the failure of the English Revolution (1642–1660) and the loss of all his hopes for a puritan commonwealth. Even as he was depicting what he named the "garden of bliss", he was sadly conscious that by the end of the poem Eden, just like the English republic, would be a thing of the past—"so late their happy seat".[5]

When Milton wrote his great epic, he was a political exile within his own land; at the restoration of the monarchy in 1660 he had only escaped execution because he was by then both old and blind. So when the poet asks near the opening of his poem, "what in me is dark/Illumine" (I 22–23), he is praying for inspired vision in a world of physical as well as spiritual darkness. To express the scriptural account of Eden in new (and inevitably fallen) English poetic words was a task of great daring—something "unattempted yet in prose or rhyme" (I 16). Milton therefore sought the authority of divine inspiration for his interpretation, asking for "celestial light" to "shine inward" (III 51–52) and asserting his confidence in the "Comforter" to guide him "in all truth" (XII 490). For, in presenting his epic interpretation of paradise, the poet was taking upon himself a demanding vocation; he was responding to no less a challenge than to "assert eternal providence,/And justify the ways of God to men" (I 25–26).

---

[4] For a lively account of seventeenth-century English Calvinist uses of the Bible, see John R. Knott Jr., *The Sword of the Spirit: Puritan Responses to the Bible*, Chicago 1980.

[5] John Milton, *Paradise Lost*, Ed. Alastair Fowler, London 1968, VIII 299, XII 642; all further references to *Paradise Lost* will be to this edition. For further discussion of the sense of loss and finality in Milton's poem, see Helen Wilcox, "'Is this the end of this new glorious world?': *Paradise Lost* and the Beginning of the End", in: Laurel Brake (Ed.), *Essays and Studies 1995: The Endings of Epochs*, Cambridge 1995, 1–15.

Milton's Paradise

How did Milton bring the Garden of Eden to life in his poem? In this short study I will draw attention to some of the most significant among Milton's interpretative and creative strategies, the first of which is that he shows us paradise from the perspective of imperfection—that is, through Satan's eyes. This is very appropriate, since we, as post-lapsarian readers, inevitably approach perfection with a similarly envious, or sceptical, attitude. Our first impression of Eden in Book IV of *Paradise Lost* is gained from a lengthy description of what Satan sees on reaching the garden. He has climbed over the garden wall in the same way as "a prowling wolf" would enter a sheep-pen (IV 183) and looks down from the tree of life in which he is perching "like a cormorant" (IV 196):[6]

> Beneath him with new wonder now he views
> To all delight of human sense exposed
> In narrow room nature's whole wealth, yea more,
> A heaven on earth, for blissful Paradise
> Of God the garden was, by him in the east
> Of Eden planted; Eden stretched her line
> From Auran eastward to the royal towers
> Of great Seleucia, built by Grecian kings,
> Of where the sons of Eden long before
> Dwelt in Telassar; in this pleasant soil
> His far more pleasant garden God ordained;
> Out of the fertile ground he caused to grow
> All trees of noblest kind for sight, smell, taste;
> And all amid them stood the tree of life,
> High eminent, blooming ambrosial fruit
> Of vegetable gold; and next to life
> Our death the tree of knowledge grew fast by,
> Knowledge of good bought dear by knowing ill.
>
> (IV 205–222)

Even Satan is struck with "wonder" as he contemplates the paradise which God has created. Building on the Genesis account of the garden's location ("east of Eden", Gen 2:8) and its many trees ("All trees of noblest kind', as in Gen 2:9), Milton attempts to suggest, from Satan's perspective, the many apparent contradictions of Eden.

[6] There is an interesting contrast to be made here between the *Vision Pauli*, in which the Spirit is said to have rested on the tree of life, and Milton's darker vision of the devil usurping that place; see Ton Hilhorst's essay in this collection.

Not only is it "heaven on earth"—the fundamental paradox of perfection—but it is also a small emblem of great plenty: "In narrow room nature's whole wealth". The most intense combination of opposites in this contained yet unlimited paradise is the fruit of "vegetable gold", a startling phrase which simultaneously suggests organic life and precious mineral, the changing and the unchangeable. In Milton's language the garden is also always "delicious" (X 746), as the sensuality of his description here makes clear. The trees are splendid "for sight, smell, taste", appealing to several senses at once; the fruit of the tree of life is "ambrosial", meaning sweet smelling as well as the food of the gods. Remembering that Satan has so recently fallen from the joys of heaven and is exiled from such "ambrosial" pleasures, Milton's language in this first account of Eden is particularly intense and burdened with longing. As the poet Arthur Lindley has recently written in a witty lyric on paradise, this freshly-created world "was good/enough to eat".[7]

Milton's interpretation of Genesis, perhaps surprisingly, places considerable emphasis on the variety and movement to be discerned within paradise. This is no neat or fixed garden, but a place of activity and adventure:

> Southward through Eden went a river large,
> Nor changed his course, but through the shaggy hill
> Passed underneath ingulfed, for God had thrown
> That mountain as his garden mould high raised
> Upon the rapid current, which through veins
> Of porous earth with kindly thirst up drawn,
> Rose a fresh fountain, and with many a rill
> Watered the garden; . . .
> . . . from that sapphire fount the crisped brooks,
> Rolling on orient pearl and sands of gold,
> With mazy error under pendant shades
> Ran nectar, visiting each plant, and fed
> Flowers worthy of Paradise which not nice art
> In beds and curious knots, but nature boon
> Poured forth profuse on hill and dale and plain,
> Both where the morning sun first warmly smote
> The open field, and where the unpierced shade
> Embrowned the noontide bowers: thus was this place,
> A happy rural seat of various view;
>
> (IV 223–230, 237–247)

[7] Arthur Lindley, "As Good as a Feast" (see the full text on p. v of this book).

Again taking Genesis as his starting point ("And a river went out of Eden to water the garden"—Gen 2:10), Milton brings alive the plain biblical statement with his energetic description of the river's movement, as suggested in vocabulary such as "ingulfed", "rapid" and "fountain". The setting for this fast-flowing "current" is dramatic and sublime, especially the unusually-termed "shaggy hill"; the phrase gives the landscape almost animal qualities, as do the subsequent metaphors of "veins" and "thirst". The sense of flux and anthropomorphic motion in this passage is encapsulated in the words "mazy error", which together suggest the complexity of a maze and the meanderings of the stream. Only after the fall, Milton implies, did the word "error" take on overtones of sin; in the perfect freedom of paradise, to err was simply to wander in (punning) "amazement" and delight. We are reminded of Northrop Frye's comment, cited earlier, that Eden is "a world . . . where we may wander as we please but cannot lose our way".

One of Milton's most fundamental political and theological principles was the freedom of the rational human being.[8] Typically, therefore, his ideal garden as depicted in the later part of the passage quoted above is not an Elizabethan "knot" garden with its formal flowerbeds and almost artificially precise ("nice") control of nature; instead he favours profusion and envisages an Eden full of contrast, a place of "various view". Within the space of a few lines he alerts us to the presence of "orient pearl" and "flowers worthy of Paradise", to "hill" and "dale", "field" and "bower", and to the warmth of "morning sun" and the cool "shade" of noon. The eighteenth-century critic Joseph Addison noted this phenomenon of variety in Milton's view of paradise, commenting in 1712 that the reader's eye can "lose itself amidst the Variety of Objects that offer themselves to Observation". He rightly pointed out that in Milton's Eden "the Scene is perpetually shifting" and we are confronted with "the sight of such Objects as are ever in Motion and sliding away from beneath the Eye of the Beholder".[9] Addison's striking account of Milton's paradise, vividly reporting how the poetic scene shifts and slides away as we try to take it in, draws attention to a vital element in Milton's

---

[8] This principle is most famously and eloquently expressed in his 1644 prose pamphlet, *Areopagitica*.

[9] Joseph Addison, *The Spectator*, ed. Donald F. Bond, Oxford 1965, III 541–2.

interpretation of the Genesis account—his sense that the fullness of perfection is so infinitely varied that it is beyond our grasp.

If Paradise is ungraspable—beyond the capacity of our imagination to comprehend—then the poet faces an impossible task in attempting to describe it adequately in human language. One of Milton's most inventive strategies for dealing with this problem was to hint at the bliss of Eden by a process of negative comparison. Eden can be likened to other beautiful or luscious gardens by means of similes, but the comparisons will always fall short of that which they are helping to describe:

> Not that fair field
> Of Enna, where Proserpine gathering flowers
> Her self a fairer flower by gloomy Dis
> Was gathered, which cost Ceres all that pain
> To seek her through the world; nor that sweet grove
> Of Daphne by Orontes, and the inspired
> Castalian spring, might with this Paradise
> Of Eden strive;
>
> (IV 268–275)

Milton here recalls two of the most beautiful settings from the classical tradition—the "fair field" of Enna, and the oracle's "sweet grove" by the river Oronte—but the passage is prefaced by the word "Not" and the reader is never in any doubt over the unparalleled quality of Eden itself. The negative similes serve other purposes, too, as is so often the case with Milton's descriptive poetry. The snatching away of Proserpine by the god of the underworld and her ultimate rescue by Ceres, for example, is an allegorical anticipation of the temptation of Eve by Satan and the subsequent "pain" which will be suffered by Christ in order to redeem her. Milton's interpretation of paradise is set here in the context of what is to come, just as it was (implicitly) in the other two passages quoted so far. The reference to Telassar in the first extract (IV 214) anticipated a nation which would stand (and be destroyed) on the site of Eden in generations to come (2 Kgs 19:12); the "mazy error" of the river in the second passage (IV 239) inevitably awakened expectations of Eve's fatal error in wandering into disobedience. Milton presents an account of Eden which is rendered all the more powerful by its use of the contrasting perspectives of sin, myth, history and experience.

Meanwhile back in paradise, one of the key factors in Milton's interpretation of Genesis was his particularly protestant emphasis on work as part of the life of Adam and Eve before the fall. Milton's God says to Adam,

> This Paradise I give thee, count it thine
> To till and keep, and of the fruit to eat:
>
> (VIII 320–321)

This was a conscious interpretative decision by Milton, since the Authorised Version of the Bible only uses the word "till" to describe the labour demanded of Adam *after* the fall: "the Lord God sent him forth from the Garden of Eden, to till the ground from whence he was taken" (Gen 3:23). But in Milton's view, work was not a punishment but a pleasure; as Adam explains to Eve at the end of their idyllic day in Eden,

> other creatures all day long
> Rove idle unemployed, and less need rest;
> Man hath his daily work of body or mind
> Appointed, which declares his dignity,
> And the regard of heaven on all his ways;
> While other animals unactive range,
> And of their doings God takes no account.
> To morrow ere fresh morning streak the east
> With first approach of light, we must be risen,
> And at our pleasant labour . . .
>
> (IV 616–625)

There is no uncertainty here about how Adam and Eve are to spend their time in paradise, nor of the appropriateness of work in a place of perfection. Work is what sets humans apart from the "other creatures" and gives us our "dignity"; in God's "pleasant garden" (IV 215) it follows that the "labour", too, will be "pleasant". Working in the garden, furthermore, ensures closeness to God, since to be busy with "daily work of body or mind" is to be in the "regard of heaven", and supplies a pattern to their existence. Alongside the glorious "wanton growth" (IV 629) and almost overwhelming fecundity of nature in Eden—which Adam and Eve have to "reform" (IV 625)—there is a compensatory sense of order as they "rest" at night after working, and rise with the "first approach of light" to resume the dignity of labour.

However, in Milton's vision of paradise Adam and Eve did not go to bed simply in order to sleep, but also to enjoy "wedded love" (IV 750). Unlike the church fathers and so many other commentators on Genesis, Milton was among those interpreters who stressed that sexual intercourse was enjoyed before the fall. His description of Adam and Eve going hand in hand to their "bower" is the celebratory climax of his account of paradise:

> into their inmost bower
> Handed they went; and eased the putting off
> These troublesome disguises which we wear,
> Straight side by side were laid, nor turned I ween
> Adam from his fair spouse, nor Eve the rites
> Mysterious of connubial love refused:
> Whatever hypocrites austerely talk
> Of purity and place and innocence,
> Defaming as impure what God declares
> Pure, and commands to some, leaves free to all.
> Our maker bids increase, who bids abstain
> But our destroyer, foe to God and man?
> Hail wedded love, mysterious law, true source
> Of human offspring, sole propriety
> In Paradise of all things common else.
>
> (IV 738–752)

Milton is fiercely critical here of those "hypocrites" who presume to think that sexual love and its attendant pleasures should be associated with a fallen rather than an innocent world, and who thereby defame "as impure what God declares/Pure". Instead he honours the "rites/Mysterious of connubial love" and presents a scene of sensual innocence—no doubt another of the perceived paradoxes of paradise—implied in the comment in Genesis that "they were both naked, the man and his wife, and were not ashamed" (Gen 2:25). Once again, Milton hints at perfection by means of contrast, here in the very practical detail that Adam and Eve did not suffer the nuisance of the removal of clothes, those "troublesome disguises which we wear". And although there is a slight difference between the roles of man and wife, in that Adam turns to Eve whereas she does not "refuse" him, the parallels in the grammar of the passage suggest a partnership of some equality: "nor turned . . . Adam", "nor Eve . . . refused".[10] The passage concludes its account of unfallen physical

[10] For fuller discussions of the issues of gender and (in)equality in *Paradise Lost*, see Diane K. McColley, *Milton's Eve*, Urbana 1983, and Helen Wilcox, "'He for God only, she for God in him': Feminist Readings of *Paradise Lost*", in: Manuel Barbeito (Ed.), *Paradise Lost: The Word, the words, the world*, Santiago de Compostela 1991, 67–84.

delight some twenty lines later with an address to the "blest pair" who "lulled by nightingales embracing slept", while roses "showered" upon their "naked limbs" (IV 771–773). Milton again elaborates the sensual completeness of paradise, where the birds provide music and the roses not only have a sweet scent but are gentle to the touch—for before the fall they were "without thorn" (IV 256). Sexual fulfilment and natural beauty are shown to combine without shame; this is the "bliss" (VIII 299) of Eden.

Although my focus in this essay has been on Milton's reworking of Genesis in the depiction of paradise before the fall, it is important to our understanding of Milton's position to ask one follow-up question: what happens to paradise when it is lost? The answer is supplied by the angel Michael in the closing section of the final book of *Paradise Lost*, as he foretells the future, including the redemption of the world by Christ, and tells Adam that, once he has left the garden, he must learn to love and trust God:

> This having learned, thou hast attained the sum
> Of wisdom; hope no higher, though all the stars
> Thou knew'st by name, and all the ethereal powers,
> All secrets of the deep, all nature's works,
> Or works of God in heaven, air, earth, or sea,
> And all the riches of this world enjoyed'st,
> And all the rule, one empire; only add
> Deeds to thy knowledge answerable, add faith,
> Add virtue, patience, temperance, add love,
> By name to come called Charity, the soul
> Of all the rest: then wilt thou not be loath
> To leave this Paradise, but shalt possess
> A paradise within thee, happier far.
>
> (XII 575–587)

Michael makes it clear to Adam that knowledge—which is itself a process of interpreting the "secrets" of the heights and depths of life itself—is insufficient on its own for a regaining of paradise. To it must be added "deeds" which are "answerable" to the knowledge he has gained, and virtues which guide those actions.[11] Then the loss of paradise will not only become bearable, but will be made good by the discovery of an even happier "paradise within". Milton's

[11] For a detailed discussion of Milton's view of the two "books" of nature and scripture, see John Reichert, *Milton's Wisdom: Nature and Scripture in "Paradise Lost"*, Ann Arbor 1992.

sense of paradise, then, is not fixed in the Old Testament context; nor is it firmly eschatalogical, as the Authorised Version would suggest, the best-known use of the term in the English Bible being Christ's words to the penitent thief on the cross, "Today shalt thou be with me in paradise" (Luke 23:43). For Milton the enduring paradise, which saves *Paradise Lost* from the tragedy implied by its title, is "within", being the eternal soul as redeemed by the second Adam (1 Cor 15).

Interpretation as persuasion

Paradise Lost is a rhetorical and pedagogical poem, attempting to persuade its readers to accept "eternal providence" and to understand "the ways of God" in the creation, loss and restoration of paradise. The chief function, then, of Milton's interpretation of the Genesis account of Eden is persuasive. All Milton's interpretative strategies—the descriptive rhetoric, the cross-reference to later biblical passages and, above all, the additions and emphases which transform a short biblical text into an epic poem of twelve books—were designed to convince the reader of God's righteousness.

With respect to his poetic reconstruction of the Garden of Eden itself, what was Milton persuading us to believe? The passages that we have read go out of their way to assert not only that paradise is good but that it is very much alive. Milton did not depict a static notion of perfection; on the contrary, his garden of Eden is growing, organic and sensual, a place of activity in terms of both work and sexual pleasure. He also conveys an impression of the potential of paradise, not only by minimising any ideas of restraint or containment, but also by emphasising the infinite variety to be found in Eden. This is further underlined, as we have seen, by Milton's expansive epic style and the fullness of his lavish descriptions of the garden. By contrast, the moment of the fall itself is narrated in blunt simplicity: "her rash hand in evil hour/Forth reaching to the fruit, she plucked, she ate" (IX 780–781).

Another persuasive feature of Milton's style, as we have noted, is his use of framing devices in the depiction of paradise. We look on as Satan "saw undelighted all delight" (IV 286), the near repetition in this phrase highlighting Milton's deliberate use of contrasts. We perceive beauty and innocence through their opposites, just as the perfection of paradise is always intensified by anticipatory hints of its imminent loss. Parallels are also drawn as frames for our understanding; Eden is compared with many other wonderful gardens and vales, but always outstrips them (and our imaginative capacities) in its variety and potential. However, one very important weapon in Milton's persuasive armoury is the belief that paradise can be recreated, both through love—Adam and Eve are memorably described as "imparadised in one another's arms" (IV 505)—and through faith which leads to the "paradise within" (XII 587).

Milton's interpretation of Genesis in his epic poem *Paradise Lost* resulted in a powerfully persuasive text whose impact across the centuries has been enormous. Individual readers have been drawn in by its rhetoric to a vicarious experience of the glories of the earthly paradise and a realisation that they, too, like Eve, would have fallen and lost that realm of perfection.[12] Further, the poem has led to many debates and reinterpretations of Genesis in readers' lives, in subsequent literary texts, critical or polemical works, and—most noticeably—in the visual arts.[13] This continuing interpretation is, in itself, a sign of the effectiveness of Milton's persuasion, for the poem above all puts the case for interpretation as the believer's active responsibility. It is, in other words, a confirmation of its own method: individual interpretation of the scriptural basis of belief is the best, and perhaps the only, means by which to "justify the ways of God to men" (I 26). This was certainly Milton's own position, as expressed in a prose treatise of 1659:

> It cannot be deni'd, being the main foundation of our protestant religion, that we of these ages, having no other divine rule or autoritie from without us warrantable to one another as a common ground but the holy scripture, and no other within us but the illumination of the Holy Spirit so interpreting that scripture as warrantable only to our selves and to such whose consciences we can so perswade, can have no other ground in matters of religion but only from the scriptures.[14]

Milton here, perhaps unwittingly, sums up the defining features of what I would call his post-Reformation paradise: rooted in scripture, interpreted in personal terms by the "illumination" of the Holy Spirit,

---

[12] See Stanley Fish, *Surprised by Sin: The Reader in "Paradise Lost"*, Berkeley 1967, for the most influential account of the experience of being "taken in" by Milton and his Satan.

[13] See, for example, Marcia R. Pointon, *Milton and English Art*, Manchester 1970.

[14] Milton, *A Treatise of Civil Power* (1659), from *Complete Prose Works*, ed. Don M. Wolfe *et al.*, New Haven 1953, VII 242.

and offered as a means of persuasion, by and of that interpretation, to the "consciences" of others. As a seventeenth-century proverb expressed it, "The perswasion of the fortunate swaies the doubtfull".[15] Clearly, the "fortunate" were not only those who could see their way to the entrance to Paradise, but knew how to interpret what they found there.

[15] George Herbert, "Outlandish Proverbs" 630, *Works*, ed. F.E. Hutchinson, Oxford 1941, 342.

REFERENCES TO ANCIENT TEXTS

I. Egyptian Texts

II. Old Babylonian Texts

III. Persian Texts

IV. Greek & Latin Pagan Texts

V. Jewish Texts

1. *Hebrew Bible*

2. *Apocrypha and Pseudepigrapha*

3. *Qumran Texts*

2. *Extra-canonical Early Christian Writings*

3. *Patristic Texts*